THE COLLECTED WORKS OF

ERIC VOEGELIN

VOLUME 11

PUBLISHED ESSAYS
1953–1965

PROJECTED VOLUMES IN THE COLLECTED WORKS

The Editorial Board offers grateful acknowledgment to the Earhart Foundation, Liberty Fund, Inc., Robert J. Cihak, M.D., and John C. Jacobs Jr. for support provided at various stages in the preparation of this book for publication. A special thanks for support goes to the Charlotte and Walter Kohler Charitable Trust.

The University of Missouri Press offers its grateful acknowledgment for generous contributions from the Earhart Foundation and from the Eric Voegelin Institute in support of the publication of this volume.

THE COLLECTED WORKS OF

ERIC VOEGELIN

VOLUME 11

PUBLISHED ESSAYS
1953–1965

EDITED WITH AN INTRODUCTION BY

ELLIS SANDOZ

UNIVERSITY OF MISSOURI PRESS

COLUMBIA AND LONDON

Cataloging-in-Publication data available from the Library of Congress

ISBN 0-8262-1282-4

⊗™ This paper meets the requirements of the American National Standard
for Permanence of Paper for Printed Library Materials, Z39.48, 1984.

Designer: Albert Crochet
Typesetter: BOOKCOMP, Inc.
Printer and binder: Thomson-Shore, Inc.
Typeface: Trump Mediaeval

Contents

Acknowledgments

Acknowledgment for permission to quote previously published material and other specific acknowledgment, including the names of translators, is given on the first page of each of the items reprinted here, as appropriate. Thanks goes to the Eric Voegelin Literary Trust for general assistance and for permission to publish items that are held in copyright by the Trust. Thanks to principal contributors to the financial support of *The Collected Works of Eric Voegelin* is given on the reverse of the title page of the volume.

It remains for me as editor to thank my graduate assistants for their general help and especially their diligence and care in preparing the texts in typescript by scanning from the variety of places of original publication or from the translators' typescripts, with special thanks to Lee Trepanier and Edward Findlay. The copy-editing for this volume is the fine work of Julie Schorfheide, the index that of Linda Webster, under the supervision of Jane Lago, managing editor, and Beverly Jarrett, director, of the University of Missouri Press—with all of whom it is a distinct pleasure to be associated in this important publishing endeavor.

PUBLISHED ESSAYS, 1953–1965

Editor's Introduction

The period covered by the material published in this volume marks the transition in Eric Voegelin's career from Baton Rouge to Munich. After twenty years in America, sixteen of them in Baton Rouge at Louisiana State University, where he became one of the original three Boyd Professors, Voegelin accepted the invitation to fill the political science chair at Ludwig Maximilian University in 1958, a position left vacant throughout the Nazi period and last occupied by the famous Max Weber, who had died in 1920. Unsurprisingly, the National Socialists had little use for dispassionate political science. The years at LSU witnessed publication of Voegelin's most compelling works, those for which he is still best known: *The New Science of Politics: An Introduction* (1952) and the first three volumes of *Order and History: Israel and Revelation* (1956) and *The World of the Polis* and *Plato and Aristotle* (1957).[1] It was also the period during which he wrote the massive *History of Political Ideas* that was put on the shelf during his lifetime as superseded by *Order and History*; it, too, recently has been published in eight volumes.[2]

1. Voegelin's career and writings are sketched in Ellis Sandoz, *The Voegelinian Revolution: A Biographical Introduction*, 2d ed. (New Brunswick, N.J.: Transaction Pubs., 2000); Eric Voegelin, *Autobiographical Reflections*, ed. with intro. by Ellis Sandoz (1989; available Columbia: University of Missouri Press, 1999); an interesting personal account of the years in Baton Rouge is given by a friend and former colleague there in Robert Bechtold Heilman, *The Professor and the Profession* (Columbia: University of Missouri Press, 1999), chap. 5; Voegeliniana is compiled most comprehensively in Geoffrey L. Price, "Eric Voegelin: A Classified Bibliography," *Bulletin of the John Rylands University Library of Manchester* 76, no. 2 (summer 1994): 1–180, which is supplemented in *International and Interdisciplinary Perspectives on Eric Voegelin*, ed. Stephen A. McKnight and Geoffrey L. Price (Columbia: University of Missouri Press, 1997), 189–214.

2. Eric Voegelin, *The Collected Works of Eric Voegelin*, vols. 19–26, *History of Political Ideas*, series ed. Ellis Sandoz (Columbia: University of Missouri Press, 1997–1999).

The themes most prominent in the fourteen items reprinted here from Voegelin's occasional pieces during 1953–1965 reflect the concerns of a transition, not only in a scholar's career, and in the momentous shifts in world politics taking place around him, but also in the development of his understanding of the stratification of reality and attendant demands upon a science of human affairs adequate to the new challenges posed by the persistent crisis of the West in its latest configurations and by contemporary philosophy. Pragmatic matters, however, occupy a central place in a number of these pieces, especially the overriding question of how Germany can move from an illiberal and ideological political order into a modern liberal democratic one. Accordingly, several of the items herein originated as talks to this or that organization on problems facing German democratization and development of a market economy amid the ruins of a fragmented culture and infrastructure in a society without historically evolved institutional supports for a viable free government or for any other satisfactory social and political order. Those accustomed to the theoretical profundity of Voegelin's writings may find welcome relief in the down-to-earth, commonsensical drift of this material addressed, as it often is, to laymen and businessmen. But, of course, Voegelin is a master architect and not a journeyman plumber, so the philosophical subject matter lurks everywhere. It tends to break forth toward the end of even the down-to-earth presentations and finds full expression in several instances as the controlling context of even the least pretentious pieces. One of the attractions of these essays is to notice just what the author brings forward as serviceable elementary guideposts under adverse conditions of intellectual disarray, social decay, and turmoil.

In *Autobiographical Reflections* at one point, Voegelin remarks: "The motivations of my work, which culminates in a philosophy of history, are simple. They arise from the political situation."[3] The complex political situation underlying the material presented here reflects the Cold War era and its ideological *dogmatomachy* and the dawning realization that, whatever its theoretical deficiencies, the sole viable form of political arrangement in mid-twentieth-century Europe is representative democracy of some sort. Indeed, one of Voegelin's motivations in accepting the Munich appointment and

---

3. Voegelin, *Autobiographical Reflections*, ed. Sandoz, 93; cf. 24–25.

2

in establishing a political science institute at the university there was his conviction that "the spirit of American democracy would be a good thing to have in Germany."[4] Ever the empiricist, Voegelin as political realist regularly brings to bear the Aristotelian recognition that circumstances dictate the concrete possibilities when it comes to resolving the question of institutionalizing political order, as he played in a modest way as educator the role of political actor during the eleven years beginning in 1958. Underlying everything published here is the great work of this period of Voegelin's life, the exploration and clarification of the philosophy of consciousness that steadily occupied his attentions and found its primary statement in "What Is Political Reality?"—originally a lecture delivered to the West German political science profession in plenary session during its annual meeting in Tutzing in 1965.[5]

While all the usual themes of Voegelin's writing are exhibited in these short pieces, certain points may be selected for preliminary notice here. The first two essays are critiques of what is most wrong with contemporary political theory as practiced by even the best scholars in the field. It addresses the Hannah Arendt of *The Origins of Totalitarianism* and the Oxford political philosophers of the time. While a range of issues is addressed in each essay, some quite sympathetically, what Voegelin finds to be most deficient in both instances is the several scholars' inattention to philosophical anthropology as the controlling reality of human affairs and of theorizing about it. In the former there is Arendt's easy conclusion that the transformation of present reality into a new age approaching the promised perfection of an apocalyptic Third Realm might not be out of the question, if only one would go about it the right way— and certainly National Socialists and Bolsheviks appeared not to have done so. Voegelin's shocked retort is blunt in substance, even

---

4. Ibid., 91.

5. Presented in lecture form on June 9, 1965, to the Deutschen Vereinigung für Politische Wissenschaft and published in expanded form in the *Politische Vierteljahresschrift* 7, no. 1 (March 1966), it was reprinted in Eric Voegelin, *Anamnesis: Zur Theorie der Geschichte und Politik* (Munich: R. Piper & Co. Verlag, 1966), as Part 3, "Was ist politische Realität?" 283–354; English version trans. and ed. Gerhart Niemeyer (1978; rpr. Columbia: University of Missouri Press, 1990); forthcoming with original contents as *The Collected Works of Eric Voegelin*, vol. 6, *Anamnesis*, trans. Gerhart Niemeyer, rev. M. J. Hanak, ed. with intro. by David Walsh (Columbia: University of Missouri Press, 2001). Several of the items reprinted in the original *Anamnesis* were first published during the period of the present volume but are, for that reason, excluded and will be part of the contents of the forthcoming *Collected Works* edition (hereafter *CW*).

as he strives to couch it in the graceful and conciliatory language of friendly criticism. Human nature is a constant and does not change just because this or that ideological revolutionary might find it a convenience: Human beings are not infinitely malleable. The project of creating a new man and of transforming present reality into a new world are root elements of modern gnostic apocalyptic revolution, of Marxian and positivist pseudo-philosophy, and of ideologies right and left. Such a fantasy fatally flaws and deforms any ostensibly rational account of reality experienced by conjuring in its stead a dreamworld, an imaginary Second Reality.[6]

The Oxford political philosophers (with a solitary exception) are treated to a related and comparably sharp critique, one at times conducted with charm and wit reminiscent of Swiftian satire, but concluding with a devastating page. In this fine essay, Voegelin evaluates the work of distinguished authors and takes pleasure in hinting of their consensus that if only the world were populated by English gentlemen, then none of the nasty contemporary political problems of German and Russian tyranny would exist. But of course the majority of mankind are not English gentlemen. And a putative political philosophy that posits the ideal constitution and institutional arrangement not merely as the envy of the world but the standard for mankind is not philosophy at all but apotheosis of a salvific civil theology, one as vitiated by gnosticism as are the more familiar ideologies of which it disapproves: Despite appearances to the contrary, liberals and Communists are "brothers under the skin," Voegelin famously held.[7] Both aspire to a transformation of reality that is impossible ontologically no less than it is unfeasible historically. The Oxford political philosophers are "incarnationists," he decides, who know the truth and are made free as Englishmen in the here and now, if perhaps not so certainly in the eternal beyond. The alternative approach to the subject Voegelin proposes is the recognition of a common humanity by which every human person participates in the analytically discernible stratified comprehending reality, a participation that is capable in rare instances of optimal actualization but one that generally falls short

6. Only the body of Voegelin's essay is reprinted here; Arendt's reply and his riposte are excluded. For these see the original, *Review of Politics* 15, no. 1 (1953): 76–85.

7. Eric Voegelin, *Order and History*, vol. 1, *Israel and Revelation* (1956; available, Columbia: University of Missouri Press, 1999), xiii.

of such realization. This substrate of political philosophizing or its equivalent he contends—as well as the ethical and political implications that flow from it, as drawn in antiquity but still usefully by Aristotle in the *Nicomachean Ethics* and *Politics*—must be the starting point for education in political philosophy as a science whether at Oxford or anywhere else. To the degree it is not, then through grave neglect the door is left wide open for vacuity of education to be filled by those with confident ideological answers to the questions of human existence and promises of eschatological fulfillment—an open invitation to power to those with the clearest of all consciences, "the totalitarian killers."[8] The authority of the philosopher to profess truth and stand for justice must be assumed in the midst of corruption, if the more routine sources of authority fall silent or abdicate this noblest of roles.

The ready accessibility of much of the other material in this volume arises from its conversational quality and informality. This is true even of the final piece, "In Search of the Ground," which in a particularly valuable way continues the philosophical reflections just alluded to by taking the abstruse underpinnings of a philosophy of consciousness and sketching them with minimal technical apparatus for a general academic audience with whom a discussion ensues. The foundation of Voegelin's own philosophy in common sense is exemplified and elucidated in this context. As he explains in a related setting: "One must never forget that all classic philosophy is built on common sense while no ideology is built on common sense—not the positivism of Comte or Marx, not Hegelianism. Realizing that is the great breakthrough."[9] This common sense, which Voegelin characterizes in its derivation from the Scottish school of philosophy of that name as "an Aristotelian ethics and politics minus the metaphysics,"[10] is both the basis of Western philosophizing and a source of the peculiar strength of Anglo-American social and political culture, he argues. In contrasting German and American students, for instance, he remarks of the latter that they "did not have the background knowledge one would expect of European students, but they had something that the European, especially the German, students usually lack—a tradition

8. Herein, "The Oxford Political Philosophers," *ad fin.*
9. *Conversations with Eric Voegelin,* ed. with an intro. by R. Eric O'Connor (Montreal: Thomas More Institute Papers, 1980), 66.
10. Ibid., 65.

of common-sense culture. In the South especially, the problem of ideological corruption among young people was negligible."[11] Thus, the twitting of stuffy xenophobic arrogance in the Oxford philosophers is complemented by reiterated commendation of the unique merits of "Anglo-Saxon" society and its political and economic institutions. The point is made that the impediments to institutionalizing the market economy and the democratic political order to which everyone aspires largely arise from the absence of cultural preconditions historically emergent in England and America but missing in Germany. The ideological destruction apparent in the German students and society more generally is deeply distressing to Voegelin, who in alluding to "value-relativism" attitudes as typical writes:

> It makes all the difference for an educator, as I can say from experience, whether one can set a value relativist thinking by asking him if he would extend his relativism also to the Ten Commandments (in America), or whether he gapes stunned because the Ten Commandments are something he has never even thought of in connection with himself and his actions (in Germany). . . . In short, value relativism is the expression and the instrument of the fanatic will to destroy reason and its order in all questions of man and society. Even though it is theoretically easy to deal with this variant of relativism, you certainly will be able to gauge the difficulties of conducting discussion when one has to introduce young people to a science whose possibility they not only deny but detest.[12]

Common sense is a leading indicator for democratic citizenship no less than for philosophical science.[13] How explain the absence in Germany? There is much discussion of the question, and Voegelin gives some surprising answers. The gnostic ideological doctrines so popular with European studentry in the early 1960s and in intellectual life generally were *then* relatively unknown and where known were found unattractive to the general run of Americans. What these belief systems consist of is explored herein in "Liberalism and Its History" and with attention to Rudolf Bultmann in "History and Gnosis." The analysis of gnostic ideology with its suppression

---

11. Voegelin, *Autobiographical Reflections*, ed. Sandoz, 90.

12. Herein, "Freedom and Responsibility in Economy and Democracy," 77 and 80 below.

13. One should not forget that the last subject addressed in *Anamnesis* is precisely "common sense"—its meaning and crucial importance; cf. Voegelin, *Anamnesis* (1966), 351–54. Some of Voegelin's political science students at Munich organized themselves into the Common Sense Club, as I recall.

of reality, especially through systems and the prohibition of questions, as the leading virus of German intellectual life is powerfully stated in Voegelin's inaugural lecture at the university in Munich in fall 1958, published as *Wissenschaft, Politik, und Gnosis.*[14] The occurrence of the formative national revolutions in England in 1688 and in America in 1776 averted incorporation of the most radical elements of gnostic modernity into the core fabric of the societies they constituted. But a much different situation prevailed when increasingly radical modernity formed the content of the French Revolution of the eighteenth century and the Russian and German revolutions of the twentieth century. As Voegelin sums up in *The New Science of Politics:*

> The German Revolution, finally, in an environment without strong institutional traditions, brought for the first time into full play economic materialism, racist biology, corrupt psychology, scientism, and technological ruthlessness—in brief, modernity without restraint. Western society as a whole, thus, is a deeply stratified civilization in which the American and English democracies represent the oldest, most firmly consolidated stratum of civilizational tradition, while the German area represents its most progressively modern stratum.[15]

In the present analyses, Voegelin elaborates the problems further. What makes German society more vulnerable than Anglo-American society to modern gnosticism is primarily the course of development taken by the religious experiences of the Reformation and its aftermath in each society. From the first sentences of *The Political Religions* onward (1938), Voegelin argues in a wide variety of ways that the susceptibility of societies to ideologies hinges on the fact that they are substitute religions that provide civil theologies announcing eschatological destiny as the matrix of social order.[16]

14. German text published in Munich by Kösel Verlag, 1959; English edition, Eric Voegelin, *Science, Politics, and Gnosticism: Two Essays,* trans. William J. Fitzpatrick, intro. Ellis Sandoz, Gateway Editions (1968; Washington, D.C.: Regnery Publishing, Inc., 1997).

15. Eric Voegelin, *The New Science of Politics: An Introduction,* foreword by Dante Germino (1952; Chicago: University of Chicago Press, 1987), 188–89.

16. Eric Voegelin, *Die politischen Religionen* (Vienna: Bermann-Fischer Verlag, 1938). The religious core of the issue is emphatically affirmed in Voegelin's 1939 preface written (after his narrow escape from Austria) from Cambridge, Massachusetts: Ethical denunciation is not "radical enough" and may even conceal the real problem with National Socialism, viz. "its root in religious experience." Quoted from ibid. (Stockholm: Bermann-Fischer, 1939), 8. This work is published in translation in *The Collected Works of Eric Voegelin,* vol. 5, *Modernity without Restraint: The Political Religions; The New Science of Politics; and Science, Politics, and Gnosticism,* ed.

The modern crisis is first and foremost a *religious* crisis, he steadily insists over the decades. His renewed firsthand acquaintance with Europe and Germany most particularly in the 1950s and 1960s did not alter this basic insight. To the contrary, we see it here being further refined and elucidated. For a wide variety of reasons that cannot concern us in a brief introduction, the development of religious sentiment in England and America took a far different course from that in the nations of the European continent and especially in Germany. The specific deficiency that opened wide the door to gnostic ideology as the new civil theology or belief system of Germany Voegelin sees in the lack of a Second Reformation such as that enjoyed by England and America during the Great Awakening of the 1730s and chiefly identified by him with John Wesley and the rise of Methodism. The source of Abraham Lincoln's "government of the people, by the people, and for the people" in John Wycliffe's Bible translation of 1384 is carried forward, he argues, even in the revivalism of the Wesleys and, with it, the vital reassertion of the "*Judaeo*-Christian" conception of the "theopolity of Israel" as the enduring pattern for Anglo-American representative democracy and constitutional government: "Out of the heroic struggles for the right political form of existence of a Christian people," Voegelin approvingly writes, "emerged . . . the great idea of civil government, namely, the idea that a national community of Christians should not make its ecclesiastical-organizational and dogmatic differences the object of political struggles and that there would be a specific civil sphere of life to which political authority is limited by its legal organization. It is such civil government that we call democracy."[17]

The effective absence of any such developments in Germany is intertwined with contrary developments, especially the powerful persistence of a Lutheran Pietism that condemns the world and politics as the devil's realm and insists that "power is evil."[18] The result is to turn the citizenry away from involvement with political affairs as intrinsically corrupt and corrupting. A further, reinforcing major influence comes with the celebrated educational reforms of

---

with an intro. by Manfred Henningsen (Columbia: University of Missouri Press, 2000).

17. Herein, "Democracy in the New Europe," 61–62 below.

18. Herein, "Freedom and Responsibility in Economy and Democracy," 73 below; also 218–19.

Wilhelm von Humboldt in the nineteenth century, engendering an anti-spiritual narcissistic individualism that channels talent in the direction of secular scholarship and science as the exclusive ways of life for self-respecting persons of talent and intelligence who are destined to compose the educated elite. "The narcissistically harmonized subject need not occupy himself with public affairs. The university, therefore, doesn't have to transmit the stock of knowledge needed for the rational discussion and transaction of public business."[19] At one point Voegelin writes:

> Humboldt expressly expounded the antithesis between the political citizen of the ancient polis and the apolitical citizens of the constitutional government of his times. In his educational ideal he decided for the second type. Only if the citizen is not politically active can he fully unfold his personality through cultural formation; and this liberal *Bildungsideal* has been implemented in the organization of the university, in its business of research and teaching.[20]

By religious as well as educational means, therefore, the political leadership of the society is systematically left by default to the less qualified and even to the dregs of society (if one considers Hitler and his associates), to opportunists and illiterates unhindered by spiritual concern or intellectual scruple, and if animated by any zeal at all then by the passion of *libido dominandi*.

Finally, a few words may be helpful in identifying Voegelin's core theoretical stance as reflected in these presentations; it is one familiar to readers of his other work, of course. That is to say, his response to the decultured horizon of the West—whether encountered among the German students and academics or more generally in personalities of the rank of Rudolf Bultmann and even Arnold J. Toynbee—is to reject the reductionist accounts of reality and to seek therapy and renewal in the great sources of classic and Christian philosophy, which must be at our fingertips, as he says. The therapy and renewal are conceived of *experientially*—not doctrinally nor in terms of reviving a tradition. The flaming statement from the Cambridge preface to the reprinted *Political Religions* is worth remembering. Good ethics is not enough; spiritual revival is requisite. "This renewal proceeds to a large extent only from great religious personalities; but it is possible for everyone to be

19. Eric Voegelin, "The German University and the Order of German Society: A Reconsideration of the Nazi Era," in *CW*, 12:18–34.
20. Herein, "Democracy and Industrial Society," 219 below.

9

prepared and to do his share to prepare the soil from which the resistance against evil will rise. On this point, however, politicizing intellectuals fail completely."[21]

Voegelin further writes herein, in a related matter, that

> communication in the substantive sense, in the sense of the Platonic persuasion, is concerned with the right order of the human psyche. The order of the soul is dependent—if we may use the Augustinian terminology—on the *amor Dei;* it will be disturbed when the *amor sui*, the love of self, prevails against the love of God. The [ideological] movements . . . of which I have spoken are a phenomenon of world-historic importance in that they are the revolt of Western society against God. This revolt has expressed itself in three great symbolic acts: (1) in the removal of the papacy as the representative of divine order from the public scene of the Western world; (2) in regicide; and (3) in deicide.[22]

Plato, Augustine, and Edmund Burke echo in this passage as sources for sound understanding of the human condition in an era of world-wide rebellion. In his critique of Toynbee, Voegelin compares the writer's *A Study of History* with a Platonic *zetema* but finds that

> the work . . . is beset with a . . . difficulty of a personal nature. A search for truth is supposed to reach its goal, that is, a view of reality existentially informed by the *philia* of the *sophon* in the Platonic sense, or by the *intentio animi* toward God in the Augustinian sense. Toynbee does not reach this goal of the love of God, but stops short at a sensitive spiritualist's and a historical connoisseur's sympathy with religions.[23]

Finally, a summarizing syllabus is usefully provided by Voegelin in another presentation, and with its quotation we conclude our introduction and invite the reader to turn directly to the full texts themselves.

3. Reason and Society

1. The postulates of classical politics: (a) Man participates in the Logos or transcendent Nous. (b) The life of reason consists of actualizing this participation and making it sufficiently important so that it becomes

---

21. Voegelin, *Die politischen Religionen* (Stockholm reissue, 1939), 8–9. It is not evident that the situation described in the final sentence has improved appreciably since it was written on Christmas 1939, I would venture to suggest; they ("politicizing intellectuals") still hope this line of analysis will disappear and tend to do all they can to silence it.

22. Herein, "Necessary Moral Bases for Communication," 54 below.

23. Herein, "Toynbee's History as a Search for Truth," 101 below.

an influence on the development of character. (c) In regard to the life of reason, men are potentially equal, but empirically (for whatever reason) they are unequal in the actualization of their potentiality. (d) Men capable of an optimum actualization are a minority. (e) A society has a de facto hierarchical structure in terms of actualizing the life of reason. (f) The "quality" of society depends on the degree to which the life of reason, actively carried out by a minority of its members, becomes a creative force in that society.

2. Additional postulates: A number of other assumptions must be added to the classic postulates. These were of course implicit in the politics of Plato and Aristotle, but only became explicit at a later date. (a) The psychic tension of the life of reason is difficult for the majority of the members of a society to bear. (b) As a result, any society in which the life of reason has reached a high degree of differentiation has a tendency to develop, along with the life of reason, a "mass belief." By sheer social expansion, mass belief may reduce the life of reason to socially meaningless enclaves or even forcefully suppress it. (c) In the case of early Jewish society, Jeremiah diagnosed this tendency as the "fall" of the people away from the "true God" to "false gods" [Jer. 10:10–14]. At the height of the spiritual flowering of the Middle Ages in the West, Joachim of Fiore conceived of a "Third Realm" in the framework of history, and this has, with a certain number of variations, become an element of mass beliefs in the West today. Plato was aware of the problem when, for reasons of political expediency, he made concessions to the "popular myth" and accepted it as a parallel to existence in philosophical form. Examples prove that mass beliefs can assume many different forms. When the situation is favorable, as in the cases of the Hebrews and Greeks, the people can retain, or revert to, a living polytheistic myth; when, as at the height of the Middle Ages in the West, no living myth exists, the search for a mass belief is directed toward immanentist symbols of the apocalyptic or secularist-ideological type. (d) The coexistence of mass beliefs and the life of reason in a society has, since the Stoics, been classified under the headings of *theologia civilis* and *theologia naturalis*. (e) The rise of ideologies to social and political power in modern society must be considered in the context of attempts to establish a civil theology.[24]

While much else of importance and interest awaits the reader of this volume, perhaps enough has been said to illustrate some of its chief themes and to suggest something of the sense of the whole.

ELLIS SANDOZ

---

24. Herein, "Industrial Society in Search of Reason," 180–81 below.

PUBLISHED ESSAYS, 1953–1965

1

The Origins of Totalitarianism

The vast majority of all human beings alive on earth are affected in some measure by the totalitarian mass movements of our time. Whether men are members, supporters, fellow travelers, naive connivers, actual or potential victims, whether they are under the domination of a totalitarian government, or whether they are still free to organize their defenses against the disaster, the relation to the movements has become an intimate part of their spiritual, intellectual, economic, and physical existence. The putrefaction of Western civilization, as it were, has released a cadaveric poison spreading its infection through the body of humanity. What no religious founder, no philosopher, no imperial conqueror of the past has achieved—to create a community of mankind by creating a common concern for all men—has now been realized through the community of suffering under the earthwide expansion of Western foulness.

Even under favorable circumstances, a communal process of such magnitude and complexity will not lend itself easily to exploration and theorization by the political scientist. In space the knowledge of facts must extend to a plurality of civilizations; by subject matter the inquiry will have to range from religious experiences and their symbolization, through governmental institutions and the organization of terrorism, to the transformations of personality under the pressure of fear and habituation to atrocities; in time the inquiry will have to trace the genesis of the movements through the course of a civilization that has lasted for a millennium. Regrettably, though, the circumstances are not favorable. The positivistic

---

This essay was published originally in the *Review of Politics* 15 (1953) as a review essay on Hannah Arendt's *The Origins of Totalitarianism* (New York: Harcourt, Brace, and Co., 1951).

destruction of political science is not yet overcome; and the great obstacle to an adequate treatment of totalitarianism is still the insufficiency of theoretical instruments. It is difficult to categorize political phenomena properly without a well-developed philosophical anthropology, or phenomena of spiritual disintegration without a theory of the spirit; for the morally abhorrent and the emotionally existing will overshadow the essential. Moreover, the revolutionary outburst of totalitarianism in our time is the climax of a secular evolution. And again, because of the unsatisfactory state of critical theory, the essence that grew to actuality in a long historical process will defy identification. The catastrophic manifestations of the revolution, the massacre and misery of millions of human beings, impress the spectator so strongly as unprecedented in comparison with the immediately preceding more peaceful age that the phenomenal difference will obscure the essential sameness.

In view of these difficulties the work by Hannah Arendt on *The Origins of Totalitarianism* deserves careful attention.[1] It is an attempt to make contemporary phenomena intelligible by tracing their origin back to the eighteenth century, thus establishing a time unit in which the essence of totalitarianism unfolded to its fullness. And as far as the nature of totalitarianism is concerned, it penetrates to the theoretically relevant issues. This book on the troubles of the age, however, is also marked by these troubles, for it bears the scars of the unsatisfactory state of theory to which we have alluded. It abounds with brilliant formulations and profound insights—as one would expect only from an author who has mastered her problems as a philosopher—but surprisingly, when the author pursues these insights into their consequences, the elaboration veers toward regrettable flatness. Such derailments, while embarrassing, are nevertheless instructive—sometimes more instructive than the insights themselves—because they reveal the intellectual confusion of the age, and show more convincingly than any argument why totalitarian ideas find mass acceptance and will find it for a long time to come.

This book is organized in three parts: Antisemitism, Imperialism, and Totalitarianism. The sequence of the three topics is roughly chronological, although the phenomena under the three titles do

---

1. Hannah Arendt, *The Origins of Totalitarianism* (New York: Harcourt, Brace, and Co., 1951), xv, 477 pages.

overlap in time. Antisemitism begins to rear its head in the Age of Enlightenment; the imperialist expansion and the pan-movements reach from the middle of the nineteenth century to the present; and the totalitarian movements belong to the twentieth century. The sequence is, furthermore, an order of increasing intensity and ferocity in the growth of totalitarian features toward the climax in the atrocities of the concentration camps. And it is, finally, a gradual revelation of the essence of totalitarianism from its inchoate forms in the eighteenth century to the fully developed, nihilistic crushing of human beings.

This organization of the materials, however, cannot be completely understood without its emotional motivation. There is more than one way to deal with the problems of totalitarianism; and it is not certain, as we shall see, that Dr. Arendt's is the best. Anyway, there can be no doubt that the fate of the Jews, the mass slaughter and the homelessness of displaced persons, is for the author a center of emotional shock, the center from which radiates her desire to inquire into the causes of the horror, to understand political phenomena in Western civilization that belong to the same class, and to consider means that will stem the evil. This emotionally determined method of proceeding from a concrete center of shock toward generalizations leads to a delimitation of subject matter. The shock is caused by the fate of human beings, of the leaders, followers, and victims of totalitarian movements; hence, the crumbling of old and the formation of new institutions, the life-courses of individuals in an age of institutional change, the dissolution and formation of types of conduct, as well as of the ideas of right conduct, will become topical; totalitarianism will have to be understood by its manifestations in the medium of conduct and institutions just adumbrated. And indeed there runs through the book—as the governing theme—the obsolescence of the national state as the sheltering organization of Western political societies, owing to technological, economic, and the consequent changes of political power. With every change sections of society become "superfluous," in the sense that they lose their function and therefore are threatened in their social status and economic existence. The centralization of the national state and the rise of bureaucracies in France makes the nobility superfluous; the growth of industrial societies and new sources of revenue in the late nineteenth century make the Jews as state bankers superfluous; every industrial crisis creates superfluity of human beings through unemployment; taxation and the inflations of the twentieth century dissolve the middle classes into social rubble; the wars and the totalitarian regimes produce the millions of refugees, slave-laborers, and inmates of concentration camps and push the membership of whole societies into the position of expendable human material. As far as the institutional aspect of the process is concerned totalitarianism, thus, is the disintegration of national societies and their transformation into aggregates of superfluous human beings.

The delimitation of subject matter through the emotions aroused by the fate of human beings is the strength of Dr. Arendt's book. The concern about man and the causes of his fate in social upheavals is the source of historiography. The manner in which the author spans her arc from the presently moving events to their origins in the concentration of the national state evolves distant memories of the grand manner in which Thucydides spanned his arc from the catastrophic movement of his time, from the great *kinesis*, to its origins in the emergence of the Athenian polis after the Persian Wars. The emotion in its purity makes the intellect a sensitive instrument for recognizing and selecting the relevant facts; and if the purity of the human interest remains untainted by partisanship, the result will be a historical study of respectable rank—as in the case of the present work, which in its substantive parts is remarkably free of ideological nonsense. With admirable detachment from the partisan strife of the day, the author has succeeded in writing the history of the circumstances that occasioned the movements, of the totalitarian movements themselves, and above all of the dissolution of human personality, from the early anti-bourgeois and antisemitic resentment to the contemporary horrors of the "man who does his duty" and of his victims.

This is not the occasion to go into details. Nevertheless, a few of the topics must be mentioned in order to convey an idea of the richness of the work. The first part is perhaps the best short history of the antisemitic problem in existence; for special attention should be singled out the sections on the court-Jews and their decline, on the Jewish problem in enlightened and romantic Berlin, the sketch of Disraeli and the concise account of the Dreyfus affair. The second part—on Imperialism—is theoretically the most penetrating, for it creates the type-concepts for the relations between phenomena, which are rarely placed in their proper, wider context. It contains the studies on the fateful emancipation of the bourgeoisie that wants to be an upper class without assuming the responsibilities of rulership, on the disintegration of Western national societies and the formation of elites and mobs, on the genesis of race-thinking in the eighteenth century, on the imperialist expansion of the Western national states and the race problem in the empires, on the corresponding continental pan-movements and the genesis of racial nationalism. Within these larger studies are embedded precious miniatures of special situations and personalities, such as the splendid studies of Rhodes and Barnato, of the character traits of the Boers and their race policy, of the British colonial bureaucracy, of the inability of Western national states to create an imperial culture in the Roman sense and the subsequent failure of British and French imperialism, of the element of infantilism in Kipling and Lawrence of Arabia, and of the Central European minority question. The third part—on Totalitarianism—contains studies on the classless society that results from general superfluity of the members of a society, on the difference between mob and mass, on totalitarian propaganda, on totalitarian police, and the concentration camps.

The digest of this enormous material, well documented with footnotes and bibliographies, is sometimes broad, betraying the joy of skillful narration by the true historian, but still held together by the conceptual discipline of the general thesis. Nevertheless, at this point a note of criticism will have to be allowed. The organization of the book is somewhat less strict than it could be, if the author had availed herself more readily of the theoretical instruments that the present state of science puts at her disposition. Her principle of relevance that orders the variegated materials into a story of totalitarianism is the disintegration of a civilization into masses of human beings without secure economic and social status; and her materials are relevant insofar as they demonstrate the process of disintegration. Obviously this process is the same that has been categorized by Toynbee as the growth of the internal and external proletariat. It is surprising that the author has not used Toynbee's highly differentiated concepts; and that even his name appears neither in the footnotes, nor in the bibliography, nor in the index. The use of Toynbee's work would have substantially added to the weight of Dr. Arendt's analysis.

This excellent book, as we have indicated, is unfortunately marred, however, by certain theoretical defects. The treatment of movements of the totalitarian type on the level of social situations and change, as well as of types of conduct determined by them, is apt to endow historical causality with an aura of fatality. Situations and changes, to be sure, require, but they do not determine, a response. The character of a man, the range and intensity of his passions, the controls exerted by his virtues, and his spiritual freedom, enter as further determinants. If conduct is not understood as the response of a man to a situation, and the varieties of response as rooted in the potentialities of human nature rather than in the situation itself, the process of history will become a closed stream, of which every crosscut at a given point of time is the exhaustive determinant of the future course. Dr. Arendt is aware of this problem. She knows that changes in the economic and social situations do not simply make people superfluous, and that superfluous people do not respond by necessity with resentment, cruelty, and violence; she knows that a ruthlessly competitive society owes its character to an absence of restraint and of a sense of responsibility for consequences; and she is even uneasily aware that not all the misery of National Socialist concentration camps was caused by the oppressors, but that a part of it stemmed from the spiritual lostness that so many of the victims brought with them. Her understanding of such questions is revealed beyond doubt in the following passage:

> Nothing perhaps distinguishes modern masses as radically from those of previous centuries as the loss of faith in a Last Judgment: the worst have lost their fear and the best have lost their hope. Unable as yet to live without fear and hope, these masses are attracted by every effort which seems to promise a man-made fabrication of the paradise they longed for and of the hell they had feared. Just as the popularized features of Marx's classless society have a queer resemblance to the Messianic Age, so the reality of the concentration camp resembles nothing so much as medieval pictures of hell. (419)

The spiritual disease of agnosticism is the peculiar problem of the modern masses, and the man-made paradises and man-made hells are its symptoms; and the masses have the disease whether they are in their paradise or in their hell. The author, thus, is aware of the problem; but, oddly enough, the knowledge does not affect her treatment of the materials. If the spiritual disease is the decisive feature that distinguishes modern masses from those of earlier centuries, then one would expect the study of totalitarianism to be delimited, not by the institutional breakdown of national societies and the growth of socially superfluous masses, but rather by the genesis of the spiritual disease, especially since the response to the institutional breakdown clearly bears the marks of the disease. Then the origins of totalitarianism would not have to be sought primarily in the fate of the national state and attendant social and economic changes since the eighteenth century, but rather in the rise of immanentist sectarianism since the high Middle Ages; and the totalitarian movements would not be simply revolutionary movements of functionally dislocated people, but immanentist creed movements in which medieval heresies have come to their fruition. Dr. Arendt, as we have said, does not draw the theoretical conclusions from her own insights.

Such inconclusiveness has a cause. It comes to light in another one of the profound formulations that the author deflects in a surprising direction: "What totalitarian ideologies therefore aim at is not the transformation of the outside world or the revolutionizing transmutation of society, but the transformation of human nature itself" (432). This is, indeed, the essence of totalitarianism as an immanentist creed movement. Totalitarian movements do not intend to remedy social evils by industrial changes, but want to create a millennium in the eschatological sense through transformation of human nature. The Christian faith in transcendental perfection through the grace of God has been converted—and perverted—into the idea of immanent perfection through an act of man. And this understanding of the spiritual and intellectual breakdown is followed in Dr. Arendt's text by the sentence: "Human nature as such is at stake, and even though it seems that these experiments succeed not in changing man but only in destroying him . . . one should bear in mind the necessary limitations to an experiment which requires global control in order to show conclusive results" (433). When I read this sentence, I could hardly believe my eyes. "Nature" is a philosophical concept; it denotes that which identifies a thing as a thing of this kind and not of another one. A "nature" cannot be changed or transformed; a "change of nature" is a contradiction of terms; tampering with the "nature" of a thing means destroying the thing. To conceive the idea of "changing the nature" of man (or of anything) is a symptom of the intellectual breakdown of Western civilization. The author, in fact, adopts the immanentist ideology; she keeps an "open mind" with regard to the totalitarian atrocities; she considers the question of a "change of nature" a matter that will have to be settled by "trial and error"; and since the "trial" could not yet avail itself of the opportunities afforded by a global laboratory, the question must remain in suspense for the time being.

These sentences of Dr. Arendt, of course, must not be construed as a concession to totalitarianism in the more restricted sense, that is, as a concession to National Socialist and Communist atrocities. On the contrary, they reflect a typically liberal, progressive, pragmatist attitude toward philosophical problems. We suggested previously that the author's theoretical derailments are sometimes more interesting than her insights. And this attitude is, indeed, of general importance because it reveals how much ground liberals and totalitarians have in common; the essential immanentism that unites them overrides the differences of ethos that separate them. The true dividing line in the contemporary crisis does not run between liberals and totalitarians, but between the religious and philosophical transcendentalists on the one side and the liberal and totalitarian immanentist sectarians on the other side. It is sad, but it must be reported, that the author herself draws this line. The argument starts from her confusion about the "nature of man": "Only the criminal attempt to change the nature of man is adequate to our trembling insight that no nature, not even the nature of man, can any longer be considered to be the measure of all things"—a sentence that, if it has any sense at all, can only mean that the nature of man ceases to be the measure, when some imbecile conceives the notion of changing it. The author seems to be impressed by the imbecile and is ready to forget about the nature of man, as well as about all human civilization that has been built on its understanding. The "mob," she concedes, has correctly seen "that the whole of nearly three thousand years of Western civilization . . . has broken down." Out go the philosophers of Greece, the prophets of Israel, Christ, not to mention the patres and scholastics; for man has come of age, and that means "that from now on man is the only possible creator of his own laws and the only possible maker of his own history." This coming-of-age has to be accepted; man is the new lawmaker; and on the tablets wiped clean of the past he will inscribe the "new discoveries in morality," which Edmund Burke had still considered impossible.

It sounds like a nihilistic nightmare. And a nightmare it is rather than a well-considered theory. It would be unfair to hold the author responsible on the level of critical thought for what obviously is a traumatic shuddering under the impact of experiences that were stronger than the forces of spiritual and intellectual resistance. The book as a whole must not be judged by the theoretical derailments, which occur mostly in its concluding part. The treatment of the subject matter itself is animated, if not always penetrated, by the age-old knowledge about human nature and the life of the spirit, which, in the conclusions, the author wishes to discard and to replace by "new discoveries." Let us rather take comfort in the unconscious irony of the closing sentence of the work, where the author appeals, for the "new" spirit of human solidarity, to Acts 16:28: "Do thyself no harm: for we are all here." Perhaps, when the author progresses from quoting to hearing these words, her nightmarish fright will end like that of the jailer to whom they were addressed.

2

The Oxford Political Philosophers

The wars and revolutions of the twentieth century bring to its end a period that begins with the consolidation of the Western national states in the fifteenth century. An upheaval of such magnitude, convulsing the whole of a civilization, affects not the institutions only but also the sentiments and beliefs that went into their building, the verities that they represent, and the body of ideas and symbols used for denoting, justifying, and interpreting them. Political philosophy today is concerned with sifting the debris, with testing in the light of contemporary experience the validity of problems and symbols still taken for granted a generation ago, and with repairing the edifice of critical theory that has become badly dilapidated in the course of the so-called modern centuries.

A brief introductory assessment of this task will properly start from the vicissitudes of the power unit that has stamped its character on the era now drawing to its end, that is, from the national state. The nation organized for sovereign dominion over its territory and population, as it emerged in Western Europe in the fifteenth century, has become the prototype of political organizations. The prototypicality expresses itself, first, in the belief that national societies should have the status of sovereign power units; and, second, in the tendency to classify all sovereign powers as nations. Since, however, in historical reality neither all candidates for nationhood can form viable states, nor all viable power units are nations, the indulgence leads to difficulties in theory and practice. When the principle of national self-determination broke the central and eastern European multinational empires, as seemed proper at the time,

This essay first appeared in *Philosophical Quarterly* 3, no. 1 (April 1953), and is reprinted here by kind permission of Blackwell Publishers.

it also broke the Concert of Europe, which had furnished the hard core of stable organization for the area of Western civilization; and, after the interludes of French continental hegemony through the instrumentality of the League of Nations and German hegemony through the National Socialist expansion, the destruction has resulted for the time being in the organization of a Soviet empire and the counter-organization of the Western powers in the NATO, now including the United States and Canada, confronting one another along a border that divides the former German national state. The object lesson of history should drive home the fact, well known to the more perspicacious thinkers of the nineteenth century, that the reality of politics is not exhausted by national states. As a consequence, a philosophy of politics that insists on being a theory of the state is rapidly moving into the shadow of obsolescence, as the theory of the polis did when the age of empire had come. The first problem to be mastered by a contemporary philosophy of politics is, therefore, a redefinition of its object in such a manner that the national state, while receiving its due, will be understood as part in a greater civilizational whole.

The prototype has been further narrowed down, especially in the twentieth century, through its absorption of the demand that a national state, with regard to its internal organization, should be something like a democracy in the Anglo-Saxon sense. In the wake of such concretization of the type further difficulties both theoretical and practical were inevitable, for the European national states have different histories resulting in different locations of political authority. A theory that insists on discussing politics in terms of Anglo-Saxon democracy cannot deal adequately even with the Western national states, and not at all with the political organization, e.g., of Asiatic civilizations. It will, therefore, be a second problem of political philosophy to separate the essential from the historically contingent and to break with the habit of treating the institutions of a particular national state at a particular time as if they truly manifested the nature of man.

The rise of the national state was accompanied, furthermore, by the Reformation. From the resulting conflicts and civil wars, governments could extricate themselves only by transforming temporal power into secular statehood, leaving the spiritual life and its organized expression free to develop in whatever direction it chose. The result was a development in the direction of immanentist creed movements, such as nationalism, progressivism, liberalism, positivism, and ultimately Communism and National Socialism. A political theory that takes it uncritically for granted that the secular national state is the one and true object of inquiry will run into difficulties flowing from this further source. The theorist will have to interpret phenomena of the adumbrated type as movements on the level of secular power politics, which they are not. He will be blind to the fact that his own secular state is not quite so secular as he believes it is, but that civil rights and democratic recognition of equality derive from an idea of man that has grown in the shelter of Stoic cosmology and Christian faith, and hence does not make sense to men who do not live in this cultural tradition. And he will perhaps engage in democratic propaganda and "re-education," an endeavor that can only arouse the scorn of gnostic sectarians who have dedicated their lives to exorcising the devil by means of revolutionary action. The contemporary phenomena compel, therefore, as a third task, a critical examination of the compact symbolism that has grown in the period of the secular state, and its replacement by a considerably more differentiated body of concepts.

The rise of the national state as well as of the immanentist creed movements was accompanied, finally, by the destruction of classic and medieval philosophical culture; in particular philosophical anthropology was destroyed so thoroughly that we have not recovered from the blow to this day. The just mentioned differentiated critical concepts, however, can be developed only by penetrating to principles; and the principles of politics are not to be found on the level of a debate about the rights of man or what institutions are best, but, as established by Plato and Aristotle, in philosophical anthropology. The recovery and further development of a critical theory of man is the fourth, and systematically most important, task of philosophy at the present juncture when we emerge from the national state with its comparative safety, simplicity, and homeliness onto a wider, uncharted, and more dangerous scene.

The task of political philosophy in our time, thus, is both negative and positive. It is negative insofar as the unanalyzed symbols in which the thinkers of the national state period expressed their convictions about the right political order must be submitted to analysis, separating the chaff from the grain, preparatory to a reconstruction of theory by critical standards. It is positive insofar as the criticism must receive its direction from the aim, however dimly

26

seen, of developing a theory that will not mistake the principles on which a special type of political institutions is based, for the principles of politics as such.

This work of criticism and reorientation, while being a general preoccupation of political philosophers in our time, has assumed a wide variety of forms according to the variety of conditions that occasion the inquiry. It has at present the general character of movements from different starting points converging toward a common goal rather than of final achievement. One cause of diversification, to be mentioned only in passing, is the advantage possessed by the sciences that are closer to the classic and Christian sources of critical theory than others. Political scientists proper are laboring under the handicap of being narrowly bound, by their subject matter as well as by the symbols in use, to the theoretical situation that must be overcome; and some of the most effective work is done, as a consequence, by classical philologists, medievalists, philosophers, and theologians. A second cause of diversification is provided by the differences of social and institutional stability in the several national states. Where the national institutions do not enjoy the authority that comes with age; where the class structure is in turmoil owing to defeat, inflation, and unemployment; and where the immanentist creed movements have made such inroads on the cohesion of national society that the movement rather than the nation has become the society that organizes itself politically, as is the case in Germany; there a science of principles will develop, and especially of philosophical anthropology, to the neglect of an analysis of institutions—although the philosopher will be at a loss what to do with his knowledge in an environment that seethes with ideological enthusiasm, has no use for reason, and hates the dianoetic excellences. Where institutions have absorbed the political experience and wisdom of centuries; where they have proved, without a break of continuity, adaptable to the political articulation of new social groups; where the immanentist creeds have not seriously disrupted the civilizational tradition, as is the case in England; there the analysis will start from the treasure of institutions, working its way cautiously toward principles in order not to lose anything of the truth that has accumulated in an organization functioning so well for so long—even at the risk of leaving principles in a penumbra where they remain indistinguishable from the state of England.

In the light of these general reflections on the contemporary situation, the revival, not to say the outburst, of political philosophy
at Oxford in recent years must be seen and studied. The noble
succession of T. H. Green, Bernard Bosanquet, and Sir Ernest Barker
is now continued by a sizable group of scholars who have responded
to the challenge of the age and who try to reformulate the problems
of political theory under the guidance of a venerable tradition. The
principal works that will form the basis of the following discussion
are Lord Lindsay's studies on democracy,[1] R. G. Collingwood's systematic study of political culture supported by his philosophy of
history,[2] the studies on the theory of the state, political conflicts,
and obligations, by J. D. Mabbott and T. D. Weldon,[3] the study on
moral philosophy by E. F. Carritt,[4] and a brilliant lecture on the
theory of the state by G. R. G. Mure.[5] To this impressive list of
works must be added the enterprise of Blackwell's Political Texts,
edited by C. H. Wilson and R. B. McCallum, as well as the series of
introductions, preceding the single volumes, especially those by R.
B. McCallum (Mill), J. W. Gough (Locke), Max Beloff (*The Federalist*), W. Harrison (Bentham), and A. P. D'Entrèves (Saint Thomas).[6]

The authors of these works do not form a school. What they have
in common is a set of inarticulate premises rather than an explicit
doctrine. All of them (with the exception perhaps of Mr. Mure?) are
willing to accept the mystery of incarnation: that the principles of
right political order have become historical flesh more perfectly in
England than anywhere else at any time. Mr. Mabbott's formulation
of the point may be considered representative. In the preface to
his book he declares it his programme "to bring out the general
principles of politics," which happen to be identical with those
"of his own civilization." If anybody should argue that he regarded
local prejudices as permanent principles, he would answer that local

1. A. D. Lindsay, *The Essentials of Democracy* (Philadelphia, 1929); *The Modern Democratic State* (1943) (New York and London, 1947).
2. R. G. Collingwood, *The New Leviathan, or Man, Society, Civilization and Barbarism* (Oxford, 1942); *The Idea of History* (Oxford, 1946).
3. J. D. Mabbott, *The State and the Citizen: An Introduction to Political Philoso-phy* (London, 1948); T. D. Weldon, *States and Morals: A Study in Political Conflicts* (London, 1946).
4. E. F. Carritt, *Ethical and Political Thinking* (Oxford, 1947).
5. G. R. G. Mure, *The Organic State*, in *Philosophy*, vol. 24, no. 90 (1949).
6. The introductions enumerated are to be found in the Blackwell Texts of J. S. Mill's *On Liberty* and *Representative Government*, of Locke's *Second Treatise*, of *The Federalist*, of Bentham's *Fragment* and *Principles*, and of Thomas Aquinas' *Selected Political Writings*.

variations in standards need not involve relativity in values. Some local standards may, indeed, be permanent principles, and he can do no more than give the arguments that in this case the coincidence is a fact. Nothing follows from this conviction for practical politics. "This does not mean that the principles here defended are immediately applicable or should be immediately imposed all over the world. It may even be the case that only in Western Europe, in the British Commonwealth, and in the United States of America have historical conditions been such as to make their application possible within any foreseeable future." Nevertheless, if other nations and civilizations should be debarred by circumstance for the indefinite future from following or even recognizing these principles, "I cannot avoid the conclusion that, in the field of politics at least, they are condemned to lasting loss and sacrifice."

This attitude has nothing to do with either complacency or jingoism. Mr. Mabbott's as well as the other studies under consideration are responsible, closely reasoned works of science. Nevertheless, the reader, while being a little envious of the happiness that such assurance must confer on its possessor, will also feel a little uneasy about a philosopher in such harmony with his environment. He will remember Plato and Aristotle, who did not hesitate to rank Hellenic political culture higher than any other but found enough of a gulf between standards and reality to make them despair that a well-ordered polis could ever be realized in Hellas. The Oxford political philosophers do not adopt the classic philosophical attitude that reality at its best is still far from conforming with principles. Their arrangement of mankind in outer circles of the "condemned" (Mabbott) or "barbarians" (Collingwood) and inner circles of Western civilization, with a further more concentric ring of the Anglo-Saxon democracies, and a distinction between "radical" and "individualist" democracy that will confer a slight edge on England over the United States (Weldon), is reminiscent of Bodin's arrangement of mankind, under a theory of climates, in outer sectors of partial goodness and a center of political virtue in France, with a concentration of this virtue in the French constitutional lawyers, and an ultimate concentration of political wisdom in the principles laid down by Bodin. While none of my distinguished colleagues at Oxford (if I may say the superfluous in order to avoid even the shadow of a misunderstanding) could ever conceive the idea of Bodin's personal apotheosis, there is alive in their attitude the Renaissance pathos of the national state that emerges as the supreme organizational form of human societies after the breakdown of Church and Empire, as well as the pathos of its humanistic thinkers. And this is not the pathos of classic philosophy; for the Greeks were no humanists.

The preceding paragraph attempted a characterization; it did not give an argument. The humanists may well be right if they do not follow the classical philosophers in developing principles based on the *bios theoretikos,* or Christian thinkers into a conception of politics orientated toward the sanctification of life. But this question can be answered only through a closer study of their argument. I shall proceed by analysing in some detail their position with regard to a theoretically central problem, to the principle of liberty of conscience. When in this manner the type of argument has been clarified, it will be possible to deal more briefly with a few further issues.

We may appropriately start from the final judgment passed by Mr. D'Entrèves on the politics of Saint Thomas. When Mr. D'Entrèves proceeds from his impeccable account to an evaluation, he arrives at the following conclusions: "We find that the matters which the State is supposed to leave to the Church are precisely those which the modern man has struggled for centuries to secure against the interference of Church and State alike: such as the pursuit of truth and the worship of God according to his conscience. There is no room for religious freedom in a system which is based on orthodoxy." "Medieval intolerance . . . was a thorough, totalitarian intolerance." On the other hand: "It looks as if, instead of providing us with a complete and elaborate system, Saint Thomas had been concerned with setting forth the principles from which such a system can be constructed. What matters is that the principles should not be betrayed. All the rest is a task for the 'prudent' legislator." "And now in our days the Church and Catholic apologists have brought that teaching even nearer to us in the battle against totalitarianism. We have learnt to appraise a doctrine which is founded upon the vindication of human personality and on the unflinching assertion of the primacy of spiritual values." Nevertheless: "It is hardly possible for the modern man to accept the system which Saint Thomas coherently founded upon (the 'primacy of the Spiritual') without renouncing that notion of civil and religious liberty which we have some right to consider the most precious conquest of the West."[7]

7. D'Entrèves, introduction to *Selected Political Writings,* by Thomas Aquinas, xxi f., xxxii f.

We sympathize with the sentiments that have inspired the judgment, and we do not doubt the correctness of the facts on which it
is based. If nevertheless we take exception to it, it is on the purely
theoretical ground that the judgment is couched in terms, halfway
between critical concepts and humanist-progressivist ideological
symbols. Mr. D'Entrèves does not attack the "primacy of the Spiritual." What he really does not like is Saint Thomas' insistence
on the use of temporal power for discrimination against Jews and
Gentiles, as well as for the criminal prosecution of heretics and
apostates. The logical flaws in the expression of his dislike stem
more immediately from the anachronistic application of the term
coherent system to a medieval "summa" that does not derive propositions from axioms but moves in the tension between reason and
faith. "Systems" are a modern invention; and I doubt that one can
properly speak of a "system" before Descartes. Hence, the reprehen-
sible demands of Saint Thomas do not follow "coherently" from the
"primacy of the Spiritual," but originate in the spheres of prudence
or political expediency, of the mores of the age, and of the Roman
Law whose revival was accompanied by a regrettable enthusiasm
for construing spiritual divagations as crimes in the legal sense.
From the recognition of spiritual perfection as the highest good of
man (in Christianity the beatific vision) there follows nothing at all,
as far as I can see, with regard to specific measures that will serve the
creation and protection of the environment most favorable to the
realization of this good. If the distinction between an inquiry into
principles (hierarchy of goods) and prudential measures is not made,
if both are treated on the same level as a "system," the result will
be that odd totalitarian intolerance of Saint Thomas, which at the
same time is concerned about the integrity of human personality,
is "the most important factor of Western civilization," and is even
an ally in the battle against totalitarianism.

Mr. D'Entrèves' formulations make, furthermore, anachronistic
use of the term *totalitarianism*. The term has arisen, in the 1920s,
within the modern gnostic mass movements. It does not denote
the measures of extraordinary atrocity that these movements use
in their expansion and domination, but the faith in human intramundane (not transcendent) perfection through political action by
groups who are in possession of eschatological knowledge about the
end of history. This substitution of human self-salvation, of something like a transfiguration of human nature through historical

action, for the Christian idea of perfection through Grace in death is, indeed, a matter of principle insofar as it can be maintained only if the whole range of experiences of transcendence is disregarded. Totalitarian politics is based on an immanentist philosophical anthropology, as distinguished from Platonic-Aristotelian and Christian anthropologies which find the ordering center of human personality in the experiences of man's relation to transcendent reality. It seems to me impermissible to apply the term *totalitarianism* to both types alike, for such indiscriminate usage would obliterate the essential difference of principles and stress the nonessential similarity of prudential measures that, in various historical circumstances, may be used for the protection of a society against spiritual disintegration.

The anachronistic use of terms, while impairing the theoretical value of the judgment, has nevertheless an intelligible purpose. Mr. D'Entrèves assumes three types of political principles: the medieval totalitarian, the modern totalitarian, and in between the preferred modern type characterized by free pursuit of truth, religious freedom according to conscience, and civil liberties. If we make the suggested distinction between philosophical anthropology (as a science of principles) and prudential measures that will, under given historical circumstances, create the best possible environment for the attainment of the highest good, the question concerning the status of the aforementioned freedoms cannot be avoided. Are these freedoms really fundamental principles, or are they perhaps no more than prudential devices? If the latter should be the case, the halo that surrounds them certainly would pale; the rude question, which can never be addressed to a principle, would have to be asked: whether they work or whether they have failed, perhaps quite as miserably as the medieval device of persecution. If, however, the distinction is not made, embarrassment will be avoided and the freedoms can be as inalienable, eternal, and ultimate as anyone desires. The cult of political institutions as incarnations of principles depends on the suspension of theoretical animation.

When, however, the rude theoretical question concerning the status of the freedoms, and in particular of the freedom of religion and conscience, is raised, we find no simple answer. First of all the apparent simplicity suggested by Mr. D'Entrèves' opposition of an orthodoxy that leaves "no room for religious freedom" to the liberties that are "the most precious conquest of the West" must be broken down. In this radical opposition of freedom and orthodoxy as the respective representatives of good and evil we recognize an instance of gnostic-Manichaean dualism. In English political thought this dualism has its venerable ancestry in Hobbes's *Leviathan* with its opposition of the "Christian Commonwealth" to the "Kingdom of Darkness"; and the tradition is both preserved and renewed in Mr. Collingwood's *New Leviathan* where the dualism, in the more secularist form of "Civilization" and "Barbarism," is erected into the principle that defines political cultures and governs the process of history. This dualistic formula, while adequately expressing the political perspective of a gnostic metaphysician, will, however, not pass the test of critical application. The thesis that there is no religious freedom under a system based on orthodoxy must be rejected. There was, of course, religious freedom in plenty during the Middle Ages, as is attested by the range of religious personalities from Saint Francis to Saint Thomas, by the range of theological speculation from realism to nominalism, by the foundation of numerous special *religiones* within Christianity, ranging from hermits to military orders, and by the great mystics from Eckhardt to Cusanus. But such concrete reminders should not overshadow the general argument that, whenever a great religious civilization unfolds, somebody must have taken the liberty to create it. Nevertheless, the thesis has a nucleus of truth; heretics were persecuted, indeed; and some varieties of religious experience were not allowed the freedom to express themselves. The gnostic-Manichaean dualism of orthodoxy and freedom must, therefore, be reduced to the theoretical question: In what respect was religious freedom expanded through insistence on the freedom of conscience? The question is all the more important because even under the new dispensation it is agreed that religious freedom has its limits. When Adamite sectarians were informed by their consciences that the naked truth of God would best be represented by walking in the street without clothes, even a Roger Williams drew the line.

Freedom of conscience in the political sense is the right to act according to one's conscience free of governmental prevention, interference, or subsequent sanction. Conscience itself can be defined as the act, or acts, by which we judge, approvingly or disapprovingly, our conduct in the light of our rational moral knowledge. Conscience in this sense is not infallible. It can err either because the facts of the case requiring our action or inaction are insufficiently known, or because an intricate conflict of obligations resists a correct solution within the time at our disposal, or because our general state of ignorance, our lack of intellectual training and imagination, our moral obtuseness and spiritual perversion, will produce false judgments. The structure of this problem has received a new precision through the distinction, developed by Mr. Carritt, between three views concerning the ground of obligation. He distinguishes the objective, the subjective, and the putative view. "The general question is whether our obligations, and consequently our duties, depend upon our actual situation, including our capacities for affecting it and the consequences of what we immediately bring about, or upon our beliefs about that situation, or upon our moral estimate of what the supposed situation demands."[8] We never know our objective duty because we are not omniscient with regard to the actual situation; we sometimes know a subjective obligation because one or more of the obligations from which we have to select our duty may be simple enough for us to know with certainty the action morally required by what we believe to be the facts of the situation; and we always know our putative duty because we always can form a moral estimate (although exposed to moral error) of what is demanded by what we believe to be the actual situation.[9] The fulfillment of putative duty is conscientious action.

At this point the difficulties begin. In order to be moral, action must be conscientious; a will that deviates from conscience is immoral. Even if his conscience is badly in error, a man must follow it. Does liberty of conscience in the political sense mean that every man must be left free to follow it, even if it advises him to organize a revolution of Fifth Monarchy men or of the proletariat? If we say No, we are back to persecution for the sake of conscience. And since the practice of Western statecraft in fact has said No, the so-called freedom of religion and conscience has never been opposed as a "principle" to medieval persecution. The difference between "persecution" and "freedom" is one of degree; some consciences that would have been persecuted in the Middle Ages are left free in the modern national state—but not all of them by far.

It would be unfair to state that the Oxford political philosophers evade the issue deliberately, but they certainly do not rush into the fray. Representative is perhaps Mr. Gough's introduction to Locke's

8. Carritt, *Ethical and Political Thinking*, 14.
9. Ibid., 26.

Letter Concerning Toleration in the Blackwell Text. Mr. Gough is fully aware that there is something odd about a toleration from which are excepted Mohammedans, Roman Catholics, Antinomians, revolutionary millenarians, and atheists; he is, furthermore, aware that Locke was not tolerant on principle but that his views were those of a Latitudinarian who had experienced strong formative influences from Dutch Arminians. But at this point the matter is left hanging, as it is left after Mr. Gough has carefully shown how Locke whittles down his principle of government by consent to consent by the fact of residence—although it would be interesting to know what Locke *did* develop if not the principles for which he is famous. Could it be that behind the formulae of freedom and toleration hides the orthodoxy of a liberal, semi-secularized Protestant church-state?

Silences are sometimes quite as noteworthy as positive assertions. The restraint with regard to the issue under consideration is remarkable, and certainly in need of explanation; for it is one of the glories of English political philosophy to have faced the question of conscience and its suppression unflinchingly in the person of Hobbes. Under the impression of the Puritan revolution one of the greatest psychologists of all times laid down the rule that men who are moved by their religious conscience to civil war, for the purpose of imposing their creed on others, are not moved by the spirit, but are guilty of pride, of *superbia* in the Augustinian sense, to the point of madness. Hobbes diagnosed passionate self-assertion, the *amor sui,* as the formative force of the Puritan conscience; he understood its dictates as a manifestation of *libido dominandi,* not of the spirit of Christ. This diagnosis tears the problem of moral conscience wide open; beyond conscience lies the spiritual personality of the man who has it. A conscience may be good in the moral sense and nevertheless thoroughly evil in the spiritual sense, as Hobbes's predecessor in this question, Richard Hooker, had already shown in his acid portrait of the Puritan, in the preface to his *Ecclesiastical Polity.* Hobbes, to be sure, was in error himself when he assumed that there was no such thing as a true spiritual orientation of the soul through *amor Dei* and that every conscientious conviction, when in conflict with the civil order, was thereby proven evil. Nevertheless, in his estimate of the movements of his time he was empirically as shrewdly right as he could be without the conceptual apparatus for the classification of phenomena of this

35

type that is at our disposal today; he could hardly classify them as gnostic sectarian movements of the type that was suppressed as heretical in the Middle Ages, but he could see that men who wanted to replace the "Christian magistrates" of England by "officers of Christ" chosen from the membership of their sects, and to deprive all Englishmen who were not members of their political rights, had somewhat strayed from the *amor Dei* in the Christian sense. And since he could not believe in spiritual reform as a cure for the evil, he devised the Leviathan that would sit as a king over the proud; the *libido dominandi* of the Puritan conscience would have to be broken by the fear of physical death, if it could not be healed by the love of God. He countered the destructive exuberance of spiritually disoriented conscience by the invention of a rigidly enforced *theologia civilis* in the Varronic sense of the word.[10] The various dimensions of the problem thus have a solid English tradition of inquiry; here is the basis on which a contemporary examination of the freedom of conscience that we actually enjoy, as well as of the dangers created by the gnostic politico-religious movements of our time, could build. And yet there is this odd restraint.

The explanation that I have to offer hinges on the conflict between civil theology and philosophy. The practice of English politics has adopted the Hobbesian recipe of a civil theology on principle. To be sure, nothing remotely resembling the narrow brutality of the Leviathan was developed. The repressive measures in the wake of the Revolution were far less radical and oppressive than those suggested by Hobbes—although some of them were quite juicy and today would be called totalitarian. And the actual range of freedom rapidly became very much larger than anything envisaged as "freedom for the press" by Milton in his *Areopagitica,* or as "liberty of conscience" by Locke in his *Letter Concerning Toleration.* Nevertheless, a civil theology it was; and this is the root of our problem. The institutional symbolism of the English polity has become accepted as the language of political discourse. And, as a consequence, contemporary political debate is only to a minor extent theoretical discussion, while to a larger extent it is a cautiously moving elaboration of civil theology and its adaptation, if possible, to the disquieting events of the age. Since, however,

10. This point has been stressed by Mr. Oakeshott in his introduction to Hobbes's *Leviathan* (Oxford: Basil Blackwell, n.d.)—in the Blackwell Texts, p. lxii—if for a moment a Cambridge man can be admitted to the Oxford circle.

history does not seem to tread the path of English civil theology, its adherents are in a difficult position. Unless one is willing to give up political theologizing altogether and to take the plunge into philosophy, one has to act with great circumspection, or the dogmatic edifice will come tumbling down. When the dogmatic symbols of the creed, such as Locke's toleration and liberty of conscience, or John Stuart Mill's improvement, are touched by critical examination, they will inevitably fall apart.[11] This is not a course to be taken lightly. The fortunes of history have granted England a breathing spell between the gnostic movements of the seventeenth and the twentieth centuries; a great political culture has grown, its durability has endowed its symbols with the pseudo-eternity of principles, and it has engendered loyalties that motivate justification rather than dissolving criticism.[12] The road from English civil theology to philosophy must be traveled; but the restraints and silences prove that the journey is not easy.

The conflict between civil theology and philosophy is the crucial issue. Its presence makes itself generally felt in the work of the Oxford political philosophers, but not in every case does it become the object of theoretical attention. In the following pages I shall discuss the more articulate responses to the issue.

I shall begin with the comparatively simple treatment accorded to the issue by the late Lord Lindsay in his book *The Modern Democratic State*.[13] Lindsay wants to give an exposition of the English *theologia civilis*, and he actually gives one of the best ever written; but he does not want to appear in the role of a political theologian and, hence, is concerned about defining "political theory" in such a manner that it becomes identical with theology. Since this attempt

11. See the excellent page on J. S. Mill's political theology, and especially on the insufficiency of his Pelagianism in the face of contemporary events, in Mr. McCallum's introduction to the *Essay on Liberty* in the Blackwell Texts, p. xix. Mr. Gough's penetrating analysis of the Lockean symbols has been mentioned previously.

12. See, for instance, the passage on the best form of government in Carritt, *Ethical and Political Thinking*, 149: "In our time and country, the most interesting form of the question is how to justify our conviction that democracy is the kind of constitution most likely to take this good form, and therefore to have the strongest claim to our loyalty, though a majority may be as unjust and is often less clever and efficient than other rulers." What is remarkable about passages of this type is the author's apparent ability to insulate himself completely against the totalitarian crisis of Western civilization, as well as against the work of the thinkers who saw the disaster coming (Tocqueville, Burckhardt, Nietzsche), to say nothing of the more recent literature on the subject.

13. I am using the American edition, with a preface by W. Y. Elliott (New York and London, 1947).

involves him in reflections on the function (or rather non-function) of a philosophy of politics, his argument is of general interest for the vicissitudes of philosophy in our time.

The task of the theorist, he rules, is the study of a historical type of state, such as the modern democratic, or the Greek, or the medieval state. As distinguished from the description of institutions, theory is concerned with the "operative ideals," the beliefs of the citizens, which sustain the state in existence. Lindsay, thus, accepts the rarely accepted insight that the representation of a truth about the meaning of human life is an essential component in the structure of a political society. He knows that what he tries to establish under the name of theory is in substance a *Geisteswissenschaft* of politics. While this programme as such sounds unobjectionable, the strange use of the term *theory* nevertheless suggests that not everything is in perfect theoretical order. For, if we give an account of "operative ideals," describing their content, telling the story of the situations from which they have grown and to which they are applied, we are writing history, a history of ideals, beliefs, or dogmas; and if we try to explore the relations of meaning between the ideals, to demonstrate their connection and consistency, perhaps to extrapolate axioms from which they can be derived logically, we are engaged in a systematic exposition of dogma. Only under the assumption that the operative ideals contain a critical theory of man in political existence, although perhaps only by implication and fragmentarily, could their systematic exposition legitimately be called a theory. Unfortunately Lindsay remains vague on the question: What is the truth of theory as distinguished from the truth of ideals? Certain it is that he only writes history, and that he expounds dogma, from the position of a believer. We are moving in the area of restraints and silences.[14]

Lindsay's intentions must be inferred from his position with regard to the classic philosophy of politics. He disposes of it sweepingly by attributing to Plato and Aristotle the creation of "ideal states," which are historically conditioned in the same manner as the "operative ideals" and hence devoid of rational truth. This

---

14. The only passage concerning the question of truth is to be found ibid., 45. In this passage Lindsay concedes that ideals deserve some consideration with regard to their "absolute worth," but then insists that "the primary business of the political theorist" is the understanding of actually operative ideals. "Political theory, then, is concerned with fact."

argument, however, is valid only if the liberal interpretation of the two philosophers as "constitutionalists" and "idealists" be considered valid. And this interpretation, which itself is part of the liberal construction of the history of ideas, is not acceptable in science. Plato and Aristotle did not create "ideal states" (the very word *ideal* has no equivalent in Greek) but developed imaginative paradigms, models of the best polis. What is "best" again has nothing to do with "ideals" but will be decided by the pragmatic suitability of the model to provide an environment for the "best" or "happiest life"; and the criterion of the best or happiest life in its turn will be established by the science of philosophical anthropology. The best life, according to the various formulations, is the life that leads to the unfolding of the dianoetic excellences, to one's existence as philosopher, to the *bios theoretikos,* or to the cultivation of the noetic self. The models, thus, are based on a theory of the nature of man, which claims to be a science. Nobody, of course, will today unreservedly agree with the results of the Platonic-Aristotelian analysis of human nature; for in order to agree he would have to ignore the advances of philosophical anthropology that we owe to the Fathers and scholastics, as well as to such contemporary thinkers as Bergson, Gilson, Jaspers, Lubac, or Balthasar; and as far as the classical models are concerned, our pragmatic interest in them will be mild, since we have little use for Greek poleis at present. Such restrictions, however, do not affect the principle established by the classic philosophers that a philosophy of politics must rest on a theory of the nature of man, and that philosophical anthropology is a science—not an occasion for idealistic tantrums. The liberal interpretation cavalierly disregards the explicit content of the Platonic-Aristotelian work; and we conclude, therefore, that it cannot be used for disposing of this problem of the *philosophia perennis.* If there should exist any doubt about Lindsay's intention when he uses it nevertheless, it will be removed when we see him classify Aristotle's concept of the "good life" as one of the ideals that vary with time. The classification emasculates the concept by denying that it has a theoretical basis. This is a radical attack on philosophy as the science of order in the soul and society. As to Lindsay's intention we conclude, therefore, that he wanted to avoid the classic tension in which the philosopher opposes his authority to that of the civil theology under which he lives; he wanted to be a theologian, and in order to act his part in good conscience he

had to annihilate the uncomfortable authority of the philosopher—
a procedure that casts a further interesting light on the intricate
problems of freedom and conscience.

One cannot, however, annihilate critical standards without in-
curring the consequences. When the theologian is victorious over
the philosopher, there will be trouble for the historian who now
finds himself deprived of the conceptual instruments for understanding "operative ideals." He cannot gain the necessary critical
distance from his object and must surrender to the stream of history.
The surrender does not make the work altogether worthless; while
swimming with the stream, one still can trace the course of events,
assemble historical materials, and discern the lines of meaning
embedded in the evolution of the "operative ideals" themselves. As
a matter of fact, Lindsay has achieved a convincing demonstration
that the English democratic idea derives from Puritan congrega-
tional life. Nevertheless, the "understanding" will fall short of
theoretical penetration. In order to demonstrate the gravity of the
issue I shall, first, give a brief summary of Lindsay's thesis and,
then, add the missing theoretical considerations.

Democracy, the thesis may be formulated briefly, is secularized
Independency. "Modern democratic theory" originates in the communities of the elect where the possession of the "call," overriding all other qualifications, makes for democratic equality. These
"communities of grace and inspiration" are essentially churches;
but the Puritans of the Left applied the procedures developed in
such communities "by analogy" to the conduct of state business. In
order to expand such a theocratic church-state beyond the confines
of a sect to embrace the nation, the idea of the "elect" must be
secularized so that every citizen will be counted as "elect" for political purposes. The national society, in fact, takes the place of the
church of the elect, while the "state" acquires the characteristic of
an "instrument" for the purposes of "society," in the same manner
as formerly the temporal power was an instrument for creating the
proper environment for a community of Christians. This ultimate
transformation found its expression in the work of Locke.

Lindsay, the theological historian, renders a sympathetic, ha-
giographic account of these origins of democracy. A philosophical
historian, while accepting the "facts," would make their meaning
transparent by relating them to a theory of human nature. A church
of the "elect," he would have to say, is a group of persons who claim

a certainty of knowledge concerning their state of grace, which is only God's; they indulge in *superbia* and arrogantly separate from the community of sinners. When they transfer their ecclesiastical procedure to political affairs, and especially when they engage in revolutionary action for millenarian purposes, they usurp the functions that Revelation 20, with a more critical knowledge of the limits of human powers, has reserved for an angel of the Lord. When finally, through secularization of the idea, the whole nation is taken to the bosom of election under the name of "society," the original sectarianism and separatism has become an ingredient of the national *theologia civilis*, as well as a force forming the national character. The way has been traveled from Christianity to immanentist self-salvation on a national basis.

The result should give pause to the philosopher as well as to the Christian—especially when he considers that these are the very immanentist principles that inspire our contemporary totalitarian movements to use "the instrument of the state" for creating the society of the millennium. A philosopher would prefer to conduct his plea for democracy (or against it, dependent on the situation) with more earthly arguments derived from the school of Aristotle.

Since philosophy is an integral part of Western civilization, a figure in the intellectual landscape that cannot be ignored, the indulgence in civil theology is hardly possible (except on a very primitive level) without constructions that will decently screen the nuisance from sight. It is not surprising, therefore, when screening operations of the same type as Lindsay's are undertaken elsewhere in the works under consideration. Of the various constructions used for the purpose, Collingwood's merits our special attention for its technical brilliance of execution, as well as for its high degree of deliberateness.

Collingwood's *New Leviathan*, as previously indicated, is a conscious revival of Hobbes's gnostic-Manichaean dualism. The author places himself squarely in the sectarian tradition. The gnostic aeons of Light and Darkness, of Truth and Lie, transformed by medieval sectarians into immanent-historical symbols, have become in the so-called modern period (which could be better named the gnostic age) the predominant mode of political thought in the various nationalisms, in progressivism, in the totalitarian movements, as well as in the civilizational creeds of Europeanism, Americanism, general Occidentalism, and the more restrictive Westernism of the

Atlantic national states. Collingwood's is a civilizational creed, more specifically a restrictive Westernism, with a strong core of English nationalism. Civilization in the historical sense means for Collingwood the creation of a "world," that is, of a geographical area inhabited by people with a common manner of life. Such a world was formed in the Roman period, has existed in continuity, although with ups and downs, to this day, and culminated in "modern Europe" or, synonymously, "Christendom." In relation to this civilizational course there appear as "barbarisms" in the historical sense all peoples and movements that threaten the existence and continuity of civilization. Collingwood deals specifically with the Saracens, the Albigensians, the Turks, and the Germans. The civilized peoples who are "sitting unshakable on top of the world" are justified in organizing preventive wars for averting the threats to civilization. Such wars would not have to be motivated by self-preservation but could be conducted "for the sake of the world at large," for "there are bodies politic, so to call them, which are so useless to the world in their parasitic imbecility and so dangerous to their more intelligent neighbors that they would better be destroyed." The counsel applies in particular to the German "Yahoo herd." The rest of mankind, since it neither belongs to the "world" nor comes under the head of threatening "barbarism," is not mentioned.[15]

The aeonic struggle between the civilizational forces of Light and the barbarian forces of Darkness expresses Collingwood's gnostic religiousness. In order to protect the resulting, rather phantastic picture of history against obvious criticisms, he invents the Principle of Limited Objective.[16] The principle means that a science should limit itself to what actually can be explored and not waste time on what resists methodical inquiry. Classical physics limited "its explanatory efforts to such facts as admitted of mathematical treatment," while the secondary qualities were set aside. Classical

15. I have included the passages on preventive warfare in the account because they indicate a strain in Collingwood that goes farther back than Hobbes. Preventive warfare against civilizationally inferior peoples was demanded and justified, for the first time in English political thought, by Thomas More in the *Utopia*. In the setting of the *Utopia* the origin of the argument in humanistic *hubris* is even clearer than in Collingwood's work.

16. I do not enter into the theoretical problems of Collingwood's philosophy of history, because they have recently been submitted to a careful analysis in Leo Strauss's article "On Collingwood's Philosophy of History," *Review of Metaphysics* 5, no. 4 (June 1952). I am in substantial agreement with Professor Strauss.

politics, represented by Hobbes, Locke, Spinoza, and Rousseau, limited itself similarly to society, "meaning that part of political life which consists in agreement between mentally adult persons for the purposes of joint action." A body politic consists of its social part, the area of free will, of joint activity, of contractual agreement, and a nonsocial part that hitherto has resisted penetration by science. This nonsocial part is "the state of nature, the natural condition of mankind." All that classical politics can say about this nature "is that it is that element in political life which is not society." Civilization, then, can be defined theoretically as the process of approximation to the state of civility, that is, of a maximum of society and a minimum of nature in the body politic; and classical politics is, therefore, the political science that deals with the civilizationally relevant part of politics.

Armed with the principle of limited objective, Collingwood can dispose of philosophy. The object of science, he argues, can only be defined in terms of science. We cannot define physics in terms of Nature or political science in terms of Politics, but must define Nature or Politics as that which is treated in physics or political science. The only political science that we possess is classical politics from Hobbes to Rousseau. The ancients can be neglected because classical politics has absorbed what was valuable in their work. And no later political science, that would have penetrated more deeply into the area of "nature," has superseded classical politics. The gnostic-Manichaean vision of history is supported by theoretical argument, insofar as classical politics is the legitimate scientific instrument for the interpretation of history and politics.

Critical reflections on this position are embarrassing because they must point out the obvious. The Platonic-Aristotelian philosophy of politics contains a good deal that is not to be found in "classical politics"; and the surplus happens to be the most important part. There is, furthermore, in existence a contemporary science of politics that seems to have escaped Collingwood's notice. It will be sufficient to mention the names of Pareto and Max Weber, and to refer to Bergson's *Deux Sources*, in order to evoke this massively existing science. The notion of "classical politics" as the one and only science of politics thus breaks down. What remains is the misuse of philosophical technique for bolstering a ramshackle theology of history and politics. It is a debasement of philosophy to the role of *ancilla theologiae*. The misdeed, however, must not be charged fully to the account of Collingwood. He does no more than what everybody does in our time when he bolsters his pet gnostic dualism with theoretical argument; his case is only clearer than many others because he had a brilliant mind and was able to articulate his position with care. And this brings us back to questions of conscience: Does ignorance cause us to hold certain beliefs with a good conscience, or does our will to hold certain beliefs cause us to remain ignorant with regard to disturbing facts? And if the latter should be the case, does the end of holding a certain belief justify the means of ignorance? Is there not a truth, higher than a civilizational creed, binding a philosopher's conscience? Is he really entitled to hold a belief concerning the meaning of history, although he perfectly well knows (or ought to know) that the meaning of history, its essence or *eidos*, is unknown because history extends into the future and hence is not a "thing" whose eidos can be known? And is, therefore, political gnosis that confers on us knowledge of the unknowable a philosophical attitude at all? And if it is not, does not our indulgence in gnostic speculation destroy the truth of philosophy? And if we are doing that, are we not actively engaged, with the best of consciences, in the destruction of the civilization that we praise, like any Communist or National Socialist?

In Collingwood's *New Leviathan* the real cause of the distressing state of political philosophy becomes more tangible than in the work of others: It is the trauma of the World Wars. The threat to national existence causes the withdrawal into the citadel of national political values, their defiant reassertion, and the condemnation of anything alien to them. Mr. Weldon's division of all political theories into organic and mechanical theories is a good example of this state of mind. Under the head of organic theory are generously pooled together Plato, Aristotle, the Catholics, Hitler, and Mussolini, while "Christianity as developed since the Reformation, and especially in Puritan England during the seventeenth century, can have nothing whatever to do with this as a political theory."[17] It is "the claim of the Protestant Reformation that in matters of faith and conduct the final court of appeal is the conscience of the individual, and no authority can be morally entitled to control or even to interfere with the operation of that conscience. . . . No

17. Weldon, *States and Morals*, 39.

Protestant doctrine of conscience can conceivably permit Society to claim the right to dictate to the individual what he ought to do."[18] The rich differentiation of political cultures in the history of mankind, as well as the work of the philosophers in grappling with the problem of man in political existence, are wiped out with one stroke. It all boils down to the difference between Protestant England and the rest of mankind. This appalling impoverishment amply justifies Mr. Mure's warning: "Today controversy concerning the nature of the State is so near to common life, so closely bound up with cruel memories and agonizing hopes and fears, that there is danger of its degenerating even in England into a mere ideological brawl."[19]

Looking at Mr. Mure's lecture on *The Organic State* we feel, however, that not all hope is lost. Here at last is a real philosopher, rushing to the defense when a particularly ignorant attack on classic philosophy arouses his wrath.[20] With excellent craftsmanship he restates the ontological principles underlying the Aristotelian theory of the polis. The state is an entity in the hierarchy of being that ranges from matter to God; the levels of the immanent hierarchy are related with each other, the higher presupposing the lower for their existence; beings on the various levels develop from potentiality to actuality, or are checked in their development; and so forth. In the hierarchy of being the state is, therefore, the condition for full actualization of human potentialities; but it is nevertheless founded on the associational life below the level of the state, and cannot supersede it without destroying human development. Mr. Mure's elaboration in detail of the conflict of loyalties between the various levels of associational life, as well as of the respective function of each level, is admirable. But what is most remarkable historically is perhaps the fact that a restatement of philosophical fundamentals in matters of politics comes as a surprise, almost a feat of heroism in a hostile environment.

I shall conclude on an Aristotelian point, which the limits of his lecture did not allow Mr. Mure to make. The polis offers the opportunity for full actualization of human nature. The fully actualized man is the *spoudaios*, the mature man, who has developed his dianoetic excellences and whose life is orientated by his

18. Ibid., 43 f.
19. Mure, *The Organic State,* 206.
20. The occasion was Karl Popper's *The Open Society and Its Enemies.*

noetic self. This is the decisive issue in a philosophy of politics, the issue that the distinguished authors whose work we have discussed studiously avoid. Under pretext of respect for the freedom of conscience they ignore the fact that conscience, however "good" it may be putatively, can only be as good as the man who has it. A theory of conscience that shies away from ontology, and in particular from a theory of the nature of man, is empty; it is a parlor game in which one can indulge as long as the surrounding society contains enough Christian substances to make at least the worst sort of good consciences socially ineffective; but even under such favorable conditions (as they still exist in England) this nihilistic theory of conscience contributes to the intellectual and moral confusion that paves the way for the best of all consciences, viz., that of the totalitarian killers. All men are equal, to be sure, or they would not be individuals of one species; but sometimes it is forgotten that the point in which they most certainly are equal is their capacity for evil. Enough of that evil is rampant; and this is no time to pat the viciously ignorant on the back for being "sincere," or abiding by their "conscience." This is a time for the philosopher to be aware of his authority, and to assert it, even if that brings him into conflict with an environment infested by dubious ideologies and political theologies—so that the word of Marcus Aurelius will apply to him: "The philosopher—the priest and servant of the gods."

3

Necessary Moral Bases for
Communication in a Democracy

Communication between human beings is the *modus procedendi* through which a society exists. The fact that the "Moral Bases for Communication in a Democracy" are in question at all, and with good reason can be made the topic of a lecture, indicates the graveness of moral confusion in our time. For if we feel the urge to discuss communications in contemporary democracy, we betray our awareness that something is problematic about our procedures of communication. Moreover, with regard to the substance of society, it is supposed to be always moral. And if we raise the question of morality in connection with our democracy, we betray the awareness that something is wrong with the moral substance that flows through the channels of communication. If, finally, we connect the two problems of moral substance and procedure of communication, as the title of this lecture does, we suggest that certain procedures of communication in our time are unfit for the achievement of moral purpose, or even destructive of morality.

The area of problems opened by these initial reflections is large— much too large to be covered in so brief a form. I shall attempt no more than passing glances at some of the great topics.

We may begin with the distinction of three meanings in which the term *communication* is used in the debate on the subject. One can, first, distinguish communication in the *substantive* sense, that is, communication that has its purpose in the unfolding and building of personality. In a second usage, communication is a technique for

This essay was originally published in *Problems of Communication in a Pluralistic Society* (Milwaukee: Marquette University Press, 1956) and is reprinted here by kind permission of Marquette University Press.

inducing people to behave in such a manner that their behavior will agree with the communicator's purposes, as for instance political or commercial purposes. This second type may be called *pragmatic* communication. A third meaning appears when the term is used in connection with media of mass communication, such as film, radio, or television. While such media are very energetically used for the advancement of pragmatic purposes, and while occasionally a valiant attempt is made to use them for the substantive building of personality, their primary function, on the fulfillment of which rests their mass use, is that of an *intoxicant*. We shall speak, therefore, of the substantive, pragmatic, and intoxicant functions of communication.

A few words of elaboration will suggest the relevance of the three types of communication to our topic:

(1) Communication in the substantive sense is one of the great problems of the *philosophia perennis*. In the dialogues of Plato it is the pervasive problem of education through persuasion. You will remember the "follow my persuasion" as the standard formula by which Socrates tries to induce other men to enter into his orbit of the love of the *sophon*, to restore the order of their souls by entering into the paradigmatic order of the Socratic soul, to establish the existential community with Socrates by sharing in common with him his desire for the divine *Agathon*. Communication in this sense is the process in which the substantive order of a community is created and maintained. To suggest the permanence of the problem it will be sufficient to recall the central position that it has in our own time in the philosophy of Karl Jaspers. Among the contemporary philosophers he has done perhaps more than anybody else to clarify the relevance of existential communication for the order of man and society. It will not be necessary to supplement the instances of classic and modern philosophy with Christian examples—you know better than I do what the cure of souls through the Spirit means for the order of a Christian community.

(2) Communication in the pragmatic sense has the purpose of inducing in the human target a state of mind that will result in behavior in conformity with the communicator's intention. The wide field of propaganda, advertising, and psychological management furnishes the instances for this type. If substantive communication be understood as the concern with building the order of the soul, pragmatic communication can be set off as a concern with the

order of behavior and action, regardless of the question whether the behavior or action will affect the substantive order positively or negatively. Pragmatic communication shall be understood as an autonomous concern with fitting another man's behavior as a means into the realization of one's own project. Such indifference toward the higher good of the substantive order does not of necessity mean that the purposes of pragmatic communication are dubious. On the contrary, the functioning of a modern industrial democracy is largely dependent on the effectiveness of well-devised and well-conducted political and commercial propaganda.

Nevertheless, when pragmatic communication has become a highly organized business with vested interests, as it has in our society, the question of its legitimacy in the light of substantive order must in the practice of its conduct remain in suspense. All too often the result will be that men at large are induced to vote for a candidate for whom they would never vote without the psychological pressures of a campaign, or to buy a piece of industrial junk that they never would buy if their good sense had not been destroyed by skillful advertising. The pragmatic success may seriously damage the substance inasmuch as the personal organization of a man's life will disintegrate under the constant stimulation of anxieties and passions through the pragmatic propaganda aimed at him in our society, while the agents of communication find themselves in the morally dubious position of destroyers of their fellowman's order. And, finally, it must be considered that the vastness of our modern industrial society, the infinite complexity of its structure, makes it difficult, if not impossible, to trace in detail the positive or negative effects that the types of behavior induced by the concentrated fire of pragmatic communication have on the substance of order. The autonomy of the pragmatic purpose has indeed become an automatism that moves by the momentum of power and profit. Moreover, the obscurity of coordination between pragmatic and substantive order, which to a large extent is inevitable in the order of magnitude of a modern society, tends to acquire a legitimacy of its own. The fact that questions concerning the coordination have frequently to remain without answers tends to be transformed into the postulate that no questions must be asked. A moral vacuum expands around the unquestioned automatism.

(3) Communication as an intoxicant belongs among the phenomena that Pascal has treated under the title of *divertissements*. In

49

his *Pensées*, Pascal has explored the anxiety of life, the *noirceur*, the blackness that pervades the soul, the emptiness that results in boredom and ultimately in despair, when the soul is not ordered by faith. In order to escape these states of the soul, man develops the *divertissements*—the diversions that intend to overcome emptiness through activity. The specific diversions treated by Pascal, the social activities of the court society of the seventeenth century, are not our concern. The problem, however, is still the same today when industrial instruments have been developed for overcoming the anxiety and boredom of a mass society. A goodly bulk of movie-going, listening to radio, and, more recently, looking at television has the character of a *divertissement* in the sense of Pascal, of an intoxicating activity that will drown the anxiety of an empty life.

The brief survey of the types of communication, and especially of the last one, leads directly to the center of our problem, that is, to the moral basis of communication in contemporary society. The development of communication as an industry for pragmatic and intoxicant purposes is certainly a symptom of moral crisis—a fact that is only obscured by the social code neither to question the moral integrity of pragmatic pressures nor to let the character of intoxicating communication become topical. In violation of this code it must be said that commercial pressure, which ensures a steady stream of production and sales by psychological enforcement of a material at the expense of a cultural standard of living, is conduct of dubious morality; and that it is an open question whether intoxication through television is not more destructive of personality than intoxication through alcohol. Moreover, the mere existence of communication as a mass industry is an important index of the degree of spiritual and moral disintegration, for the mass media have not created the situation in which they function successfully—although certainly they do nothing to improve it. Their success is practically a quantitative gauge of the state of society, for men in the mass would not use the media for purposes of intoxication unless they were in need of it. And this state of things, finally, is of specific importance in a democracy, because the human beings whose personality is formed, or rather deformed, by the mass media of communication are the voters whose wishes must be satisfied by the elected representatives. Hence, the disturbances of this kind have an impact on the functioning of contemporary democracy, which they did not have in an absolute monarchy of the seventeenth century and which they do not have in the same measure in a Soviet dictatorship.

The mass media of communication in the widest sense, including the previously mentioned types as well as the various products of the press, can flourish in a state of disintegration, but they have not created it. The indifference to the implications of their functioning (hardly affected by the worries that have induced the organizers of this meeting to choose the present topic), the taboos on their appropriate characterization, and even the defense, under the cant of "freedom," of their destructive effects, are deeply rooted in what we call, with a certain pride, the "pluralistic" nature of our society. As "pluralistic" we understand a society in which the formation of opinion is left, through the use of various means of communication, to private initiative, as distinguished from a "unitary" society, in which mass opinions are formed through various types of governmental action. The pluralistic society is supposed to be the type that facilitates the peaceful struggle of opinions, with truth prevailing in the end (although this end seems to be always just around the corner), while a unitary society quite obviously is a bad thing.

The distinction between the two types of society is so highly esteemed that undoubtedly it must have some merit. Nevertheless, it will hardly do justice to the concrete structure of pluralistic societies, as represented by the national states of Western civilization. The struggle of opinions for mastery over the minds of men is, in historical concreteness, not peaceful at all. It is so little peaceful that, in fact, the periods of peace are no more than interludes in the bloody war of opinions that has racked the Western world now for more than four hundred years and is still going on all around us.

I shall now turn to the second topic of this lecture, to the actual structure of opinion in contemporary society, to that pluralism of opinion that supposedly is the guaranty of peaceful advances toward truth. The contemporary structure is the result of the waves of political movements that have rolled off since the Reformation. In these waves a certain pattern can be discerned. A movement like the Reformation was countered by the society, against which it was directed, by organized resistance, by a "counter-Reformation." The clash between the opposing camps brought the eight civil wars in France in the sixteenth century, the Thirty Years War in the seventeenth century, and the English Revolution. And the centuries of war were followed by the great peace settlements of Westphalia in 1648 and Utrecht in 1713. This pattern of (1) movement, (2) countermovement, (3) wars, and (4) peace settlement, now, repeated itself in the next great wave, beginning with the French Revolution. The terminology, to be sure, changed in accordance with the secularist complexion of this second wave. The "revolution" (the term came into use on this occasion) was countered by "reaction," "conservatism," and "counter-revolution." But the clash between revolutionary forces and the conservative alliance again resulted in the period of the great wars that came to their conclusion with the Congress of Vienna (1815). At present we are in the middle of the third wave that began, in the nineteenth century, with the movement of Communism. In the measure in which the nature and success of this third movement became more distinct, the countermovement crystallized and began to acquire such self-designations as "liberalism" or the "free world." The wars between the two camps, cold and not so cold, are still going on, and a peace settlement is not yet in sight. The pattern just described certainly characterizes the successive waves of movements, but concretely it is disturbed by additional factors. The concept of the pattern fits perfectly only the first wave, that of the Reformation. In the second wave, beginning with the French Revolution, the pattern is complicated by the entrance of Russia into world politics. And in the third wave, the phases of the pattern are seriously disturbed through complications arising from within and from outside Western civilization. From the inside, the problem of a National Socialist Germany blurs the alignments of the opposing camps; again from the inside, the complexion of the alliance changes profoundly through the appearance of the United States as a world power; and from the outside, it is again the growth of Russia to a new order of magnitude that complicates the simplicity that the pattern had on the occasion of the first wave.

The waves of the movements are not an affair of ancient history, for every one of them has left its sediment of intellectual and political positions in the texture of contemporary civilization. In a sense, all of these waves "coexist" today; their sedimented positions are alive, and the struggle between the movements and countermovements is still going on in our time. What we call the struggle of opinions in our "pluralistic" society is concretely the war of the movements that reaches into our present. The moral climate of the age, the problem of communications in our democracy, can be understood only if we penetrate beyond the euphemistic assumption of a rational debate, conducted among searchers for truth with peaceful intentions, to the blood and stench of the war that is conducted now for four-and-a-half centuries, with no end visible. Especially is such penetration necessary if we want to understand the otherwise confusing shifts of alliances—so confusing indeed that many a political intellectual has come to grief because he did not catch up in time with the game that was played. For as the waves of movement succeed one another, former enemies become friends when faced by a newly arising, common danger; and even the new enemy will join the ranks of the established powers, when the next threat raises its head. The bitter foes of the Reformation and counter-Reformation discovered, underneath their Protestantism and Catholicism, a common Christianity, when the French Revolution faced them with the cult of reason. And with the rise of Communism, not only Catholics and Protestants could cooperate in Christian-Democratic parties, but even secularist liberals could discover the ground they had in common with Christians. This pattern of the realignments, however, suffers from the same disturbances as the pattern of the movements itself. Under the pressure of the National Socialist danger, the enemies of the third wave were drawn together in a common front, through the Popular Front policy inaugurated by Stalin in 1934 and continued into the Resistance movements of the Second World War. And while this unnatural alliance broke apart with the end of the National Socialist danger, it has left in its wake the struggle for the soul of large sectors of Western democracies, which expresses itself, especially in France and Italy, in the discrepancy between a stagnant, if not decreasing, membership of the Communist Party and the strength of the Communist vote.

These are the hard facts concerning the texture of opinion in contemporary democratic societies. We are not dealing with human beings who hold this or that opinion as individuals, but with Christians and secularists; not with Christians, but with Catholics and Protestants; not with plain liberals, but with Christian and secular liberals; not with plain secular liberals, but with old-style liberals of the free-enterprise type and modern liberals of the socialist type; and so forth. This rich diversification of socially entrenched and violently vociferous opinion is what we call our pluralistic

53

society. It has received its structure through wars, and these wars are still going on. The genteel picture of a search for truth in which humankind is engaged with the means of peaceful persuasion, in dignified communication and correction of opinions, is utterly at variance with the facts. And at the center of this serious situation, in which differences of opinion lead to war rather than to peaceful understanding, we find our problem of communication.

Communication in the substantive sense, in the sense of the Platonic persuasion, is concerned with the right order of the human psyche. The order of the soul is dependent—if we may now use the Augustinian terminology—on the *amor Dei;* it will be disturbed when the *amor sui,* the love of self, prevails against the love of God. The movements, now, of which I have spoken are a phenomenon of world-historic importance in that they are the revolt of Western society against God. This revolt has expressed itself in three great symbolic acts: (1) in the removal of the papacy as the representative of divine order from the public scene of the Western world; (2) in regicide; and (3) in deicide.

The removal of the papacy from its place in the public order of the Western world is the symbolic result of the first wave of the movement. When the treaties of Munster and Osnabruck were negotiated, the curia was not admitted, although the redistribution and secularization of ecclesiastical principalities were an important item on the agenda. The protests of the curia did not even receive an answer. With 1648, the papacy disappeared from the diplomatic scene of European order. The anti-papalism that became manifest on this occasion had considerable consequences in the area of communications inasmuch as Milton wanted to reserve the freedom of the press in England to Protestant opinion, while Locke excluded Catholics explicitly from tolerance in the English Commonwealth. The political disabilities of Catholics continued in England into the nineteenth century; and the social disabilities continue in the Anglo-Saxon countries to this day.

While the removal of the papacy from the public order of the West has hardly been recognized as the first of the great acts of revolt, the connection between regicide and deicide as symbolic acts of the revolt against God is well understood. I beg you to refer to an excellent, recent study on the subject, to Albert Camus' *L'Homme révolté.* The execution of Charles I was not an outburst of republicanism against a tyrant, but the attack on "divine kingship," on the king as the representative of transcendental order in the community, and his replacement as a source of authority by the community of saints in the Puritan sense. And for the meaning of the community of saints, again I beg you to refer to the literature on the subject, especially to Hooker and Hobbes. The decapitation of the king, then, was followed by the decapitation of God—in the cult of the French Revolution, in the declaration of the death of God in Hegel's *Phenomenology,* in the replacement of God by the superman through Marx and Nietzsche.

The symbolic acts of revolt could not be undertaken without apology, they could not make sense unless prepared by the growth of a new intellectual climate. And the terms of their justification have become the language symbols in the struggle of opinions in our pluralistic society. I must briefly dwell on this issue, for the morality of communication is intimately connected with the truth of its contents. Morality is inseparable from rationality of discourse— "rationality" understood in the substantive sense of truthfulness. If the language employed in communication is irrational, the morality of the communication itself will be impaired in the measure of its irrationality. From this infinite field of problems, I shall select for consideration the movement of ontological reduction with regard to the accepted source of order in man and society. By this movement is meant the transformation of our conception of society by moving the substance of order from the Logos, through the levels of the ontological hierarchy, down to organic substances and drives. ·

In the classic and Christian conceptions of society, the substance of order is understood to consist in the *homonoia* of its members. Men are members of society insofar as they participate either in the *Nous* in the classical sense, or in the *Logos* in the Christian sense. This conception of social order was predominant well into the seventeenth century. Only then, in the *Leviathan,* Hobbes eliminated the divine *summum bonum* from the hierarchy of being; and since with the *summum bonum* the rationality of order had disappeared, he dramatically introduced the *summum malum,* the fear of death, a passion, as the new force that would inject reason into the order of society. The issue has never been restated with such clarity as on this occasion of its first appearance in Hobbes. By the eighteenth century, the new situation of a society without the order of a divine *summum bonum* is already taken for granted; and the search for ontological substitutes of order, only half-conscious of the implications of the enterprise, is well under way. The main phases of the search are well known. The Age of Reason has received its name, not because it was particularly reasonable, but because the thinkers of the eighteenth century believed to have found in Reason, capitalized, the substitute for divine order. The construction was unstable, because human reason in the immanentist sense, that is, a reason without participation in the *ratio aeterna*, is devoid of ordering substance. One could talk about reason, and proclaim that certain truths were self-evident, as long as the contents of order still found social acceptance by the momentum of tradition; but the question of validity could not be deferred forever. In the course of the attempts to find a more solid basis for the new immanentist creed, the reason that had been voided of substance was endowed with the meaning of rationality in the pragmatic sense of adequate coordination of means and ends. The restriction of the meaning of reason, however, made only more painfully clear the vacuum created by the abolition of the highest good as the source of rational order. Where should the indefinite chain of means and ends in action find its anchorage, when the Logos of order had disappeared? Utilitarianism seemed to have found an answer in the self-interest of man who would see to it that his actions were useful to him, not harmful. But the conception of order through the greatest good of the greatest number, or through a balance of enlightened self-interest, or through the more specific balance achieved by the pursuit of economic profit, proved at variance with the disorder and human suffering created concretely in the societies that experienced the beginnings of the Industrial Revolution. Since the love of God was taboo, Comte invented the autonomous love of man, and coined for this newly discovered sentiment the term *altruism*. The self-interest of man, which now acquired the connotation of egotism, could be supplemented by the new altruism as a stabilizing force of order in the utilitarianism of a John Stuart Mill. The attempt to substitute the useful for reason was followed by further steps of ontological descent—to the technological forces of production with Marx, to the racial structure of human groups with Gobineau and his successors, and finally to biological drives in depth psychology. The substance of order, thus, moved down in the ontological scale from God, through reason, pragmatic intellect, usefulness, production forces, and racial determinants, to biological drives.

This sliding down of the substance of order over the ranks of the ontological hierarchy holds as much interest for the historian as it does for the philosopher. For from the eighteenth century to the present, the ontological reduction has been completed. The range of theoretical possibilities to find substitutes for the *summum bonum* is, on principle, exhausted. This observation does not imply that new variants of the earlier steps of reduction cannot be developed and find temporary acceptance; nor does it suggest that the firmly entrenched earlier reductions will lose their power as social creeds in the near future. Nevertheless, the fact that the reduction has run its whole gamut must not be belittled. This fact is for the social scientist the most important index that "modernity" has run its course.

I shall now draw some conclusions from the brief sketch of selected topics.

Morality is inseparable from rationality. The connection will be clarified by the definition of *conscience* given by Étienne Gilson: Conscience is the act of judgment by which we approve or disapprove our actions in the light of rational moral principles. In order to act rationally, a man must know who he is, in what kind of a world he lives, and what his station is in the order of being. A man who is confused about the essentials of his existence is incapable of rational action; and if he is incapable of rational action, he is incapable of moral action.

If "opinion" is characterized by the conceptions of the nature of man and the order of society that have arisen in the course of the ontological reduction, the knowledge of the essentials of existence is badly disturbed. And if the disturbances of this type determine the climate of opinion, as they do in our "pluralistic" society, the opinions communicated are irrational, while the acts of communication are deficient in morality to the extent of their irrationality. Communication, even if it is substantive by intention, will be not formative but destructive of personality if the conception of order it communicates moves on one of the levels of the ontological reduction. Moreover, the type of pragmatic communication that we have distinguished acquires a new and sinister meaning in this situation, insofar as communication becomes *essentially* pragmatic when it moves on the level of substitute substance. It cannot function as persuasion in the Platonic sense at all, but only induce conformist states of mind and conforming behavior. And finally, since human nature, even under the attack of pragmatic communication, remains what it is, resistance to the purpose of the communicator must be expected from the resources of a soul that is essentially open toward God. Communication, once it has become essentially pragmatic, can no longer rely on the persuasiveness of the reason it has decapitated. In order to achieve his purpose, the pragmatic communicator must therefore rely on the arsenal of psychological tricks—*suppressio veri* and *suggestio falsi*, repetition, the "big lie," and so forth—to create the emotional diversions that will prevent his target from questioning the substantive authenticity of the communication. For this reason, essentially pragmatic communication is inevitably forced in the direction of intoxication.

4

Democracy in the New Europe

Today we celebrate the inauguration of our Academy for Political Education. You have heard the essentials about the motives and purposes of this founding, about the hopes we place in it, from an authoritative source. I ask you to follow me now briefly in some thoughts on the political situation in which the Academy is called upon to work.

We live in a free and democratic society, and we want to see that it remains free and democratic. But freedom and democracy is not something that can be guaranteed once and for all through installing a constitution. We had a democratic constitution before. But it was paralyzed in its functioning by a majority bloc from the right and left; and it was swept away by a force that did not arouse the resistance of an organized counterforce. Certainly, not all who contributed their conscientious share of enthusiasm and efforts to this catastrophe wanted the consequences. Only too often we heard them stammering: "That is not what we intended"—expecting one would pat them on the shoulder for the thought after the deed. But to the citizen of a democracy, the thought after the deed is not allowed; he must think beforehand, and he must know what he is doing. That sounds harsh—and it not only sounds so, it is harsh indeed. A democracy is no Cockaigne in which the peaceful citizen can pursue his affairs and enjoy the economic miracle; rather it is a state of daily, well-exercised, and habitual vigilance and discipline in the fundamental questions of political life. Democracy is possible

Translated from the German for this edition by Manuel Brieske, this text originally appeared in *Gesellschaft-Staat-Erziehung* 4, no. 7 (1959), as the published lecture delivered at the inauguration of the Bavarian Academy for Political Education, a bipartisan, publicly supported institution for scholarship and teaching in civic education in Munich.

only where civic virtue exists. And the first of virtues, without which all others lack a proper basis for action, is sound knowledge of the principles of social coexistence among free men in a free society.

But where do we find these principles? The catchwords of political life—to which also belong "democracy" and "freedom"—do not give them to us. Expressions that have become such clichés that a Soviet politician can use them as easily as a democrat require precise reflection about their meaning, that precisely in their name freedom and democracy not be destroyed. How does one break through the encrustation of propaganda-abuse to the essence of the matter again?

We can rediscover the meaning by recalling the grandiose expression that the belief in democracy found in the classical speech of its great statesman whose 150th birthday the Western world is celebrating this year [1959]—in Abraham Lincoln's *Gettysburg Address*. It was delivered in 1863 in the third year of the Civil War, which was about the abolition of slavery. It was proclaimed on the battlefield of Gettysburg in honor of the men who were killed in action so that the founding of a people in free humane existence would not be shattered. And when one now hears Lincoln's peroration one should also remember that in this very building where we are gathered there is the Scholl Siblings Memorial.[1]

> We cannot dedicate—we cannot consecrate—we cannot hallow—this ground. The brave men, living and dead, who struggled here have consecrated it. . . . It is rather for us to be here dedicated to the great task remaining before us—that from these honored dead *we* take increased devotion to that cause for which *they* gave the last full measure of devotion—that we here highly resolve that these dead shall not have died in vain—that this nation, under God, shall have a new birth of freedom and that government *of the* people, *by the* people, *for the* people, shall not perish from the earth.[2]

Due to the *Gettysburg Address*, the formula of the "government *of the* people, *by the* people, *for the* people" has become so

---

1. Encouraged and supported by philosophy professor Kurt Huber, Sophie and Hans Scholl organized the student resistance movement *Weisse Rose* at the University of Munich. The White Rose gradually extended its activities (mainly the distribution of anti-Nazi leaflets calling for the reintroduction of democracy and personal freedom) to central Germany before the Scholls and other members were arrested by the Gestapo, Hitler's secret police. In a mock trial, Sophie and Hans Scholl were sentenced to death and executed February 22, 1943.—Trans.

2. Emphasis added by Voegelin.—Ed.

famous that its authorship is attributed to Lincoln. Today, we no longer sense its full gravity because we no longer remember the importance it had in the tradition in which Lincoln found himself and out of which he took it. Let us therefore recall its original, complete version. It is to be found in the prologue to Wycliffe's Bible translation of 1384, and it reads: "This Bible is for the Government of the people, by the people, and for the people." With this phrase by John Wycliffe, which has continued to live on in the Anglo-Saxon tradition up to today, the spiritual motif of Western democracy becomes visible to which there is no independent parallel outside the Western culture-sphere with its depth-dimension in the Judaeo-Christian tradition. The people that can govern by itself and for itself is not any people in an ethnic sense, not any people regardless of its cultural maturity (*Kulturstand*). It is the people that experienced its birth under God, that can also lose its life in this status, and that—remember Lincoln's address—necessitates a rebirth to be able to govern. The English reformers of the fourteenth to the eighteenth century, from Wycliffe to John Wesley, who were political as well as ecclesiastical reformers, achieved the essential for the democratization of the West when they took the life of the Christian community and of the community-constitution to be a model for the existence of citizens in a national society also in secular matters.

This attempt has not occurred without severe conflicts and derailments. I spoke earlier of the *Judaeo*-Christian tradition deliberately. For the attempt to transform the community into a nation or—since the reforming community does not encompass the nation—to coerce the nation into the limits of the community could not follow the Christian tradition in the narrow sense with its distinction between spiritual and secular authority. Although the reformers were Christians, their political dream as inspired by their study of the Bible was the theopolity of Israel: the idea of God's chosen people and its rulers under God and His law. The enterprise of the dreamers (*Träumer*) in Israel (as they are called in the Anglo-Saxon tradition) was bound to lead to the great conflicts with the cultural ethos (*Kulturgehalten*) of the English nation climaxing in the emigrations, civil wars, and persecutions of the seventeenth century. Some of what had acute relevance then is forgotten today— for instance, the projects to make the legislation of Moses the civic law of England instead of the common law. Other occurrences had world-historical consequences, such as the emigration of Puritan communities to America to organize themselves as God's people in the new Canaan according to the biblical model. Out of the heroic struggles for the right political form of existence of a Christian people emerged, at the end of the seventeenth century, the great idea of civil government, namely, the idea that a national community of Christians should not make its ecclesiastical-organizational and dogmatic differences the object of political struggles and that there would be a specific civil sphere of life to which political authority is limited by its legal organization.

It is such civil government that we call democracy. We must recognize its characteristics if we want to know which conditions it is subject to in its functioning; which conditions we are to establish for it to function; and where the struggle for democracy is to begin if its functioning-conditions are threatened.

The idea of the civil government demands that organized authority be limited to the protection of a sphere of life, understood as being "natural," of free, independent men. To this "natural" sphere belong the cardinal goods of life, freedom, and property. Beyond the protection of these goods of the natural sphere by means of civil and criminal law, organized authority is to be employed only for the protection of the society as a whole against external enemies. The life-spheres of reason and of spirit in principle have to remain outside the civil sphere affected by power and authority. The spiritual sphere is governed by freedom of belief and freedom of consciousness; the sphere of reason, by freedom of thought and freedom of discussion.

The separation of the spheres of life into political and nonpolitical, however, is possible only if the members of the society are prepared not to turn the questions of spirit and reason into a political issue, only if there are no groups in society that want to take advantage of the authority of the state to impose their beliefs and ideas upon their fellow citizens. A democracy is therefore *in principle not tolerant;* it can be tolerant only toward those who are willing to submit to the conditions of the civil government.

In which direction democracy is to be intolerant depends on the historic circumstances. At the end of the seventeenth century, Catholicism and Puritanism were regarded as the enemies of the civil government. And Locke's *Two Treatises of Government* were directed against the "ecclesiastical polity" of the Elizabethan era.

In our time, the gnostic mass movements—especially National Socialism and Communism—are the enemies of democracy. On no account should democracy be understood as that regime that leaves the enemies of democracy the freedom to organize its overthrow. As Justice Robert Jackson, in a U.S. Supreme Court decision, formulated the principle: The Bill of Rights is not a suicide pact.[3]

This formulation was directed against Communism. Let us turn to casuistry for a moment—for, in the short history of the Federal Republic, we had to face such a question before, on the occasion of the banning of the Communist Party. The ban was, according to the principle of civil government, generally correct—besides, it was constitutionally covered. One could only raise the reservation about the decision that the Communist Party was not politically relevant enough to deserve a ban; that no interest in need of protection existed; that democracy was not sufficiently jeopardized to warrant the precedent of a ban. For, of course, we have to be aware of the fact that men are men indeed; that in every society of a certain extent there is a so-called *lunatic fringe*; and that one should not throw the pathos of democracy into the scale every time a fool or fanatic cannot, by any means, hold back something anti-democratic. Tolerance and intolerance of democracy require cautious casuistry.

Beyond all doubt is the case when unmistakable anti-democratic parties reach a strength that renders the functioning of the parliamentary system impossible, as was the case in the Weimar Republic. On the democratic parties of the 1920s rests the severe guilt that they, due to a lack of democratic knowledge and resoluteness, allowed the anti-democratic parties at the left and the right initially to gain strength illegally without banning them; and as a ban was scarcely possible to issue without risking civil war, they did not risk civil war; that they did not recognize the point where the coziness of the national community (*Volksgemeinschaft*) in an ethnic sense ends and the seriousness of a people in a civic sense has to assume its rights. This civil war would have been bitter but

---

3. Voegelin originally mis-spoke by attributing this sentiment to Associate Justice Frank Murphy. In *Terminiello v. City of Chicago*, 337 U.S. 1, 37 (1949), Associate Justice Robert H. Jackson, in a dissenting opinion, stated, "There is a danger that, if the Court does not temper its doctrinaire logic with a little practical wisdom, it will convert the constitutional Bill of Rights into a suicide pact." Cf. Eric Voegelin, *The New Science of Politics: An Introduction* (Chicago: University of Chicago Press, 1952), 144, where the matter is correctly attributed.—Trans.

certainly not as bitter as the alien rule (*Fremdherrschaft*) of the National Socialist sectarian movement, as World War Two and its consequences.

A remarkable provisional solution was found recently for the problem of a parliamentary paralysis through the Communist Party in France with the new de Gaulle constitution. By changing proportional suffrage to a single-member-constituency system (with the need for election coalitions), as well as by some constituency geometry, the parliamentary representation of the Communist Party has been forcefully reduced to a minimum. Against the doubts raised here, too (that one should not play too much with the election law so that manipulation not become a habit with every change in government), there was utilized in this case the argument of expedience with reference to the election law. The election law, however, is not an autonomous sphere with its own laws of justice. It does not have the purpose of giving every ethnic group with special interests or a distinctive *weltanschauung* the opportunity to disturb the political business of the nation through its representatives in parliament. The election law is an instrument for giving *large* parties the opportunity to conduct such business with workable parliamentary majorities on the basis of the people's mandate.

Since questions of general suffrage are all too often discussed dogmatically and not pragmatically (as they ought to be treated), perhaps I should recall the procedure of American presidential elections. The two-tier suffrage is so constituted that in a two-party system a very small majority of the popular vote can translate into a very large majority of the electoral vote. And if a party split occurs so that three candidates run for office, then it can even happen that the candidate with only a plurality of the popular vote again gains an overwhelming majority of the electoral vote, as was the case in Woodrow Wilson's election. This resonance effect, incorporated into the suffrage and capable of turning a minority candidate into a plebiscite leader of a people, provided the man has the necessary stature, is not at all regarded as unjust but as one of the great advantages of this electoral system. It is in general not that important for the people which party wins the election campaign if surprises from neither one (in a negative or positive sense) are to be expected. Thus, so long as the civil government as such is stable, suffrage manipulations of this kind are not at all a contemptible means for strengthening the ruling authority in a democratic state.

The idea of civil government, its theory and its constitutional practice, was created in England; the American republic of 1789 was founded on its principles; then, in the course of the nineteenth century, the continental European nations developed their constitutions in light of this model. And although this model in concrete cases, through ideological movements of the last century that have not yet faded away, is today still jeopardized in many ways, we can nonetheless maintain that civil government has become the specifically Western form of political order.

With this ascertainment the issue is nevertheless not yet settled. To the contrary, it opens up the perspective toward the future of government and the tasks still ahead of us. For democracy has been developed within nation states as the political organization of the nation, and today we face the task of activating democracy for the organization of Europe and, beyond that, for the Western world encompassing also America and the British Commonwealth. From this task arises an intensification of duties for citizens of a civil government in each of the Western peoples. For as long as the nation states were relatively closed communities, the vicissitudes of their constitutional history could be regarded as their internal matters—even though, at that time too, only to a certain degree—so long as the events did not affect the interests of the other peoples. The organization of the new Europe, which is in being, requires, nonetheless, reliable continuous cooperation among the governments; and successful cooperation is impossible if it permanently stands in the shadow of some kind of ideological nonsense (*Ideologieunfug*) in one of the partner states. The stability of civil government within the European nations, in every single one, has become the condition for the survival of all of them. The iron suppression of ideological nonsense is today the condition for bare existence.

The federative joining together of the European states system has become a necessity beyond discussion because over the last 150 years the scale of societies necessary for an independent, free existence has changed significantly. Such a world historical change in scale did not occur today for the first time: When the Mediterranean empires of antiquity were founded—the Persian, the Macedonian, the Roman—the time of the Greek polis had expired; when in the fifteenth century the Western nation states were organized the end of the freedom of the Italian city-states had come; and now the time for the Western nation states has run out.

Although the problem is not a new one, it is only today that it, in the last hour, is being tackled seriously. Already Napoleon, in 1802, realized that: "There are only two nations [in the world]—Russia and the Occident."[4] His vision of a European empire under French hegemony was motivated by the concern for the future that he saw determined by powers the size of Russia. Up until the founding of the German Reich in 1871 the journalistic debate over the problem had not come to a rest; and Bismarck, too, remained conscious of the constantly precarious existence of his founding in Russia's shadow. Only at the turn of the century, at the time of the vigorous outburst of German population growth and industrialization, could this ominous shadow be forgotten, although it continued to fall across Europe, as events have shown. In Hitler's policy again, as in Napoleon's, the concern about scale in relation to Russia is to be found as a motif. This motif gave Churchill grounds for fear when the National Socialist armies had conquered France: He considered it possible that Hitler could have a fit of political intelligence and treat the French respectably so as to win their cooperation in a federative continental European empire. His fears were groundless. The failure of these two great attempts, the Napoleonic and the Hitlerian, ought to remind us that a unification of Europe is linked to the style of Western political form grown over the centuries, i.e., to the style of civil government. A unification cannot be brought about by nationalist and ideological imperialism. Today, we attempt it for the third time, in the federative form in which alone it can succeed, with the backing of the American military and economic power for the transition period. If this attempt does not succeed this time, or if it experiences such serious delays and disturbances that the American backing is withdrawn as being hopeless and too expensive, then it requires no particular prophetical skill to predict the end of a free European civilizational society.

The problem of scale developed a dangerous sharpness, which it did not have a hundred years ago, through the evolution of industrial technology and, subsequently, through the transformation of the old agrarian societies into industrial societies. The respective stage of industrial technology requires for its optimal utilization by a society a certain size of territory and population, of capital and market. We all know, and I need not explain it, that the European

4. Cf. Voegelin, *New Science of Politics*, 116.—Ed.

nation states are too small in all these respects to allow for optimal utilization of the technological state. A modern economic constitution necessitates the scale of the American or Russian society. A European society would also belong to this scale. Since, furthermore, the power potential of an industrial society increases not by linear ratio to its size but by a multiple toward the smaller society, European unification has become by virtue of the state of technological development a power-political necessity.

These harsh necessities, however, have a pleasant aspect as well with regard to the future of democracy. Concluding, let me dwell on this positive side for a moment.

The civil government as a permanent stable government is only possible in a society of free and independent people. And to man's freedom belongs a material basis, which allows him sufficient freedom of movement, thought, and education, to participate in public life—and above all to experience public life as something that concerns him personally. I fall back upon Jefferson's vision of the American democracy to elucidate the problem.

Jefferson dreamt of an agrarian-economic America. The majority of the citizens were to be farmers on free soil. Through family work with only minor help from land-laborers, small communities were to obtain through good management everything necessary for their lives. In rural county-cities a population of artisans, small merchants, teachers, doctors, and jurists were to take care of further needs of this modest society. The development of industry, of metropolises, and of an urban proletariat were to be avoided at any cost, and for this Jefferson pictured as a deterrent the young industrial cities of England. America was to become a real republic, a society of modestly living but sincere and free citizens. This dream did not become reality and nobody regrets that today, but it needs to be recalled so as to point out the concern for the vision of the free society.

The development of technology and industry caused, as its first consequence, the emergence of the industrial proletariat Marx was able to observe in England. The possibilities of a free society seemed to be submerged by the revolutionary inflammable material that accumulated in working-class neighborhoods of the large cities. Social welfare legislation of the late nineteenth and the twentieth century addressed the immediate danger by creating a modest security status for the laborers, but the danger still continues to smolder today. Only the last half-century and, above all, the last twenty years have shown a new possibility for the solution of the social problems in the industrial society. The constant and considerable increase in labor productivity due to technological development (approximately 3 to 5 percent annually) has increased labor income in such a way that there remains an income surplus beyond the necessities of daily life—in America called nonessential income—which facilitates for everybody the setting aside of considerable savings reserves and even the beginning of a moderate creation of wealth through investment. During the recent American recession, accompanied by a very alarming increase in unemployment, consumer goods sales, for the first time in the history of economic crises, did not fall off remarkably; apparently the reserves are already high enough so that temporary unemployment no longer affects the necessities of life.

But with this the social problem of the industrial society has changed radically. The standard of living for all is so high and so well secured that nobody has to wage class-struggles to extract from an inadequate supply of goods the necessities for oneself and one's family as the subsistence level. The struggle-front (*Kampffront*) has shifted from the conflict of interests between laborers and entrepreneurs, from poor and rich, to the community of interests in exploiting technological productivity. And this radical shift, which had been quantitatively long in preparation, became qualitatively apparent only during the last twenty years. When I went to America in 1938 nonessential income, the phenomenon that today puzzles economists, sociologists, and politicians, did not exist. On this new productivity-basis, it has come within the reach of the possible and even become reality what Jefferson foresaw as possible only under the conditions of an old-fashioned agrarian economy: the material security for all, but with a far higher level of consumer and capital goods (*Güterausstattung*) within modern industrial society. The possibility of a civil government in an industrial society can, based upon the American experience, be considered as assured.

What was possible in America is also possible in a united Europe, if we are willing and prepared to adapt to the conditions of a large-scale industrial society. And some adaptation will indeed be necessary. For increase of productivity means developing new technological processes and rendering old ones obsolete. Factories, mines, and whole industries that had become unproductive need to

68

be closed down to make room for more productive ones. A certain percentage of temporary and structural unemployment, of changes in work place and place of residence, of retraining into new professions and skills, is the relentless concomitant of exploiting technological productivity for the common good. Europe's well-worn security psychology will have to make room for a new attitude of adaptability and flexibility as it has developed in America as a self-evident, free attitude and as it is being forced upon the population of the Soviet Union by the less pleasant method of coercion. Education for democracy in the new Europe, thus, will, in one essential part, have to consist of spelling out to the broad masses of the people the nature of industrial society and its conditions and of developing attitudes of mobility and adaptability.

I have now arrived at the end of my remarks. They could but sketch out the complex issue in broad outline. But one has probably noticed that great tasks are ahead of us requiring a lot of work and discipline until we reach the goal of a free, powerful, and secure Europe with a sound welfare basis for all. And one has probably also seen that the tasks are not hopeless. To the contrary, the goal is in reach of the younger generation among those gathered here. But the realization of these tasks requires all the help we can possibly muster. And such help is extended to us today by the Bavarian state and the founding of the Academy for Political Education. I wish the Academy and its director the best for the success of this undertaking.

5

Freedom and Responsibility in Economy and Democracy

You just heard a brilliant lecture on the virtues of the entrepreneur. Following the remarks about the virtues of the entrepreneur, I shall now add my reflections on the virtues of the citizen.

By *civic virtue* is meant the right behavior of man in political society; and this right behavior is possible only if it is grounded in sound knowledge. But Germany especially lacks sound knowledge of right behavior. What I am going to present to you concretely concerning this question stems from my experiences with students. They come from all over Germany; and even if they are perhaps not a cross-section of the whole German people, at least they are a cross-section of that part which, in upcoming years, will speak vociferously, which will act for better or worse, and will have an influence. I will attempt to give you some ideas about how things look for this representative cross-section; what difficulties emerge for education for democracy, for education for freedom and responsibility; and what difficulties students have in acquiring the knowledge they have to acquire to become democratic citizens.

The questions that concretely emerge may be divided into two groups. First, I will address the particularities of the historical-political situation in Germany: Why is it that installing democracy and educating for democracy is more difficult in Germany than elsewhere? Following this I shall, secondly, add reflections on misunderstandings that circulate among the younger generation as matters of principle. These reflections should be of significance

Translated from the German for this edition by Manuel Brieske, this article originally appeared in *Die Aussprache* 10 (1960) and is published here by kind permission of Arbeitsgemeinschaft Selfständiger Unternehemer e. V. (ASU) in Bonn.

even beyond the student generation, since a fair amount of what the young think and articulate they must have heard from the older generation.

I

But let us first look at the difficulties originating from the German historical-political situation.

German constitutional history is distinct from that of other Western nation-states above all in that it does not have the secular, sometimes centuries-old depth of Western democracies. There are no established, respected traditions which, for example, made it impossible even for a Roosevelt to fill the Supreme Court with justices in 1937 to bring about decisions more favorable to his New Deal legislation. Germany lacks institutions capable of arousing emotions of such depth because its constitutional history has been brief, only since 1871, and it has experienced those powerful disturbances with which you are familiar.

A further characteristic of the German situation leading to difficulties in education is the lack of a national revolution that would give the institutions, however resilient they may be, the emotional foundation of a great and final decision. Consider that the English institutions, despite all the reshaping they have experienced, go back to the Puritan revolution of the seventeenth century and the Glorious Revolution of 1688/89; that in France, where the situation is more complicated than in England, the Revolution of 1789 is the decisive factor in the ethos and pathos of democracy up to today; that the American Constitution goes back to the War of Independence and has its roots even further back in the English Puritan revolution. The great revolutions of the West lent their signature to the national institutions and their development for centuries. There are no comparable occurrences in German history. The German democracy on the national level has, with due respect for older regional developments, not been founded by a German revolution. Following lost wars, it was twice institutionalized by external pressure—now, the second time, with greater energy, resorting to more vigorous measures and shattering older resistances more thoroughly. But the internal revolution that should come along with the externally forced democratization and could give the institutions their emotional depth has not taken place yet. As I can tell from the younger people—i.e., from their majority, since there are also pleasant exceptions—the consciousness of being a citizen of a democracy lies emotionally on the surface, and the knowledge about domestic and foreign policy duties and the consequences of this status has hardly developed. The internal revolution still has to be made up for in Germany.

One important aspect of the German historical-political situation is particularly distinct from the Anglo-Saxon. Unlike in England, no Second Reformation took place in the eighteenth century in Germany. Through the spreading of the Methodist Church and its influence on other churches, the second reformation, initiated by the appearance of John Wesley in England, has also included America. This reformation became socially effective, with enormous consequences barely understood in their significance on the Continent. For in the critical period of the Industrial Revolution and the forming of the industrial proletariat, the second reformation carried Christendom in England to the people; it Christianized the working population and small middle class and thereby virtually immunized them against later ideological movements. A comparable phenomenon does not exist on the Continent, above all not in Germany. This absence in Germany resulted in the nineteenth century in the labor force's susceptibility to Marxism and in the twentieth century in the middle class's susceptibility to National Socialism and other secularist ideologies. The German labor force was almost as immunized by Marxism against later ideologies as the English and American ones against Marxism by the second reformation.

The lack of a second reformation in which Christendom might have seized the new social strata is aggravated by the development of Protestantism from the old Protestant orthodoxy in the eighteenth century to pietism and, in the nineteenth century, to liberalism. German pietism is a broadly enmeshing phenomenon; it has penetrated the people's character and shaped its form—even if not altogether pleasantly. Only one German pietistic trait need be emphasized here, namely, the propensity to insulate an existence understood as Christian from the profane, impure sphere of the political. This propensity can take very different forms, as, for example, the stance of the devout subject who leaves the business of politics to the secular authority; or the Kantian insistence that the only good in the world may be good will; or the educational-liberal idea that the cultural integrity of the individual may be jeopardized if a man becomes active as a political citizen; or the form of Christian or secular existentialism. On the whole, this propensity's result for Germany has been the destruction of the classical and Christian ethic as the power shaping the order of society. The destruction has even touched ethics as an organized body of knowledge. Thus in organizing the Institute for Political Science in Munich, I found out that there are no parallel student editions of Greek text and German translation for the classical standard works (of Aristotle's *Ethics* and *Politics*); we had to fall back on French and English parallel editions. There seems to be no need for these kinds of editions in Germany.

Among the most serious consequences of this withdrawal from the profane sphere is that the wrong attitude toward the problem of power has become characteristic of Germany. Friedrich Christoph Schlosser in the nineteenth century popularized the dictum "power is evil." This phrase became common property of the educated bourgeoisie; and its authority was intensified by Jakob Burckhardt's taking it up and further popularizing it. Let me juxtapose this formula with the phrase by Lord Acton that gained similar popularity in the Anglo-Saxon culture-sphere: "Power corrupts; absolute power corrupts absolutely." Here you encounter a radically different attitude. Power in a good sense is inevitable to create and maintain the order of society. Since at the same time power is a temptation for its holder, it must be subjected to control. We subject it to control by having an opposition in parliament that keeps a close eye on the government (what the opposition unfortunately does not always do to a desired extent), by placing the actions of legislation and administration under the right control, and by leaving open especially for the citizen a sphere of fundamental rights into which legislation and administration are not to intrude. Hence, power itself is morally neutral—one can use it for better or for worse—but it is always a temptation for man, which is, after all, in accordance with his nature. With that, however, we touch upon a question of anthropology that, again, is not clearly seen under the influence of the pietistic sectarianism in Germany. We touch upon the thesis, which is self-evident to classical and Christian ethics, that although man has the potential to become good, he can also miss this possible development—*every* man, politicians included—so there is no particular reason for being irritated when it comes out only too

73

often that politicians are men, too; *every* man is included, even the little man who at a safe distance from the temptations of power is filled with moral indignation at corrupt politicians (or what he takes to be their corruption). May I again remind you of an Anglo-Saxon politician, Alexander Hamilton, who in his cynical way formulated the phrase "Men are rascals." If we adopt this healthy cynicism, we will bear with equanimity those occasions when a holder of power possibly abuses it (since one has always to reckon with this human possibility), and we will be more keenly aware of our civic duty. For by participating in political life, we take care that this abuse does not exceed an inevitable minimum. In any case, the pietistic propensity to keep out of politics because power is evil and politics is a dirty business verges in a democracy on high treason.

To the complex of abstinence from politics, in which pietism has been a historically shaping influence, finally belongs also the German jurists' positivism, often decried and, since National Socialism, heavily accused. The jurist, so goes the charge, saw his professional duty in exactly knowing and in conscientiously applying positive law as it lay before him in the form of the statutes; as for the moral content of the law and the principles of justice, he regarded that as lying outside his scientific judgment; he was proud of having nothing to do with politics, especially with the jurisdiction of the nation, and of only moving correctly within the limits drawn by the law; he was the compliant tool of any regime, democratic as well as totalitarian. If the charge is brought in such unconditional generality, it certainly is unfair—one could draw up a respectable list of great jurists who do not fit into this scheme. But however one extends this list, for the jurist profession as a whole there is only too much truth to the charge. In the political life of the nation the German jurist indeed does not have the authoritative position of the English and American jurist, whose ethos is nurtured from the judicial creation of law (*richterliche Rechtsschöpfung*) of the common law tradition and whose legal articulation of fundamental justice goes back with uninterrupted continuity to the *jus divinum et naturale* of the Middle Ages. His authority has been severely damaged by the great codification movement since the eighteenth century, which gives precedence to codified law over the adjudicator of the law. But the injury was aggravated by a voluntary retreat from critical-philosophical penetration of the given legal code. Let us juxtapose this situation with the Anglo-Saxon idea of jurisprudence as an art of politics; let us remember that Woodrow Wilson said of the American Supreme Court that it was a permanent constitutional convention; and let us hope, since fundamental rights and an extensive catalog of other subjects have been made litigable, that, in due course, the *Bundesverfassungsgericht* gains something of the authoritative character of a permanent constitutional convention.

Finally, to the difficulties of the political-historical situation belongs the relationship to National Socialism. The difficulty ought perhaps to be seen in a slightly different way than you are used to. For in the foreground, there is always the complaint about the concealing of the past—and indeed it is astounding what the young people do not know about it, since apparently they have not been informed either in school or in conversations in the parental home and in their conversational circles. However, one can conceal the problem of National Socialism not only by veiling but perhaps even more thoroughly by an extensive, accusatory portraying of the atrocities. Both methods—and the second perhaps even better than the first—conceal the intellectual confusion that let National Socialism emerge and that essentially, even though subdued by disillusion, is today [i.e., 1960] still the same as in the 1920s. For the understanding of this thesis, consider a simple case: If the number of gangsters in Chicago and their crimes increases significantly, nobody would presume that this occurrence was to be traced back to a mystical mutation of the cosmos, but one would ask oneself what is wrong with the police and the courts. What kind of corruption exists in the bureaucracy that facilitates such an increase in crime? For there are gangsters and National Socialists as human types everywhere; in every numerically large society they will be found in a certain percentage. The problem lies in how to keep down people of this type socially; how to prevent them from coming to power in society. Totalitarian movements of the kind of National Socialism, however, cannot be kept down unless the society exhibits that automatic resistance that, due to clear knowledge of correct democratic behavior, immediately turns against the concrete instances of its violation. It does not diminish the dreadfulness of National Socialism if one realizes that those democrats who did not prevent its rise are to blame for its emergence, nationally and internationally. And the intellectual confusion by which totalitarian movements can become socially powerful still persists.

75

II

With this assessment I continue to the second part of my reflections, the misunderstandings regarding the principles of social order. What do the young people not know that they should know so as to be a citizen in a democracy, so as to resist automatically phenomena such as National Socialism?

Let me again start out from the concrete situation. When I came to Munich two years ago, students were surprised and disappointed that political science was more than a mere compilation of facts, and also more than the voice of uninformed conversations among people of various ideological convictions so popular in Germany; that indeed there was a political science, that it was founded by Plato and Aristotle in antiquity, and that the founding's principles were still valid today, even if much new insight has been added in the course of two thousand years. The basic information—that a science of how to act correctly did not exhaust itself in establishing correct statements regarding the assignment of means to ends, but that it also regarded the correctness of the ends; that there was a hierarchy of goods and a rational theory of the highest good: in brief, that a theory of politics presupposed a theory of the highest good—turned out to be particularly provoking.

What is so provoking about these elementary statements? What stirs up sentiments and resentments so deeply? Among the variety of arguments being advanced in discussion, two emotional centers of resistance are clearly discernable. The first is the resistance to the possibility that, in questions of human action, particularly political ones, one can distinguish objectively between right and wrong. Any attempt to acquire rational principles of action with a general binding nature is considered authoritarian and dictatorial. The second is the resistance to the transcendence-problematic that inevitably arises from the theory of the highest good, for the question of the highest good as the ultimate purpose of human existence is inseparable from the question of man's destiny. This question, in turn, is posed by life ending in death. With whatever philosophical or religious dogmatic formula one may take hold of the problem, human action in the world is thereby affected; it gains or loses its weight in that it is action toward ultimate purposefulness beyond life. One cannot discuss any basic question of politics—be it in the classical or Judaeo-Christian area, in the Islamic or Chinese, in the Indian or modern-ideological—without touching on the transcendence problematic. However, as soon as the transcendence question is raised in discussion, ideological rebellion erupts among the students. We face a situation where, to a substantial sector of the younger generation, the culture of classical and Christian ethics (and we do not have any other) is so radically ruined that a political-scientific education meets the greatest difficulties because the general cultural preconditions of scientific discussion do not exist and will first have to be re-established.

The destruction of culture by ideologies is an international phenomenon; it is no German monopoly. You may ask yourselves, therefore, why I emphasize the point so strongly in this context. This is because ideologies are much more dangerous to Germany than to other Western nation-states, since, as I mentioned earlier, in Germany the counterpoise of secular institutions founded by revolution is absent. Certainly, you will find the same assortment of ideologies in America, France, or England as in Germany, but it is an important difference whether the ideologies in the psychological make-up of the student are counterbalanced by the culture of institutions and political mores. It makes all the difference for an educator, as I can say from my experience, whether one can set a value relativist thinking by asking him if he would extend his relativism also to the Ten Commandments (in America), or whether he gapes stunned because the Ten Commandments are something he has never even thought of in connection with himself and his actions (in Germany).

From this vantage point of a lack of balance by the weight of tradition, mindlessness (*Denkunarten*), errors, dubious theories, etc., which could by themselves through a brief word of correction be moved out of the way, evolve into fantastic powers of disruption in the educational enterprise, because their removal requires on every occasion disproportionate time and effort at the expense of the original matter to be dealt with. A constant source of disruption is the stance, originating in the liberal era, that in fundamental questions about the nature of man and society everyone has a right to his own opinion; in defense of this position the constitution is even quoted that it guarantees everybody the right to freely express his opinion. Against this view it has to be laboriously explicated that, while the constitution protects the freedom of expression of opinion against state intervention, it does not furnish those opinions everybody holds with a truth-content nor does it lend them immunity from critique. It has to be further explicated in detail why and that opinions, views, convictions, ideologies, vantage points, *weltanschauungen*, etc., are a dubious possession. One has to fall back onto the beginnings of the history of philosophy to explain that all political science starts with the distinction between *doxa* and *episteme*, between opinion and knowledge. And finally, one can attempt to make the young person understand that in fundamental questions of existence he has no right of opinion, that instead he is a human being like anybody else and, therefore, he is obliged like anybody else to think and to speak the truth.

This is not to say that the young people were insincere, that they had no will for truth—they merely want truth to be identical with what appeals to them at the moment. With this I touch on the disastrous legacy of pietism, on the depraved habit of justifying various views and actions by referring to conscience and responsibility. Consider the enormity of this attitude. Conscience is man's obligation and ability to examine his actions and their consequences in accordance with rational moral principles. This examination requires, first, knowledge of the principles and, second, the exact understanding of the situation in which the action intrudes. And juxtapose these obligations with today's praxis in which the conscience and the responsibility are conveniently invoked when somebody has the intention to commit an unprincipled and irresponsible deed. The reference to the conscience has developed in our society into an order-destroying form of deception, into a demagogical trick with which the person concerned cuts off rational argument and wants to force respect for his irrational, subjective will.

In dealing with the students the situation is aggravated in that the destruction of rational ethics in Germany has eaten deep into academic life so that the students can refer to highly regarded authorities for sanctions of their opinions. I think here particularly of the disastrous effect that Max Weber's distinction between *Gesinnungsethik* (ethics of intention) and *Verantwortungsethik* (ethics of responsibility) still has today as the last word of wisdom in these questions. A *Gesinnungsethiker*, according to Max Weber, is a man who acts politically with reference to his convictions or intentions without regard for the consequences; a *Verantwortungsethiker* is a man who carefully considers the consequences of his actions and who is prepared to accept responsibility for the consequences. As types occurring in social reality these two figures are drawn exquisitely—we recognize that. As theoretical instruments for treating the questions of ethics and politics for which they were intended they are an embarrassing document reflecting the spiritual and intellectual low-point of the time when Max Weber conceived them. Today they probably have significance only as evidence of the radical destruction of public knowledge about fundamental questions of human and social order at the beginning of the century. This is because the *Gesinnungsethiker* is obviously the ideologue who has transformed the conscience into an order-destroying form of deception. And for the *Verantwortungsethiker*, to whom Weber's sympathies belong, it does not look much better. This is because, although he is fully aware of the consequences of his actions, he assumes he nevertheless has no rational guidelines for his actions; so too, his acts are unprincipled and irresponsible— unless the tradition in which he acts (and Max Weber surely thought of this) contains a residue of reason. However, it would be malicious impropriety to conjure up the shade of this ingenious man only to hold against him today that he could not cope with the problems of rational ethics during the miserable time in which he lived. With his type creations he still shows more significant achievements than any other thinker of his generation. I had to speak about him because today, although the intellectual-historical and political situation has changed radically, Weber's types are still used by highly regarded thinkers (who should know better in their capacity as professors) in discussing current political questions in apparent ignorance of classical political science. I wanted to make you aware of the terrible pressure of the "past Germany has not yet come to terms with"—in a different and far deeper sense than the conventional one—under which the young generation still lives today, and of the resulting resistance we have to overcome in educational efforts.

To conclude I would like to point out some factors that make themselves felt as continuing sources of disruption in seminar work. They stem from the ideological milieu in which the students grow up. Three factors should be emphasized as especially destructive of academic work: value relativism, existentialism, and neo-positivism.

Value relativism posits in its radical form that the social science researcher act within the values dominant in his society and time.

There are no objective criteria according to which problems could be recognized as relevant and no objective theoretical principles upon which to base a discussion of the problems. What is considered to be important according to the society's values should be treated as important. Relativism of this type, as you can imagine, enjoys great popularity, since it legitimizes any subjective political position as having the same right as every other, and it extends the right to each ideological apology to give itself airs as science. The relativist position would perhaps not be worth any attention if it only remained a matter of dispute among ideologues themselves. But value relativists transform their demand into the thesis that objective science is impossible and that any attempt to pursue it rests on a purely subjective evaluation of the ideology-enterprise. In short, value relativism is the expression and the instrument of the fanatic will to destroy reason and its order in all questions of man and society. Even though it is theoretically easy to deal with this variant of relativism, you certainly will be able to gauge the difficulties of conducting discussion when one has to introduce young people to a science whose possibility they not only deny but detest.

A second kind of nonsense strongly represented among students is existentialism. I say "nonsense" deliberately; for even if the analyses of existence by the existentialists are of utmost importance in terms of intellectual history, the implicit assumption is that thereby everything relevant has been said concerning an investigation of human nature. At the same time, the way classical and Christian ethics is ignored as if it never existed is a further philosophical scandal. Without thereby trying to decrease the positive achievements of existentialist thinkers in their limited field, the disastrous effect of reducing human nature to the problematic of man's existence, factually justified by nothing, needs to be stressed. Inspired by existentialists, this neutrality attitude, the attitude of resoluteness in openness toward being approaching us ("We are committed, we just don't know to what," it has been ironized), seriously disturbs the willingness to get involved in the particular factual problems of politics.

And, finally, neo-positivism should be considered as a social science trend with several subvariants, under whose title empiricism narrows down the research area of political science to subjects that are quantitatively accessible. This phenomenon is well known.

There is no objection to these methods and their application—even if, in the face of numerous individual investigations, the question arises of what value the accumulated material so flawlessly ascertained methodologically and worked through is to our knowledge. The dubiousness of this trend starts, as in the two other cases, only at the point when its advocates conduct themselves as science commissars and decree that problems evading quantitative treatment cannot be the object of potential scientific investigation. In the praxis of science this decree means that the entire problem area of classical and Christian theory has to disappear.

Brief as the characterization of these three factors unavoidably had to be, you should have noticed the common trait causing the disruption—it is the negativism, the arbitrary narrowing down of the area of discussion in political science. The investigation is to be restricted in such a way that rational principles of action cannot become thematic. It is the attitude of dogmatists and dogmatic adversaries who protect their position by being up in arms against reason and who want, at any cost, to prevent the rational discussion that would uncover the scandal of their attitude. Rational discussion, however, is the lifeblood of a democracy. And with this I return to a fundamental consideration that you still will remember. You will have noticed that I carefully abstained from any critique and accusation of totalitarian movements: for democracy is not primarily endangered by totalitarian movements. The primary danger is the intellectual climate in which movements like National Socialism and Communism can grow. And the primarily dangerous climate surrounding us is created by those intellectuals ("thinkers" or "philosophers" would not be the right word) who in their political attitude stand not at all on the left, radical wing of the anti-rational gnosis, but who declare their support for democracy. We will have to deal successfully with this primary danger to democracy, if we want to survive as democrats.

Freedom and responsibility are vain words if rational knowledge is prohibited, if we are not allowed to contemplate rationally the rightness of our actions. We have to fight the prohibition of questions regarding ideological premises that intellectuals try to force upon us; we have to regain the social freedom barely still existing today to cultivate the science of right action. To regain this freedom is democratic civic duty. It is more; it is human duty. Let me point out the great principle of the classical science of politics that is today almost forgotten: *Episteme,* science and knowledge, is an intellectual virtue of man. Correspondingly: Ignorance is a vice, an "arch-lie," which destroys man and his order. The struggle against knowledge—about whose dimensions and dangers I have attempted to give you an idea so far as it was possible—is rebellion against the existence of man in freedom.

6

Liberalism and Its History

The task of sketching the history of liberalism, although modest, is for methodological reasons difficult. For we stand before the question of whether there is even such a thing as liberalism as a clearly definable subject and whether this subject, should it not be clearly definable, can have a history. We touch here upon a general methodological problem. Toynbee, for example, opens his great work with the question whether England has a history; he concludes that the English nation as a society is so closely related to the society of Western civilization that one cannot write an English history without going into the entire history of Western civilization. It is in this sense that there arise the questions of how liberalism is to be delimited and whether it has a history. And they arise more acutely because the case of liberalism is much more complicated than that of England. For even if some phases of English history, for example the Reformation, can be dealt with only in relation to the general European history of the Reformation and counter-Reformation, still there are long periods of isolated, specifically English history. In the case of liberalism, a narrowing of the subject to national societies—German, French, English, or American—is hardly justifiable. For all the regional phases of liberalism are only parts of a common Western movement; and furthermore, this movement can only with difficulty be isolated from other movements that run parallel with it in time.

Originally published in *Review of Politics* 36 (1974) and translated from the German by Mary and Keith Algozin, this essay "is adapted by the editors from a lecture delivered to the Bavarian Catholic Academy, and published by it (Würzburg, 1960)" (ibid., 504).

I

The methodological questions must be raised, because in the course of the past thirty years the image of what liberalism is has changed completely. If you look at an older standard work such as Guido de Ruggiero's work of the 1920s, you will find that at that time, at the close of the liberal era, liberalism still appeared to be an easily definable phenomenon. But if you look at the more recent literature, you will find that the prototype of Ruggiero's work has just about disappeared—today the questions of liberalism are posed in broader contexts. Let me characterize briefly three of the more recent works to see in which direction the investigation moves today.

Consider first the work of Franz Schnabel, the Munich historian, *Deutsche Geschichte im 19. Jahrhundert*, which appeared in 1934 (4 vols.; reprint, Freiburg im Breisgau, 1948). The second volume contains a thorough, penetrating treatment of liberalism. Here, while there is a chapter devoted to the type-concept of liberalism, the historical presentation can describe the phenomenon of liberalism only in the context of its struggle with other movements of the nineteenth century—reaction, restoration, conservatism, socialism, etc. It becomes evident that liberalism is no independent phenomenon; its essence can be adequately described only in terms of its confrontation with other phenomena.

Two decades later, in 1955, Joseph Lecler's work appeared on the *Histoire de la tolérance au siècle de la réforme*. In this excellent monograph on the history of tolerance in the age of the Reformation there is a noteworthy investigation of the genesis of liberal attitudes from religious conflicts. From the conflict between the churches, and from the conflict of both churches with the state, there grew a new attitude of tolerance between the churches and of both churches toward the state. Lecler traces the beginnings of the liberal attitude to a situation in which the older treatment of liberalism does not usually seek them, namely, the desire for tolerance that grew out of the experience of the religious wars—the insight that the truth of Christendom cannot be saved by the churches exterminating each other for the sake of dogma, the insight that the churches must somehow live together in one society.

Finally, in his new work on *Die Dritte Kraft* (Frankfurt am Main, 1960), Friedrich Heer draws an important line of spiritual history from the enlightenment of Erasmus's time at the beginning of the sixteenth century to the present. Using this "third power" approach, Heer presents the history of a movement that repeatedly sought to stabilize a liberal order between revolution and reaction, between the left and the right wings of the surrounding political movements of Europe. There emerges the picture of the secular political movement of which liberalism is a phase.

These brief indications show to what extent there has been articulated today the framework of problems into which liberalism must be fitted. The context that surrounds and gives meaning to liberalism goes far beyond what one commonly understands by the classical liberalism represented by John Stuart Mill.

II

The picture of liberalism changes because liberalism itself changes in the process of history. And it changes because it is not a body of timelessly valid scientific propositions about political reality, but rather a series of political opinions and attitudes that have their optimal truth in the situation that motivates them, and are then overtaken by history and required to do justice to new situations. Liberalism is a political movement in the context of the surrounding Western revolutionary movement; its meaning alters with the phases of the surrounding movement. Its field of optimal clarity is the nineteenth century, which is preceded and followed by fields of decreasing clarity in which it becomes increasingly difficult to establish its identity. We can best gain access to this constantly changing field of meaning if we seize the expression "liberal" at its point of historical and political origin.

Even if, as we have seen, the beginnings of liberalism can be traced back to the early sixteenth century, the word *liberal* is nevertheless a relatively late creation. It appears for the first time in the second decade of the nineteenth century when a party of the Spanish *Cortes* of 1812 called itself the *Liberales*. This was a liberal constitutional party that formed a front against attempts at restoration. From this beginning the expression "liberal" entered the general European vocabulary, and soon there occurred throughout Europe the formation of liberal groups, parties, and movements.

The first use of the expression indicates the problems of liberalism. The new attitude is so tightly bound up with the attitudes it opposes that the entire complex of attitudes becomes a unity of meaning that overshadows each of its elements. In the decade from 1810 to 1820 there arise, parallel with the idea of liberalism, the ideas of conservatism and of restoration. With Chateaubriand's *Le Conservateur* we have conservatism, and with Haller's *Restauration der Staatswissenschaft* of 1816 we have the idea of restoration. Within a decade those three symbols arise that henceforth designate movements and parties, run parallel, are interrelated, and are held together in a unity of meaning by the fact that they are three modes of reaction to the phenomenon of revolution. The meaning of the three modes of reaction is defined in relation to the revolution, so that only in its context can the four labels—revolution, restoration, conservatism, and liberalism—be understood.

But even having gained this insight, we still cannot state the meaning of the four symbols precisely, as in a conceptual definition. For in the historical process the elements of the movements develop even relative to each other and change their meaning. Let me indicate some changes of meaning.

In the first place, today "liberal" has become almost equivalent to "conservative," and, indeed, this is because the movement of liberalism has been overtaken by new, more radical waves of revolution, in opposition to which it plays the role of conservatism; just as formerly, in the decade from 1810 to 1820, conservatism was conservative in opposition to revolution and to liberalism. Raymond Aron, for example, answered the question about his political attitude by saying he was liberal, that is, conservative. The same could be said of the economist Friedrich A. von Hayek: He is liberal, that is, conservative with respect to socialism, Communism, or any other variant of the phase of revolution that has overtaken liberalism. The prototype of the "old-style liberal" is today considered conservative.

Another change of meaning has occurred in America. In the American political vocabulary "liberal" generally means, not the European liberalism of the nineteenth century, which today is considered conservative, but on the contrary, a politically progressive attitude. Roughly speaking, one can say that in America the Republican Party is called conservative, the Democratic Party, liberal-progressive. But what is conservative in the Republican Party is its liberalism in the older European sense—that is, its opposition to socialism, to excessive state intervention, etc.; while the Democratic Party is liberal insofar as its program tends toward the welfare state, state capitalism, and a decided emphasis upon the interests of the labor unions. The shift of meaning toward the left goes so far that "liberal" is often used as a synonym for "pink" or "fellow traveler." This change of meaning became possible in America because European liberalism of the old style scarcely existed there in a distinct form as a political movement; and it did not develop because America lacked the opponent that liberalism confronted in Europe. In the first half of the nineteenth century, during European liberalism's heroic time of struggle, America did not have to battle the movements of restoration, a surviving monarchical principle, or a politically active church allied with the state. It becomes clear that liberalism can take on various functions and shades of meaning according to the social context.

A very remarkable new change of meaning has occurred in liberalism since the Second World War. If you look at the political fronts of the postwar period—in West Germany, France, and Italy—you will note a political force that before the war did not exist to this massive extent: The principal parties are closely connected with the Catholic and Protestant churches. Through mutual assimilation, liberalism and this new force came into broad agreement. The liberals who were overtaken by the revolution became conservative; and the conservative Christian organizations liberalized themselves considerably. There became possible a common front against the common danger. But again, the social context has its effect, and the direction of the development is not unambiguous. When parties of Catholic or Protestant affiliation become the bearers of liberalism then rigidly secularist liberals may become still more secularist and more anti-clerical—may, as in France, move even more sharply toward the left, since the liberal position is now occupied by conservatives, may even tend toward the Communist Party, although they are by no means Communists. Especially in France and Italy, Communism took over the anti-clerical function of the older liberalism, because the old liberals shifted toward the right and became conservative, occasionally with distinctly Christian overtones.

But even this does not exhaust the complications. I noted before that all the symbols—liberalism, conservatism, restoration—can be understood only as modes of reaction against the revolution. In France itself, again in the decade from 1810 to 1820, liberalism appropriated the symbol of revolution and made it its own. Let us consider this shift of meaning. In 1815 the liberal Charles Comte (not to be confused with Auguste Comte) founded the *Globe*. In this periodical Comte developed the program of a liberalism whose task it would be to carry on the *révolution permanente*. What is this permanent revolution? Comte believed that there were terrible social wrongs under the ancien régime and that the revolution occurred because necessary reforms were not implemented at the proper time. If not enough is done to satisfy the demands of social justice the result is revolution. If in the future we wish to avoid a repetition of the horrible events, then what the revolution achieved by unhappy means must be achieved at the proper time through the less unpleasant means of reform. The revolution must become permanent in the sense that a permanent, flexible politics of reform buys off revolutionary terror. Even though it changed its name, Charles Comte's idea lived on in liberal politics, and by way of the reform liberalism of the nineteenth century, it became what today in America is called "peaceful change." The idea of peaceful change—a policy of timely adaptation to the social situation that, in the age of the industrial revolution, changes very quickly—has become today a constant in all shades of liberalism. From this point of view liberalism becomes a method for carrying on the revolution with other, less destructive means.

This liberalism, plausible and tempting as it sounds, is weak because it greatly underestimates the motives and forces underlying the revolution. In fact, liberalism did not buy off the terrors of revolution at all but rather was forced to play the conservative role in the age of totalitarian regimes. Indeed, Charles Comte saw correctly that in liberalism there is something of revolution, but that revolution goes very much farther than liberalism wants. This becomes evident in the course of the *révolution permanente* in the twentieth century. Trotsky took up the idea during the revolutionary phase that recently overtook liberalism. He was an acute analyst of the revolutionary movement; he knew that what is called revolution (whether today's Communist revolution or yesterday's French Revolution, the entire significance of which is understood only today) is a movement—and that a movement lives in that it moves. The radical revolutionary must make the revolution into a permanent condition; there can be no compromise or stabilization of the achievements at a definite point. For as soon as a plateau of stabilization is permitted, the revolution is over. To keep a revolution alive one must carry it on further; it thrives on unrest, it needs a permanent opponent; it must meet obstacles to be overcome by its assault, etc. If there are no more obstacles, no more imperialists or deviationists, the revolution dies for lack of things to attack. Revolution can end only if it has reached its goal. And this is precisely the insight expressed by Trotsky in his idea of the *révolution permanente:* Revolution in the modern sense has no intention of producing a stable condition; revolution is the mental and spiritual condition of an act that has no rational goal. The revolution can be permanent because its formal goal, which in Communism is a society whose members have become supermen, cannot be realized. Revolution becomes permanent when the revolutionary posits a goal that *ex definitione* cannot be reached because it requires the transformation of human nature. The unchangeable nature of man constantly places obstacles in the path to the paradisaical goal. If the goal of the revolution is defined by a gnostic philosophy of history, then revolutionary action has no rational goal. Trotsky understood this situation, although he expressed it differently.

I have dealt with this shift of the meaning of *révolution permanente,* not to present a historical curiosity, but because the problem of permanent revolution is involved in liberalism. For Charles Comte's idea that the goal of the revolution could be achieved through a constant process of reform, without the unpleasant side effects, belongs in the gnostic-utopian class. It is intimately related to the eighteenth-century progressivist idea as held by Kant and Condorcet, that a final state of rational humanity can be achieved in a process of infinite approximation. But this cannot be achieved, for man is not only rational but much else besides. Therefore it is no accident that the Communist revolutionary took up again the liberal's *révolution permanente.* For in liberalism also there is the irrational element of an eschatological final state, of a society that will produce through its rational methods, without violent disturbances, a condition of everlasting peace. Liberalism too is a part of the revolutionary movement that lives to the extent that it moves. From Charles Comte to Trotsky there runs a line of growing insight that the reform movement, to which liberalism also belongs, is a unique state of affairs insofar as its final goal cannot be actualized.

The interweaving of liberalism, revolution, and restoration will become clearer with a brief reflection on Charles Comte's more

89

illustrious namesake, Auguste Comte. In the third volume of his work on *La Jeunesse d'Auguste Comte* (Paris, 1933), Henri Gouhier has provided a noteworthy study of "Revolution and Restoration." In this study Gouhier raises the question whether Comte was a liberal, or an executor of the French Revolution, or a phenomenon of the restoration. And he shows very subtly that this question can be answered positively in each case. For the French revolutionary movement went to an extreme, stopped, and then became retrogressive; the extreme under consideration here is that which overtook liberalism in the more recent revolutionary phase. What is at issue here can best be seen in two figures, Robespierre and Hébert. During the revolution Robespierre was the representative of deism; he wanted to establish a cult of the *Être suprême,* the supreme being. Hébert believed deism was too great a concession to Christianity and clericalism; he wanted a *culte de la raison.* For Robespierre that was too atheistic. Of the two men, Robespierre was the conservative revolutionary, while Hébert was the radical revolutionary who wanted to discard completely the spiritual content of Christianity, even in the pale form of deism. And now let us examine Auguste Comte's position in the context of this tension between conservatism and radicalism. In relation to Robespierre, Comte was revolutionary; he did not want to return to deism and the cult of the *Être suprême.* He became the founder of a new religion, the *religion de l'humanité.* Thus he was the successor of Hébert; he wanted to deify reason and to organize the new humanity in the spirit of deified reason; he was the executor of the revolution, a radical revolutionary against all the restorationist and liberal movements of his time. On the other hand, however, Comte could also be seen as conservative, for he did not at all want to renew the terror. Indeed he wanted to overcome not only the ancien régime but also the revolutionary populism of the commune of Paris, whose representative Hébert had been. He sought a new way to unite the spiritual content of the revolution with a conservative organization. He wanted a temporal power of industrialists united with a spiritual power of intellectuals under the pontificate of Comte. This is the afterimage of a medieval society, with the managers in the place of the feudal princes, and the positivist intellectuals in the place of the clergy. In view of later events, one could say that this is the model of an industrial fascism under the leadership of a gnostic sect. Seen from this point of view, Comte was a conservative. And finally, there is the Comte in whom the liberals of his time took satisfaction. In the first, so-called intellectual, phase of his work he attacked metaphysics and religion from his scientistic position. Liberals like that. That was the phase in which Comte gained the friendship of John Stuart Mill and Émile Littré and became internationally influential. John Stuart Mill in particular fused into his liberalism much that he borrowed from Comte. But liberal friends were frightened and angered by the second, so-called religious, phase of Comte's work, in which he wanted to produce a world organization of positivist intellectuals and found the authoritarian organization as a new church. There occurred a break between Comte and the liberals. For our purposes now it is important to establish that there never were the two phases in the life and work of Comte. Gouhier has demonstrated that the ideas of the so-called second phase were contained, at least in outline, in the early writings of the 1820s. Comte proceeded according to plan and gradually developed the total concept of his early period; the liberal, the conservative, and the revolutionary Comte are an integral personality. For the liberal historians of the second half of the nineteenth century, however, this phenomenon was so frightening and incomprehensible that they invented the two phases and went so far as to ascribe the second phase to a mental illness. The division into two Comtes continues even into the twentieth century: the first Comte, the founder of sociology, still inspires the neo-positivist social sciences; the second, the religious Comte, has been replaced by Marxism. What frightened the liberals into their defensive constructions was the radical revolutionary element in Comte, which made all too painfully evident the gnostic content of liberalism also.

The behavior of the liberals toward Comte occasions a fundamental reflection. Comte was pleasing to the liberals so long as he attacked theology and metaphysics and opened the perspective of a sociology analogous to physics. He knew, however, that an imitation of the methods of natural science in the social sciences is no substitute for spiritual order and its theological-metaphysical symbolism. He was aware that he had to posit an alternative spiritual order to replace the spiritual order he attacked as untrue. There lay beyond the thinking he had in common with the liberals his understanding of the spiritual dimension which also, and above all, must find its fulfillment. Comte was, in fact, a genuine revolutionary of the spirit; he knew it was not enough to attack spiritual authority; and because of this consciousness of the problem, he was a more important thinker than any liberal has ever been. With this differentiation between Comte and a mere liberal we hit upon the reason why liberalism must unavoidably be overtaken by the spiritually much-more-powerful revolution. One can't get away from the revolution. Whoever participates in it for a time with the intention of retiring peacefully with a pension that calls itself liberalism will discover sooner or later that the revolutionary convulsion to destroy socially harmful, obsolete institutions is not a good investment for a pensioner.

III

We have spoken of the revolution of the spirit of which liberalism is a phase, and we have seen that more recent authors trace the beginnings of the movement back into the sixteenth century. Classical liberalism of the nineteenth century has its place in this encompassing movement. Naturally, it is not possible to give here a synopsis of the history of the movement; the subject is so vast that an investigation of details would reveal nothing more than the futility of the attempt. An outline of the model must suffice.

The revolutionary movement runs its course in great waves. In each of these waves there can be distinguished, first, the actual outbreak of revolution; second, the countermovement and organization of the resistance; and finally, a period of quiescence and adjustment, of stabilization at a new level, until the next outbreak. We can now distinguish three such waves since the sixteenth century. The first begins with the Reformation, which begets the counter-Reformation. The second wave begins with the French Revolution, which calls forth the countermovements of reaction and restoration. The third wave clearly begins with the Communist revolution. The corresponding countermovement is not so clearly defined, however, since the third wave has reverberated far beyond its Western center and become worldwide in its effect. The resistance assumes forms as different as the massive rightist reaction, within the West, of Fascism and National Socialism (which have their own revolutionary character), the resistance movement of the free world against Communism (which can, however, join in alliance with Communism against the revolutionary character of Fascism and

National Socialism), and the opposition of a neutral "third world" (which cannot be clearly outlined, since it is overshadowed by the movement of liberation from Western colonialism).

To each of these waves of movement and countermovement there corresponds a phenomenon of stabilization. With the exhaustion brought on by the religious wars there emerges a unique ideology of stabilization, the so-called natural law. It is an attempt to base a new order of Western humanity upon insights gained independently of revelation and the dogmas of the churches. Hugo Grotius formulated the intention most clearly perhaps when he said he wished to base the principles of natural law upon axioms as infallible as those of mathematics. By its very nature the attempt to construct the truths about human and social order *more mathematico* had to fail—the century of natural law was inundated by the next wave of revolution. After the revolution and the organization of the resistance in the wars of coalition, and after the period of reaction, there again follows a period of stabilization. The age of liberalism can perhaps best be characterized as this period of stabilization that corresponds to the age of natural law after the first revolutionary wave. Nothing can be said yet about the stabilization after the third revolutionary wave—the warlike confrontations between revolution and resistance are still in process, and the complications have become worldwide. But within the Western world the outlines of a stabilization can be seen in the combination of a liberal concept of economics with a politics of the welfare state. This stabilization has the further characteristic that the spiritual degeneration fostered by ideologies, although in no way overcome, has been remarkably alleviated by its tendency to draw upon the sources of Christianity and of *ratio.*

IV

We have regarded liberalism as a phase of the revolutionary movement; now we should define its content. We may use as our guide the classification of the four aspects of liberalism in Franz Schnabel's *Deutsche Geschichte:* the political, economic, religious, and scientific aspects of liberalism. This classification is oriented primarily toward the German form of liberalism; to some extent other points need to be emphasized if it is to be applied to other Western nations.

93

The *political* aspect of liberalism is defined by the liberal opposition to certain abuses, which are to be eliminated. Liberalism is above all against the old-style police state, that is, against the encroachment of the executive upon the judicial and legislative domains; in constitutional politics liberals demand the separation of powers. Secondly, they oppose the old social order, that is, the privileged position of clergy and nobility. At this point can be seen the weakness of a political attitude that is tied to the situation; we will have more to say about this later. In time, when the rising working class becomes politically capable of directing it, the attack on privilege turns against the liberal bourgeoisie itself. In the course of the revolutionary movement the attack cannot end until the society has become egalitarian. And finally, liberalism turns against the tie between church (no matter which one) and state; the movement becomes anti-clerical.

Economically, liberalism means the repeal of the old legal restrictions that set limits to free economic activity. There should be no principle and no motive of economic activity other than enlightened self-interest. It is assumed that actions undertaken in rational, anticipatory self-interest will lead to harmonious order in society.

A third front is the *religious.* This must be distinguished from the anti-clerical attitude whose goal is the separation of church and state. Beyond this constitutional demand, liberalism rejects revelation and dogma as sources of truth; it discards spiritual substance and becomes secularistic and ideological.

Liberalism's *scientific* position cannot always be separated from its religious position. Its essence is the assumption of the autonomy of immanent human reason as the source of knowledge. Liberals speak of free research in the sense of liberation from "authorities," that is, not only from revelation and dogmatism, but also from classical philosophy, the rejection of which becomes a point of honor, because of its medieval association with scholasticism.

V

In all of these four aspects liberalism has run into difficulties. The programmatic battle could always be waged with success up to a certain point, only to fall into a new difficulty, more serious than the one overcome. We must now look more closely at the phenomenon of liberalism being overtaken and mired down.

The weakness of political liberalism is its belief in the redemptive value of a constitutional model constructed in opposition to absolute monarchy and the police state. The pillars of the construction are the demands for basic human rights, the separation of powers, and universal suffrage. The three requirements are not systematic axioms; rather, their conjunction is historically contingent. The basic human rights are the sediment, become statute law, of the *jus divinum et naturale,* which obligated the rulers of the Middle Ages and the Renaissance, even if their fulfillment of the obligation left much to be desired. Using the image of sunken cultural treasure, one could say that they are a list of what has been salvaged of the ruler's duties, whose religious and metaphysical foundation is no longer permitted in a time when spiritual substance is lost. The demand for the division of power, which is often taken as a principal item of the liberal constitutional program, has an ambiguous status. In Europe north of the Alps it becomes the center of attention after the end of the seventeenth century. Montesquieu praised as a model English constitutional practice in the decades after the Glorious Revolution; and the ideas of the mixed constitution and of the balance of powers, partially influenced by the concept of equilibrium in the new mechanics, contribute their theoretical dignity. Nevertheless, English constitutional practice very soon developed away from the division of powers toward the sovereignty of parliament. When in 1789 the principle of the division of powers was incorporated into the American Constitution, it was no longer present in the English constitution. Actual English constitutional practice was made known to a wider public only after the middle of the nineteenth century by the work of Walter Bagehot, *The English Constitution* (2d ed., rev.; New York, 1877). Therefore, one can hardly speak of the division of powers as a fundamental demand within liberalism; it is rather a fashionable model, whose destiny and claim for support are conditioned by the current situation of information or ignorance. Finally, universal suffrage was originally in no way a political goal of the liberals; it was a populist element, and the older liberals sought to uphold in opposition to it the suffrage principle of property and education. Only under massive political pressure from below did it develop gradually into a liberal demand.

A constitutional model that is so manifestly historically contingent must lead unavoidably to difficulties and cause severe damage when it is dogmatized into a worldview and its elements are raised to articles of faith. The catastrophe of its exportation to non-Western societies plays itself out for all to see, but we need not look that far. Within the West itself, Europe has been led to the brink of destruction by the international propaganda against, and destruction of, political structures that do not correspond to the model of the liberal national state and by the insanity of introducing the model without transition into societies that had not produced it. Especially the misunderstanding of basic human rights as including the privilege to ideologically destroy the existing order has had deadly consequences in societies without a mature political tradition, such as the German. Today the eschatological fire of the model is, if not extinguished, considerably dampened. We know today that societies do not become free through liberal constitutions, but that free societies produce liberal constitutions and can function in their framework—a relation to which John Stuart Mill pointed emphatically.

Closely connected with the failure of the constitutional model is the collapse of the economic model. In its English conception the economic model was originally bound to the situation of a relatively low concentration of population and a predominantly agrarian economy. The model of the natural condition, out of which Locke developed his constitutional construction, was the American pioneer society, in which every head of household is a landowner and husbands his piece of land with his family, making a living, and producing a surplus. In the *Second Treatise of Government*, Locke formulates the model drastically: "In the beginning all the world was America" [§49]. This archetype survives vigorously in the Jeffersonian resistance to industrial society. The original harmonious balance of citizens of equal economic potential was destroyed by the development of industrial society. A new power structure came into being with which the original agrarian liberalism had not reckoned. When society differentiated into capitalist and worker, the model of the society of free, equal citizens was overtaken by a reality that pressed toward the crisis of class struggle. There arose the social-ethical problematic, which after long political struggles led to the massive introduction of socialist elements into the liberal economic structure.

The overtaking by history of the antireligious attitude of liberalism is so well known that a brief indication will be sufficient. The liberal attack was directed against dogmatism and the authority of revelation. If only these influences on thinking and public life could be removed, then the free human being would order society rationally with his autonomous reason. However, if in practice Christianity is successfully driven out of men, they become not rational liberals but ideologues. The undesirable spiritual order is replaced not by liberalism but rather by one or the other of the emotionally as-intensive ideologies. The liberals did not foresee this, because their conception of immanent reason had already so badly deformed the image of man that the problematic of the spirit and its transcendence had disappeared from the field of vision. Politically, the ideologizing of man, which was powerfully co-caused but not intended by liberalism, has the result that the liberal constitutional model can no longer function. If the majority of voters are Communists and National Socialists, they can form the majority bloc that makes the functioning of the constitution impossible, as we have seen in the Weimar Republic.

The scientific problematic of liberalism is very closely related to the religious. Technically, to be sure, the questions about this area are much more complicated. We must be satisfied here with a few hints. As far as I can judge, the concept of autonomous, immanent reason causes no damage in mathematics and in the mathematicized natural sciences. But in the sciences of man and society it destroys the subject matter, for man is the *imago Dei* and participates with his essence in transcendent Being. If one defines immanent reason as the essence of man, ontology as the fundamental science is destroyed, and a rational social science adequate to the subject is no longer possible. The result is the decay of the social sciences that characterizes the late liberal period and that is now being overtaken by the restoration of *ratio* and of ontology. An example of the decadence that is being overtaken today is the method of value relation and the value relativism which, as ideology, has had as much worldwide success as Marxism, positivism, or psychoanalysis. The essence of value theory is the transformation of the objective hierarchy of goods, with its *summum bonum* of transcendent completion, into human value posits. The subject of the social sciences is held to be constituted by relation to current values, while the validity of these values can be established only by posit. As long as the method is used in a tradition-laden milieu, the danger is not so obvious, since the "values" remain relatively close to the traditional objective hierarchy of goods. But if the method is applied in a society undermined by and infested with ideology, the result is as many definitions of the subject as there are ideological value posits. Science collapses into an apology for various ideologies. The extreme consequence was brought to my attention on the occasion of an address in Heidelberg, when, during the discussion I was opposed by a young man from the Alfred Weber School who insisted that in order to remain objective the social scientist must conduct his science in the spirit of the time, for there are no criteria for choosing and ordering the subject of inquiry other than the values recognized at the time. When he places himself outside the spirit of the time and introduces ontological criteria, then that is subjectivism. Thus, only if one subjectively and arbitrarily joins some ideology of the time is one objective; if one attempts to find objective grounds for judgments concerning social order, one is subjective. Examples of similar opinions could be given from the realm of neo-positivist social science. In the face of this radical destruction of social science we stand today before the problem of its reconstruction through the restoration of a critical ontology.

VI

Permit me to summarize the result of these observations. As a phase of the revolutionary movement, liberalism has left behind a sediment in contemporary Western society. Part of this sediment is the trend toward the separation of church and state, which originated in the sixteenth and seventeenth centuries, prior to the liberal period in the narrower sense. While it did not always necessitate the formal separation of church and state, as it did in America, the trauma of the religious wars called forth the resolution that under no circumstances were organizational or dogmatic conflicts between churches ever again to be permitted to achieve such high political rank in public affairs that the society would be split into parties of civil war.

Implicit in this resolution is an attitude of tolerance insofar as the outbreak of hostilities can be avoided only if a religiously pluralistic society is accepted. There has been implemented a positive policy of religious freedom and freedom of conscience for everyone, limited only by the mores of the society and the penal law. A sect of Adamites, for instance, who are informed by their conscience that the naked truth of God is best represented when one goes walking naked on the street, will scarcely be tolerated. The case is not fictitious—it gave Roger Williams great concern in his religiously liberal Rhode Island. Polygamy, too, is scarcely to be permitted—the Mormons had to give up polygamy when Utah was to be accepted into the United States. Within the indicated limits, religious tolerance was allowed to hold sway; and where it is still in doubt, it is allowed to establish itself.

Another part of the sediment left by liberalism is a certain resistance—activated slowly yet decisively in concrete cases—to those social phenomena that were the specific objects of liberalism's attack during its time of struggle, especially tendencies toward a dictatorial constitution, and attempts to implement socially an organized spiritual authority.

Finally, we may mention two more phenomena, which cannot be called part of the sediment left by liberalism since they point, on the contrary, to the transformation of liberalism under the pressure of historical events; however, they are today so deeply embedded in liberalism that they belong to the form it has taken in contemporary society. The first is the absorption of social-ethical demands into classical liberalism. This has produced that amalgam that we know under various names—New Deal, welfare state, *Soziale Marktwirtschaft*, etc. The second phenomenon is liberalism's becoming filled with Christian substance. We must be careful not to maintain that the manner of recapturing the Christian substance is always the most fortunate and promises lasting success. Yet the phenomenon is so vigorous that in the period after the Second World War the parties close to the churches could become supporters of liberal politics in three of the principal continental nations—Germany, France, and Italy.

In the light of these considerations we can say that, on the one hand, liberalism decidedly has a voice in the political situation of our time; on the other hand, however, today the ideas of autonomous, immanent reason and of the autonomous subject of economics are scarcely alive and fruitful; thus, the classical liberalism of the secularist and bourgeois-capitalist stamp may be pronounced dead.

7

Toynbee's *History* as a Search for Truth

History as a humane study is defined by Toynbee as a concern with the lives of civilizational societies in both their internal and their external aspects. "The internal aspect is the articulation of the life of any given society into a series of chapters succeeding one another in time and into a number of communities living side by side. The external aspect is the relation of particular societies with one another, which has likewise to be studied in the two media of time and space."[1] That is the well-known, much debated definition that crystallizes the conception of historical reality as a manifold of civilizational courses. I have quoted it because I want to make it the starting point for reflections on Toynbee's use of definitions. Only when their use is understood can the question of their validity be raised.

A Study of History, as it lies before us in its completed form, is an inquiry concerning the truth about the order of history. It is an inquiry in the classical sense of a *zetema,* a search for truth both cognitive and existential. Definitions in the course of a *zetema,* however, are cognitive resting points, which articulate the view of reality that has been gained at the respective stage in the existential advance toward truth. As a consequence, the validity of the definitions has two dimensions. In the one direction, they must be tested against the data of reality to which they purport to refer; in the other direction, they must be measured by the existential level reached in the search for truth. Moreover, the two dimensions of

---

Originally published in *The Intent of Toynbee's History,* ed. Edward T. Gargan (Chicago: Loyola University Press, 1961), this essay is reprinted here by kind permission of Loyola University Press.

1. Arnold J. Toynbee, *A Study of History,* 12 vols. (London: Oxford University Press, 1934–1961), 1:46.

validity are related to one another, insofar as the question which is a datum of reality depends for its answer on the existential level reached. What is relevant on a lower level may become irrelevant on a higher level, and vice versa. Hence, the definitions that articulate the view of reality achieved in earlier stages of the *zetema* are liable to be superseded by definitions reached at higher existential levels. In an existentially authentic *zetema* we are faced, therefore, with a series of definitions, the later ones qualifying and superseding the earlier ones; and under no circumstances must they be pitted against one another on the level of a logic of the external world, which ignores the logic of existence. As a matter of fact, the search for truth about the order of history has steadily advanced through the volumes of the *Study* to higher existential levels; and the earlier definitions correspondingly have been modified, if not invalidated, from the newly reached positions.

While the retrospective qualifications and invalidations of earlier definitions, inconvenient as they may be for a reader who identifies truth with information, are the inevitable mark of an authentic *zetema*, the work of Toynbee is beset with a further difficulty of a personal nature. A search for truth is supposed to reach its goal, that is, a view of reality existentially informed by the *philia* of the *sophon* in the Platonic sense, or by the *intentio animi* toward God in the Augustinian sense. Toynbee does not reach this goal of the love of God, but stops short at a sensitive spiritualist's and a historical connoisseur's sympathy with religions. Hence, the *zetema* had not come to its end when the author wrote his proud *Finis* at the physical end of his work.[2] The peculiar lack of finality now has found an extraordinary literary expression insofar as at the climax of the search, in the exploration of the universal churches, "Mr. Martin Wight" is introduced as the partner of a dialogue in which the author speaks his last-but-one word against the intellectually and spiritually superior position of his critic. I have put "Mr. Martin Wight," who is a real person,[3] in quotation marks in order to signify the function of his criticisms within the *zetema* that was not completed by Toynbee himself. One is tempted by the idea that "Mr. Martin Wight" might have been a product of Toynbee's imagination, a figure designed to cast light a

2. Ibid., 10:144.
3. Ibid., 238.

few steps ahead on the path, the *epanodos,* which the author did not choose to ascend further. That would have been a fascinating literary device to invalidate a position that the author had left behind. But "Mr. Martin Wight" is real, and his introduction in the notes and annexes casts the light that reveals as penultimate the position which Toynbee chooses to make his last one. Nevertheless, it also reveals the author's awareness that he is indeed engaged in a *zetema,* even if he balks, like the prisoner in the cave, at the ordeal of light and refuses to let himself be dragged all the way up to its mouth. While the admission of an alter ego in the person of "Martin Wight," to be sure, is existentially not equivalent to the personal completion of the ascent, it is something like an act of atonement. For we cannot, when engaged in a search for truth, stop where the view is pleasant and declare a way station to be the summit without betraying the Guide who has brought us thus far. And his critic charges Toynbee unequivocally, and justly, with the hubris of having transformed, in his treatment of the universal churches, the divine mystery of history into the manageable topic of a humane study,[4] so manageable indeed that the author can tender advice to the "four living universal religions" on what to do in order to get some peace on earth.

The nature of the humane study as a search in the Platonic sense must be recognized when dealing with Toynbee's definitions. They are resting points in the inquiry, as we have said, liable to be modified when the ascent has enlarged the horizon. Nevertheless, while their position in the search must be taken into account when gauging their cognitive import, they lose their character as instruments of cognition no more than the paradigms of the best polis in Plato's *Republic* lose it because they are the stepping stones in the ascent from the depth of the surrounding corrupt society to the vision of the Agathon. Especially with regard to the first definition, to which we now must return for a moment, he is clear about its purpose to wrest critically solid ground, in both the cognitive and existential senses, from the sophistic corruption of historiography through nationalism and Western civilizational hubris. As far as the cognitive aspect is concerned, the definition comes at the end of an elaborate exposition of the reasons why civilizations, rather than national states or mankind, are the "intelligible fields of

4. Ibid., 7:745

historical study," the "social atoms";[5] and as far as the existential aspect is concerned, the definition is followed by an analysis of the motives that induce Western historians to construct a unilinear development of human civilization, as well as by an exposition of the dubious intellectual devices used to support the construction.[6] About the cognitive validity, in particular, there can be no doubt, for Toynbee's conception of history at this first stage rests squarely, as does Spengler's, on the broad empirical basis established by their great predecessor Eduard Meyer. Among the historians of the nineteenth century, Meyer was the first to transfer the categories of the unilinear history of mankind (Antiquity, Middle Age, Modern Period) to a single civilization, the Greco-Roman, as the true unit of history; he was motivated by the expansion of knowledge to civilizations, especially the Babylonian, which were intelligible units of history although they had remained beyond the horizon of the Western unilinear construction. A revision that had been impending ever since the great break that lies between Bossuet's and Voltaire's conceptions of history had now become inevitable under the pressure of rapidly increasing empirical knowledge. At the first stage of his work Toynbee is the executor of this necessity. And whatever modifications the first definition will have to suffer in the further course of the *zetema*, it will remain valid enough to bar the return to the construction it has superseded.

The second stage of the *zetema* is extremely complex, especially in the cognitive dimension, as evidenced by the fact that it fills five and a half volumes. In order not to get lost in the wilderness of concrete details, I shall isolate the epistemological issue.

The humane study is, by definition, concerned with the chapters in the lives of the societies called civilizations. They are members of a species insofar as they reveal regularities in their course from genesis and growth to breakdown and disintegration. The exploration of these regularities, as well as the construction of adequate type concepts for their description, would encounter no difficulties other than the normal ones in the work of science, if the societies were given in the manner of botanical specimens. Unfortunately they are not because of the nature of historical sources. The courses of the various societies, whose membership in the species may be assumed, are not equally open to inspection by the historian; and he

5. Ibid., 1:17–50.
6. Ibid., 149–71.

must proceed, therefore, in practice by establishing the presumed type on occasion of the societies for which the sources flow most richly, that is, for the Greco-Roman and Western civilizations. Once the type is tentatively established on this limited basis of maximal illumination, it can be used for classifying such data as are available for the course of other civilizations. Moreover, for several of the societies the sources flow so thinly indeed that on their strength alone the society would not even have been recognized as a member of the species. Hence, the construction of type concepts, which should be based on the civilizational courses, slides over, in the practice of the operation, into the entirely different task of identifying societies as members of the species through the application of the type concepts, developed from the limited basis, to data that are assumed to be fragments of civilizational courses of the same type. This procedure has its hazards. And the question to what extent it has been successful by critical standards is a matter that can be decided in detail only by the specialists in the various historical fields. I must confine myself to the judgment, without giving reasons for it on this occasion, that Toynbee's "operations" as he calls them have been surprisingly successful; and that they have been illuminating, as have Spengler's, even when energetic exceptions will have to be taken in the detail.

From the very success in making history a humane study of civilizational courses, however, emerge the problems that mark a second stage insofar as they are incompatible with the first assumption about civilizational societies as the intelligible fields of study. For in the process of identification and exploration the presumed "social atoms" prove to be no closed monads, nor do they confine their relations to concussions befitting well-rounded atoms. Especially in the time sequence of civilizations, the majority of the later societies are related to earlier ones in various modes of "filiation," and some of them have offspring in their turn. The field of atoms, thus, is transformed into a genealogy of civilizations, running through three generations from the emergence of the species to the present. That genealogical structure of the field of civilizations is in itself an intelligible field of study, not identical with any of the societies taken singly. Yet the point might be pressed that it still comes under the "external aspect" included in the first definition. The matter becomes critical, however, when Toynbee considers the mode of affiliation that he names apparentation and affiliation. In some instances societies develop in their stage of disintegration a trinity of symptoms, called the universal state, the universal church, and the heroic age. The dominant minority of the disintegrating civilization creates in its last effort the universal state, extending over the whole civilizational area and suppressing the further internecine wars among the communities of the society; the internal proletariat releases in this situation its energies into the creation of a universal church; and the external proletariat, boring into the dying civilization, develops the ephemeral institutions and cultural phenomena of its heroic age. That is specifically the complex of symptoms to be found in the disintegration of the Greco-Roman civilization. Of the three phenomena, the universal church, however, transcends the society in which it has arisen insofar as it becomes the transmitter of civilizational heritage through its formative influence on the peoples who are to become the ethnic stock of the affiliated Western society. This service, the "chrysalis function," as well as the fact that the universal church in the cases of apparentation and affiliation outlasts the society in which it has arisen, definitely points toward the existence of "intelligible fields of study" other than the civilizations themselves.

During the execution of his program in the first six volumes of *A Study of History*, Toynbee was only dimly aware that in fact he was invalidating the programmatic definitions of the stage. He did not meet the problem with adequate revisions of his concepts and definitions. Nevertheless, at the end of volume 6 he recognized the problem in metaphorical form. The movements beaten by the alternating rhythms of Yin and Yang are not the cycle of a treadmill. "The perpetual turning of a wheel is not a vain repetition if, at each revolution, it is carrying a vehicle that much nearer to its goal." The civilizations, when they dissolve, "regularly leave behind them a deposit of universal states and universal churches and barbarian war-bands . . . [W]e shall find reason to believe that these three objects of study are something more than by-products of social disintegration . . . [T]hey must be independent entities with a claim to be studied on their own merits." We cannot afford to ignore this new question, for it "holds the key to the meaning of the weaver's work; and a yearning that *tantus labor non sit cassus* will not allow us to rest without trying to unlock the secret of this mystery."[7]

7. Ibid., 6:324–26.

One cannot but be moved when reading these pages. A giant work has been completed. The societies, whose courses are the concern of history according to the programmatic definition, have been successfully explored; and the result is the insight that the wheels of civilization carry a vehicle that is not itself a civilization toward its goal. The whole labor would be wasted unless the study of history be expanded to the "independent entities with a claim to be studied on their own merits," because they, and not the civilizations, hold the key to the meaning of history. In the metaphors of these pages, Toynbee has achieved a new insight in the cognitive sense, because he has reached a new stage in his *zetema* in the existential sense. For this is the crossroads at which he could have taken the way of Spengler into the tragic experience of civilizations as a spiritually unrelieved, organic rhythm of birth and death, of growth and decay. When, in universal states and churches, lie recognized something more than by-products of a disintegrating civilization, he was informed by a sensitiveness for the presence of the Spirit in history that is so signally absent in Spengler. Moreover, this sensitiveness must have been sharpened through the labors of his study. For anybody could have told him, by way of intellectual prognostication, and certainly he could have told it himself, that he would arrive at this spiritual crossroads when he conceived history as nothing but a manifold of civilizational courses and their relations. That sooner or later, when engaged in a study of this kind, he would have to confess himself either an existentialist of the nihilistic variety, or a philosopher and Christian. But apparently this spiritual issue was not as vividly present to him at the beginning of the *Study* as it was at the end, or he would never have formulated the first definition.

Between the publication of volumes 4 through 6 in 1939 and of volumes 7 through 10 in 1954 lie fifteen years and a world war. A theoretical situation that had remained in a state of spiritual awareness, not matched by intellectual penetration, at the end of volume 6 has been articulated by conceptual instruments in volume 7.

The new position is concentrated in the reclassification of societies that constitute intelligible fields of study. At the bottom, as in the first stage of the *Study*, are the primitive societies that are excluded from the historian's concern and left to anthropology. At the next level we find the primary civilizations (Egyptian, Sumeric) that have emerged from the primitive stage of society.

The primary civilizations fulfill their destiny in begetting the secondary civilizations (Hellenic, Sinic), who in their turn beget the higher religions (Christianity, Hinduism, Mahayana). The number of intelligible fields of study has increased to four species of society, arranged chronologically and genealogically on "an ascending scale of values."[8] This reclassification is possible and necessary because the metaphoric vehicle that is carried toward its goal by the wheels of civilizations is now identified as "the chariot of Religion."[9] The "history of Religion"[10] is now history proper, and the various societies must be characterized and classified on the scale of values according to their function in the "progress of Religion."[11] Looking back from this last position to the first one, Toynbee himself summarizes the devastating effect of the change:

> Now, however, that our Study has carried us to a point at which the civilizations in their turn, like the parochial states of the Modern Western World at the outset of our investigation, have ceased to constitute intelligible fields of study for us and have forfeited their historical significance except in so far as they minister to the progress of Religion, we find that, from this more illuminating standpoint, the species itself has lost its specific unity. In our new list of societies arranged in a serial order of ascending value, the primary and secondary civilizations appear as separate categories, differentiated from one another and located on different qualitative levels by the difference in value between their respective contributions to the achievement of bringing the higher religions to flower. As for the civilizations of the third generation, they are now right out of the picture.[12]

This drastic revision is, however, accompanied by the warning that the earlier thesis of the philosophical equivalence of all civilizations is not abandoned. The thesis "is assuredly true as far as it goes; and it has not played us false so long as we have been dealing with the civilizations themselves, in their geneses, growths, breakdowns, and disintegrations, as the ultimate objects of our inquiry."[13] The results of the first six volumes, thus, remain valid in spite of the change of position.

The work that has begun with the definition of civilizational societies as "the intelligible fields of historical study" ends with

8. Ibid., 7:448.
9. Ibid., 423.
10. Ibid., 420.
11. Ibid., 449.
12. Ibid.
13. Ibid.

the declaration that they are unintelligible. The definition thus is as invalidated as a definition can be. Nevertheless, the execution of the program contained in the definition preserves its validity intact on its own level of operations. I need not elaborate to make it clear that whatever the substantive merits of the new position may be, the conceptual work leaves much to be desired.

What has happened in the course of the inquiry can best be understood through a confrontation of the original plan of the work with the form it has actually assumed. The *Study* was originally meant to be published in three "batches" of volumes. The first batch was supposed to contain the genesis and growth of civilizations; the second batch their breakdown and disintegration, including the universal states, universal churches, and heroic ages as the most significant symptoms of disintegration; and the last batch was to bring in the contacts between civilizations in space and time, supplemented by three studies on special problems. This plan of publication corresponded to the definition of history as the human study of civilizations in both their internal and external aspects: The study of civilizational courses was contained in the first two batches; the study of the relation between the societies in the last batch. In fact, however, only the first batch fulfilled the program outlined in the preface to volume 1. For between 1935, when the preface to the second edition still referred to the same plan, and 1939 occurred the existential advance of the inquiry that induced Toynbee to include in the second batch only such elements of the universal state, the universal church, and the heroic age, as were indispensable to round out the picture of disintegration according to the first plan, and to defer the main treatment of these subjects to the last batch. The completed *Study* as a whole, and the last batch of volumes in particular, suffer, therefore, from severe misconstruction, insofar as the plan, as it was conceived on the first existential level, was retained to cover the studies executed on the last existential level.

The misconstruction has, in fact, penetrated the subject matter so deeply that one can no longer clearly separate the blocks of the first plan from the studies of the last level. One might be tempted, when looking at the tables of contents, to decide that the studies on the contacts of civilizations in space and time, as well as the three supplemental studies, belong to the first plan and complete its execution that was broken off at the end of volume 6. In that case one could isolate the studies on the universal states, the universal churches, and the heroic ages from the rest of the *Study* and consider them an independent work representing Toynbee's view of history on the last existential level. But a close reading of the text reveals that the last batch of volumes is written in its entirety from the new position; lines that would separate sections of the first plan from the new interpretation can no longer be drawn. As a consequence, neither has the plan of the first level been completed, nor has the last level found an organizational form of its own. What that form might have been can be surmised, if volume 7 be considered a work standing for itself. Here we find a clear division of subject matter into universal states and universal churches. In the part on universal states the civilizational course is considered under the aspect of its services to the flowering of religions, under such titles as "The Utilization of Provincial Organizations by Churches," "The Use of Capital Cities as Seminaries for Higher Religions," "The Roman Army's Legacy to the Christian Church," and "Imperial Citizenships and Ecclesiastical Allegiances." In the part on universal churches, then, religions are considered under the aspect of their holding the key to the mystery of history. Nevertheless, volume 7 is not intended as an independent work, and one can legitimately extract no more from its construction than an increased understanding of the incision between volumes 6 and 7 of the *Study.* As a convenience of language we shall in the following reflections refer to volumes 1–6 as the first part, and to volumes 7–10 as the second part of the *Study.*

Once the substantive problem of the *Study* has been discerned behind the veils of misconstruction, the meaning of the *zetema* and its results come into view. Barring all the qualifications that would be necessary in the light of the preceding reflections we may say succinctly that the first part deals with the history of civilization, while the second part deals with the history of religion; or, if we use the classical terminology, Toynbee has written a profane history followed by a sacred history. The two parts together reflect an Augustinian project of historiography, as distributed over Orosius's *Historia contra Paganos* and Saint Augustine's own *De Civitate Dei.*

The return to the Augustinian conception of history is an event of considerable importance; and in view of the misconstruction of the *Study* we must ask, therefore, whether it was intended by

Toynbee at all, and if so, on what level of awareness. There is some evidence of his awareness to be found in the "Acknowledgments and Thanks" of volume 10, when he speaks of Ibn Khaldun who "gave me a vision of a study of History bursting the bounds of This World and breaking through into an Other World"; and then continues: "Saint Augustine, in his *De Civitate Dei*, gave me a vision of the relation in which those two worlds stand to one another."[14] This piece of evidence must not be neglected, but neither should it be overrated. In order to find a basis for judgment, let us consider the first and last appearances of the metaphorical vehicle of progress that moves through Toynbee's study on the wheels of civilization without the horsepower of concepts.

Its first appearance[15] is surrounded by a plethora of metaphors and mythical symbols. There is the shuttle on the loom of time that brings into existence a tapestry in which there is manifestly "a progress towards an end"; the chain of challenge-and-response releases the Promethean *élan* of social growth; the cycle of withdrawal-and-return transforms a personality and enhances its powers; the cycle of reproduction has made possible the evolution of all higher animals up to man; and even the repetitive "music of the spheres" dies down to an undertone in an expanding physical universe. The *sacra necessitas* of the cycle must be assumed, therefore, to coexist with an element of freedom in human affairs. Toynbee himself considers his view as a combination of Spengler's belief in the element of recurrence in human affairs and Einstein's belief in an element of uniqueness and irreversibility in the movement of the stars. All this, of course, does not sound in any way Augustinian.

On the occasion of its last appearance, the vehicle is accompanied by the symbols of "The Law of God" and the "Laws of Nature." " 'The Law of God' reveals the regularity of a single constant aim pursued unwaveringly, in the face of all obstacles and in response to all challenges, by the intelligence and will of a personality," while the "Laws of Nature" display the "regularity of a recurrent movement." Both concepts can be held simultaneously. The courses of civilizations, with their breakdowns and disintegrations, are transcended

in the cumulative spiritual progress of Religion through learning by suffering. This cumulative progress of Religion—which is the

14. Ibid., 10:236.
15. Ibid., 4:34–38.

spiritually highest kind of experience and endeavor within the range of Man on Earth—is a progress in the provision for Man, in his passage through This World, of means of illumination and grace for helping the pilgrim, while still engaged on his earthly pilgrimage, to attain a closer communion with God and to become less unlike Him.[16]

That language sounds closer to Saint Augustine's conception of the Church as the flash of eternity into time—but obviously it is not quite the same.

If now we use the two aggregates of symbols, which belong respectively to the second and third stages of the *zetema*, and try to formulate a judgment, we can do it best in terms of the tension between the immanent logic of the *zetema* and Toynbee's unwillingness to pursue his search to the end. By its immanent logic the search would lead Toynbee to a position, resembling the Augustinian, however differently he would have to articulate it in the light of our vastly increased contemporary knowledge in matters both historical and philosophical. And if we compare the first and last appearances of the famous vehicle, we can recognize, in the change of the symbolic atmosphere, the pressure of the search. Toynbee, however, is unwilling to give way; and under the prodding of "Mr. Martin Wight's" criticisms he becomes explicit on his reason—at least the overt one: His knowledge as a historian had not only shown that all attempts to formulate spiritual truth in intellectual terms had ended in failure, but convinced him that the feat could not be accomplished at all.

> Even if it were psychologically feasible, by agreement, to discard the classic theology of the four living higher religions and to substitute for it a newfangled theology expressed in terms, not of an Hellenic or an Indic philosophy, but of a Modern Western Science, a successful achievement of this tour de force would merely be a repetition of a previous error which would invite the same nemesis.

And in retrospect from his *Finis*, written June 15, 1951, he continues: "A scientifically formulated theology (if such could be conceived) would be as unsatisfying and as ephemeral as the philosophically formulated theology that was hanging like a millstone round the necks of Buddhists, Hindus, Christians, and Muslims in the year A.D. 1952."[17] When "Mr. Martin Wight" then prods him further and argues that, if he wishes to communicate in matters

16. Ibid., 9:174.
17. Ibid., 7:494–95.

concerning truth, he cannot escape his formulations being "the proper work of Reason," he replies that he can escape following the example of Plato. For Plato "yokes Reason and Intuition to his winged chariot side by side, without ever trying to disguise either of them in any trappings that belong to the other. In my belief it is because he drives this pair of horses in double harness that he succeeds in flying so high. I appeal to Plato's example."[18]

At this point the debate must cease. For here we are facing, on the part of Toynbee, a dilettantism with regard to questions of reason and revelation, philosophy and religion, metaphysics and theology, intuition and science, as well as communication, that could easily be overcome by anybody who wanted to overcome it. The situation on the level of overt argument points to the more deeply seated difficulty that Toynbee is sensitive to the word of God insofar as it has become historically tangible in dogmatic symbols and ecclesiastic institutions, but that he does not hear the word as spoken to him personally. It would be tactless and completely out of place to touch upon this personal problem if Toynbee himself had not placed it before the public by concluding his *Study* with the now famous prayer that begins:

> Christe, audi nos.
> Christ Tammuz, Christ Adonis, Christ Osiris, Christ Balder, hear us, by whatsoever name we bless Thee for suffering death for our salvation.[19]

This public prayer rises, not from man to God, but from the united religions to their historical symbols.

The imperfections of the work, thus, originate in the unwillingness to complete the *zetema* in spite of a clear knowledge what its end would have to be. What could have become a study of history along Augustinian lines has ended with a misconstruction. For history of religion is no more a *historia sacra* than the historical language symbols are the spiritual word spoken by God to man.

---

18. Ibid., 501.
19. Ibid., 10:143.

8

Prospects of Western Civilization

J. Madaule: Today we are going to broach a subject that is particularly close to our hearts and one about which we have not really ceased thinking, even when we were talking about other things. Professor Voegelin was willing to be in charge of beginning the discussion.

Mr. Voegelin: You all know that part of the great work of Mr. Toynbee, which is entitled "Prospects of Western Civilization" [in volume 9 of *A Study of History*.] I have here the intention neither of summarizing it, nor of discussing it; Mr. Toynbee will tell us himself if his thoughts, in this regard, have or have not evolved since the publication of his book. My intention is only to present some theoretical reflections which seem to me all the more necessary since, when the prospects of Western civilization are talked about, it is not at all sure if the same thing is always understood.

In the first part of the work, Mr. Toynbee has given us a theory of civilizations and of cycles of civilizations. In the second part, corresponding to volumes 7 through 10, it seems that the point of view of the author has evolved, since, as has been already noted even here, the unit of observation is no longer civilization, but rather religion, and the classification of civilizations appears to be constituted according to their contribution to the development of universal religion. In this respect, it is certain that the third civilizational

Translated by Peter Buttross Jr. for this edition from "Les perspectives d'avenir de la civilisation occidentale" in *L'Histoire et ses interprétations; Entretiens autour de Arnold Toynbee*, ed. Raymond Aron (The Hague: Mouton, 1961), 133–51. Reprinted by kind permission of Mouton de Gruyter GmbH & Co., Publishers, Berlin. This is one of fourteen roundtable discussions regarding Arnold Toynbee's work held, under the direction of Raymond Aron, between July 11 and July 19, 1958, at the International Cultural Center of Cerisy-la-Salle.

generation, particularly our Western civilization, plays only a rather mediocre role. One can see the problem which is before us and the importance of our initial choice of that which concerns the idea that we are able to have of this civilization and its future.

In order to try to resolve it, permit me to introduce a distinction between the properly scientific domain and that which I would willingly call "pre-analytical." It is not necessary to be a philosopher of history to pose political problems. We are all of us bound to an existence which each day demands that we resolve concrete problems. It is that which I call the "pre-analytical," by analogy with the "pre-predicative" as Husserl defines it in *Experience and Judgment,* in order to designate the world in which we live and which is given anterior to scientific rationalization. The term *analytical* is understood, on the other hand, in the sense in which Aristotle employs it when he distinguishes the *Topics* from the *Analytics,* that is to say, when he opposes to the theory of science the problems of argumentation which are posed beginning with premises which are no more than "areas" of rhetoric.

Thus daily life binds us to "topical" discussions beginning with premises unanalyzed and considered, however, to be indubitable. Such is the case when we speak of the prospects of Western civilization without knowing exactly what a civilization is. And nevertheless we all know that of which we speak: It is of something which affects us directly. The question is to know if it is possible, on such a subject, to go beyond the level of the "pre-analytical," the domain of this existential rhetoric by which we justify our desires, our plans, our worries, our agonies. There are numerous works of political science which place themselves, totally or partially, at this rhetorical level; and I would even dare say that this is the case with Marx, at least for the extended segments of his work.

In the sense of passing beyond the "pre-analytical," there was the grand attempt of Aristotle himself at giving a scientific analysis of man and of the city or polis, of approaching the essence, the nature, the *ousia,* by way of a chain of more or less rigorous concepts. We know that Aristotle defines man as a "political animal," that is to say, as a living bi-dimensional being who lives, inseparably, for himself and for the social group to which he belongs. But the final failure of Aristotle comes from the fact that the social group that he considers is limited to the polis and that he does not envision, except in passing, the notion of a general history of humanity, marked by the cyclical appearance of grand personages such as Zoroaster and Plato. No more than Plato himself does he envision historicity in the modern sense, which implies a unilinear conception of becoming.

This new conception appears, on the contrary, with Polybius, who sees in the Roman conquest the goal, the "end" (the *telos*) toward which all history is oriented. Humanity becomes the center of his thought, no longer the "city" or Greek civilization. Polybius admits that this end was already approached by the great empires, by the Iranian and Macedonian conquests, and that Rome is in the process of effectively realizing it. He considers history as *theoria*, the scientific knowledge of this accomplishment. The term *oecumene* designated up until then a certain cultural milieu; Polybius makes of it an object of "practical" action and the word is going to take on, with the Romans, a juridical significance for the purpose of designating membership in an empire with universal tendencies.

In the oldest Christian literature, the same term is loaded with a third significance; in certain Pauline texts, it designates humanity as the object of mission. When this mission is accomplished, Christ will return to earth and the ecumenical humanity of the mission will take its place in the Kingdom of God. These prospects appear more and more distant; ecumenism takes on then two opposing aspects. For certain ones, the ecumene becomes purely spiritual; it signifies total humanity to the extent that it has received the Word. But for others, it is going to signify the institutionalized church, the one that is protected by a central power, by a great empire. The contamination of these two conceptions will issue, under its extreme form, in Islam. But already the Augustinian ecclesiology makes of the terrestrial church the representation, in time, of the heavenly city. The *Civitas Dei* is located beyond history, but it belongs to history through the mediation of the church. Thus ecumenical humanity participates in transcendent processes; and, in a sense, it escapes history since it is associated, in its being and in becoming, with a reality which goes beyond it. It remains, however, through the visible church, dependent on human time.

Thus appears, so to speak, four blueprints of humanity: the humanity of the mission, the humanity of the Second Coming, the humanity represented on earth by the church militant, the accidental and purely earthly humanity. Now, the only humanity that may be conquered and politically organized is this accidental and purely earthly humanity. It is not the humanity of the mission, much less that of the Second Coming, but it is not either, in spite of certain appearances, the humanity of the church as representing the City of God on earth. However, the big dream of the man of today in the East and in the West is at the same time to "evangelize" all of humanity and to organize, politically, an earthly empire. And that, in certain fashion, is a Western constant. The notion of "empire," under its ancient form, is still visible in *The Universal History* of Bossuet. But beginning in the fifteenth century we see appear, in a parallel fashion, the new idea of an earthly future for a humanity that would unite and liberate itself by its own power.

When we speak of the prospects of Western civilization, are we thinking of a "civilization" in the limited sense in which Toynbee understands it, do we have in view the Polybian image of a world on the march toward universal empire, the Pauline image of a humanity of a mission living in wait of the Second Coming, or are we rather making allusion to the great revolutionary movement which was sketched out during the Renaissance in order to make man master and possessor of Nature? Are we speaking of ecumenism in the Christian sense, or in the pragmatic sense—as object of conquest and organization, a scientific analysis of political processes?

If we stop at this last interpretation, if we retain, as an essential character of Western civilization, the development of "reason" and of "science," the ambiguity is far from being alleviated. Plato and Aristotle, in effect, taught the Western world that one can rationally attain to the apprehension of essences. But of what "reason" is it a question? An action can be qualified as "rational" when it implies a certain adaptation of means to ends; "reason" can be understood in the "analytical" sense of Aristotle; but the word *reason* can also refer to the idea of a comprehensive view of the realm of being.

Now history shows us, in this realm of being, a progressive differentiation between the domain of transcendent Being and the domain of immanent being, but participating in the *Lex aeterna*. With a Saint Thomas this differentiation leads to its maximum; and it is this that I consider to be the highest degree of "reason." But it might well be that we are today on the down slope, on that of regression, where we see the confusion between the two domains of Being reestablish itself. The Christian idea of a perfect life, of *visia beatifica*, finds itself then immanentized and tends to be confused with the revolutionary idea of a perfection of humanity in history itself. We find again then the theme of the "metastasis" of man, of the appearance of a really new humanity. But what characterizes the modern world is the preeminence, in this transforming action, of the political factor. The two great protagonists of our present history are dominated by a common faith; they believe in a *telos* of humanity, they are conscious of a mission to fulfill.

Such projects are unrealizable. The constitution of being cannot be changed. When the action of men and governments is dominated by eschatological dreams, it becomes impossible to define a rational policy; one can no longer do anything but adjust means to predetermined ends. The political style which dominates is of a tactical order. Surely, in this regard, there is a big difference between the manner in which the Americans conceive of the establishment of the American Way of Life and the manner in which the Russians await the universal reign of Communism. The U.S.A. is content to react to events, to adapt as it can to events which often surprise her; the Russians have a more offensive tactic, more anticipatory. But neither are adapted to present reality. Is it possible for an American politics still dominated by the idea of the chosen people to adapt itself to a historic situation where there are no declarations or promises made to a chosen people, but simply the human condition? Is it possible for a Communist government to find again, beyond the myth, the simple reality of man?

That is the problem that I indicated a moment ago by evoking the end of the ideological and metastatic age, the possibility of finding again contact with reality in the classical sense of the term.

J. Madaule: Mr. Voegelin has led us to a level of reflection which perhaps goes beyond the more limited problem that we were thinking of asking today. But without a doubt we are going to question him on what he understands exactly by terms like "reality in the classical sense."

R. Aron: In fact, I have several questions to pose to Mr. Voegelin. During his exposé he called to mind the two attitudes, let us say messianic or gnostic—that is the word he has used in one of his books—millenarian, we may also say, which characterizes, in a certain fashion, American politics and Soviet politics. I would like to know if he thinks that these two attitudes represent, in the present world, fundamental factors and if he thinks that the future of Western civilization calls for the abandonment of these two messianisms or for the reconciliation between them. Does he not believe that, under their present form, these messianisms are the transposition, in mythical language, of a perfectly authentic reality, which is the transformation of the natural world by the power of science and technology? In the twentieth century, can we speak of a simple return to former gnosis? Does not the "metastasis" about which Mr. Voegelin has spoken to us rest today on facts hard to deny—on a real capacity of transformation of man by man?

Undoubtedly, the belief in a veritable metamorphosis of human nature often retains a semi-mythical character. But could we not say that the degree of adherence to these new messianisms is inversely proportional to the actual aptitude of man, to his true capacity of transformation of nature? The people most sensitive to the millenarian myth—are they not precisely those for whom the transformation of nature by science is yet to come; while to the extent that this transformation is effectively realized, the call to messianism would lose its intensity? For in fact, the capacity of science and industry to free man from servitude to his environment is not a gnostic dream; it is a living reality and could today still be it even more so. I wonder if, along the same line of thinking that has been presented to us, we could not ask what is today the genre of spiritual attitude which can be combined with this power of transformation, without degenerating into these messianisms which divide mankind at the exact moment when it should be united? . . .

L. Goldmann: The messianisms are older than industrial transformation.

R. Aron: Undoubtedly, but the historical origin of ideas prejudges nothing as to the authentic significance that they are able to take on at a given moment of history. The messianisms correspond to one of the permanent types of representation of the world that is encountered all through history; but the form that they take today is inseparable from the really demiurgical power of science and technology.

E. Voegelin: That is an incontestable fact.

L. Goldmann: It seems to me that in the background of Mr. Voegelin's exposé is the philosophical idea of a "natural" attitude to which he would wish that mankind return today, and which is defined, if I understood correctly, by the absence of messianism. This attitude corresponds to a definitive "truth," immutable, tied to the primary affirmation of the transcendence of Being. It is starting from there that Mr. Voegelin sees in the appearance of messianisms a sort of regression, decline, estrangement from the "real." I would like to know on what such a judgment of value is founded. For, in short, one could see in the messianic attitude a "natural" attitude and, on the contrary, in the idea of transcendence, a phenomenon of decline.

E. Voegelin: I do not believe that it is a question of value judgments in the sense in which Mr. Goldmann understands it. It seems to me that my analysis is founded on objective criteria. I have defined the "reason" as maximal distinction between the domains of being. Can it not be said, in the most objective fashion, that as soon as this distinction between immanence and transcendence is renounced, we are on the road of regression?

L. Goldmann: Perhaps, but first on the condition of demonstrating that several domains of being actually exist, and that the realm of transcendence is not a mere illusion.

E. Voegelin: I cannot answer you on that point without entering into a difficult metaphysical discussion; I will only say that there is, historically, an experience of transcendence. Now, faced with such an experience, you have a choice: Either you accept it as a participation in transcendent Being, or you must develop a psychology of projection, of the type of Feuerbach's.

L. Goldmann: There are better ones than Feuerbach's, in the same sense. . . .

E. Voegelin: Whether this psychology be that of Feuerbach's himself or one of the improved forms of which you are thinking, I say that, in order to accept it, it is first necessary to prove that the experiences of transcendence are not what they claim to be. Now these experiences are historical facts, and it is necessary to begin by accepting them as such.

L. Goldmann: I acknowledge that I do not follow you exactly, for in fact there are in history thousands of experiences that a critical analysis has reduced, after the fact, to the level of illusions. When you yourself speak of that which you call a gnosis, you bring about reductions of that sort. Socialist messianism refers back to a sort of religious experience, but to an experience without transcendence. Why would you object to it *a priori*, when it surely constitutes a historical fact like the others?

E. Voegelin: For an epistemological reason which seems to me totally valid: because it is a question of a derivative type of experience, not of an original experience.

L. Goldmann: But it is exactly there that I discern what I called a value judgment. Why would messianism without transcendence not be the original form of religious experience, with messianisms with transcendence not making up, on the contrary, degenerate forms. The chronological order of appearance does not correspond to the order of declining reality. Science comes after magic, and nevertheless, one can in a sense consider magic as a degenerate form of science.

E. Voegelin: One cannot abstract from the historical order in which the problems appear. There is no atheism before theism; it is theism which is the condition itself of the ulterior development of atheism.

L. Goldmann: Of course, but I am simply saying that religion has no need of transcendence, in the precise mode of superhuman. I see religion as a fundamental fact, which is found, implicitly or explicitly, in all of civilization. But it is not necessary that this religion bind itself to the idea of the superhuman. You have said that modern civilization was not the creator of universal religion. It seems to me, on the contrary, that socialism is a universal religion, that it implies a perfectly authentic religious experience, and that one does not have the right to object to it as a mere degeneration when it in fact integrates all that was valid in previous experiences.

J. Madaule: That is an immense problem that we could perhaps reserve for another discussion.

R. Aron: We cannot reserve it for another time, for it is at the very center of Mr. Voegelin's exposé. Our colleague has told us, in effect, that, in that which concerns the establishment of a universal religion, Western civilization is totally sterile, that it gives a place only to derivative ideologies, of secondary value. It seems then that, for him, the decline of the modern West is directly linked to the opposition of authentic religion and false ideologies.

E. Voegelin: I did not use the word *decline*; I only spoke of an analytical regression from reality.

R. Aron: May I ask you then what historical meaning you give to this analytical regression from reality?

E. Voegelin: In order to answer you, permit me to call upon Bergsonian categories. There are periods when the soul is open to transcendence, and periods when the soul is closed to this transcendence. It is not for the historian as such to say why such a period of closure succeeds such a period of openness. I have simply described a fact. And if I have suggested that we are perhaps at the end of the period of closure, I have nevertheless not wanted to pose here as a theologian of history.

R. Aron: Whatever might be the vocabulary you use, I find nevertheless the idea of decline in the background of your perspective.

L. Sebag: Permit me to pose the problem in other terms, but which will perhaps permit us to find what is at the very heart of our discussion. It is absolutely certain, in our day, that the problem of the future prospects for Western civilization is more often posed in terms of decline. On the one hand, the West has been confronted by a certain number of other civilizations, which have progressively demanded, if not a central place, at least an equal ranking with Western civilizations; on the other hand, during the course of the twentieth century, the political supremacy, and even technology, of the West has come up against the lively ambitions and the successes of a certain number of countries belonging to other traditions. When one spoke of the "decline" of the West, one often considered the first of these aspects, not the second; one thought of the decline of certain traditional values of the West without equally posing the problem of a decline of Western society in its totality. Such is, I believe, the case with Spengler and with many authors who have entered upon the study of the process of a rationalist, technical, scientific civilization—that is to say, upon the study of all that is linked to the appearance of the industrial society as such. But this appearance itself has been considered rather as a deviation from the true Western tradition than as the historical outcome of this tradition.

Now, I think, on the contrary, that the founding of this industrial society—which tends today to become the universal social type— is the ultimate outcome of Western society as such, that it was historically possible only through the existence of Judaeo-Christian values which, under different forms, prepared the arrival of it. In this perspective, it is evident that the U.S.A. and the U.S.S.R. fully, authentically belong to this Western civilization and that these two powers express in a fundamental way the most profound aspirations of it. It is noteworthy that if there is today a challenge to Western civilization from other civilizations, it is in the very name of the values that these other civilizations have borrowed from the West. And that is a paradox we should stop to consider. For, in fact, if we consider the essential problem of our time—that of the relations between the industrialized countries and those that are crassly called the "underdeveloped" countries—it is certain that these not as yet industrialized countries, or insufficiently industrialized countries, demand precisely an equality in standard of living with the strongly industrialized countries, and that they demand it precisely in the name of values which have been permitted by this industrialization and this elevation in the standard of living. They do not at all ask for a return to a traditional wisdom, which certain Western esthetes admire so much, but the formation of a scientific and technical elite, the birth of a rationalist mentality—all that complex of elements which characterizes industrial society and which today is spreading itself throughout the entire planet.

The questioning of Western civilization appears, then, it seems to me, like the limit of its triumph. In order that this questioning were possible, it was first necessary to have conquest, colonization, the introduction by military and economic means of a new form of power, often hardly welcomed; but afterward it is in the name of this new form of power, in the name of this civilization, accepted as a universal fact, that the people—conquered or indirectly enslaved— demand their independence. The situation is very different from the one that was able to come about, for example, at the time when the Roman empire was crumbling under the shock of the barbarians. Whatever might have been the influence on these barbarians of a certain number of Greco-Roman values, one can speak, however, of an opposition between two value systems, and of a possible synthesis which took place in the Middle Ages. Today, there is only one value system, and the problem is the same for all of humanity:

to complete and to universalize industrialization, technology, and, at the same time, to reduce that which may be very roughly called the quantum of inhumanity which has accompanied the birth of industrial civilization.

We find ourselves, therefore, back at the problem which was posed, in somewhat different terms, by both Raymond Aron and Arnold Toynbee: i.e., to know which is the value system which can not only be reconciled with this new complex but can express it in the most adequate way. This is a problem all the more essential since, for the first time in history, we can, we must even, think in terms of the planet; we are witnessing a general collation of all human cultures. One can even ask if the value system which would best express the spirit of industrialized society would not in fact be the radical historicization of our condition—placing into the equation all types of language, all types of institutions which have been created by men in the course of history and in all countries.

A project of this type appears, with Hegel, in the beginning of the nineteenth century. It is a question of collating all the discourses which it has been possible for man to engage in concretely in multiple historical situations; and it may be said that, for Hegel, the true discourse of man of the universal society is exactly this collation of the entirety of languages. In the same sense, one would be able to call to mind the "Imaginary Museum" of Malraux, where, for the first time, the collation of all possible artistic styles is realized—that collation which even definitively shapes the artistic conscience of Western man.

In closing, I would like to point out that I thought I discerned in the problematic of Professor Voegelin a certain ambiguity, which stems from, I believe, a misreading of what properly belongs to our modern industrial civilization. He retains, in effect, from the ideology belonging to this civilization only the negative traits, so to speak. He admits that past societies have been able to create universal religions, while we were only capable of creating ideologies, that is to say, unilateral knowledge which does not succeed in integrating the human condition in its totality. But one would be able to maintain—totally on the contrary—that the preceding value systems wanted to be universal and that they were not, while the mankind of industrial civilization is building a system which not only seeks to be universal, but which is not able to be constituted as such without realizing the ordering of the entirety of discourses held by all men of all civilizations.

E. Voegelin: Permit me to raise the objection that you are using a great number of symbols which are not, I believe, true concepts. The expression "system of values" is one of the *topoi*, one of the "commonplaces" of our civilization, but it is a "pre-analytic" notion, which is found at the level of what I have called existential rhetoric. The object of science is precisely to go beyond this level and to attempt the analysis of rhetorical notions. Instead of such an analysis, you are returning to the pre-analytic level, and you are talking about the discovery of a system of values for industrialized society. The analysis must consider the true problems of the human ecumene under all its aspects; the analysis must define the essence of man, the essence of societies, the essence of historical life, and determine if there is, or is not, a history of humanity, etc.

L. Sebag: Surely; but beside problems dealing with the general essence of society, one can also ask just what is the essence of this particular society in which we presently live. I have wondered what were the forms of compatibility between culture and society, not in itself, but in a determined situation, which is ours at this moment, not in a little far off canton, but on the scale of the entire planet. To do that, I am in no way placing myself at the level of what you call existential rhetoric, for, if one takes no matter what cultural problem of our time, one sees that the structure, which I have tried to define, is always found to be immanent in the original intention which is capable of animating the different levels. I cited art as an example. The possibility of Western man opening himself to the totality of artistic styles—even of achieving an art founded principally on the collation of all these styles—more profoundly defines our present culture than all the ideologies of which you have spoken. I refer you, for example, to a work like *Doktor Faustus* of Thomas Mann. If we try to characterize the problem which is posed to Leverkuhn, the musician whom Mann made the hero of his book, we find that he is faced with an immense amount of musical material, and his last work calls us to a veritable transformation of this material: Beginning with Gregorian chant, it ends in twelve-tone music. That last work, the one which expresses his ultimate message, is thus made of the whole of the musical materials which man has successively or simultaneously created.

That is only an example, but a significant one, I believe. As to the whole of the social structures in which we are involved, it seems to me that you have not given a sufficient account of the positive character—I use the word with no value judgment—that they present. Raymond Aron spoke to the point when he answered you that, even if one admits to the existence of certain messianisms, it is necessary to recognize that this general movement, which runs through the entire history of humanity, receives, in present society, a new content the specificity of which must be analyzed.

R. Aron: Since Mr. Voegelin so strongly distinguishes concepts from the *topoi*, since he reproaches his challengers for remaining at the level of existential rhetoric, I would like to ask him if it is possible, according to him, to have a scientific analysis of the structures belonging to a modern society, of industrialized society. Beginning from the essence of human societies in general, does he admit only species, the differentiation of which is of little interest to him; or does he admit of a diversity which would be itself an object of scientific analysis?

E. Voegelin: One could, undoubtedly, respond that the nature of man does not change, but that nature has a history.

L. Goldmann: How do you prove that?

E. Voegelin: We are not here on ground that allows of proofs in the proper sense of the term. The term *nature* is a philosophical term and, by definition, nature is precisely that which does not change.

L. Goldmann: And if, on the contrary, I define the nature of man by change?

E. Voegelin: The idea of a human nature that would change resembles, for me, the idea of a square triangle.

R. Aron: Admitting that you can define the nature of man as a reality that does not change, is it necessary to say the same regarding the nature of societies?

E. Voegelin: The nature of man in society does not change, insofar as nature, but there is a place, however, for an amplitude, for a historic development. That which you understand by a change of nature is simply history. But the problem of nature is always there, and it is this nature which is the object of analysis.

L. Goldmann: But since you admit that nature has a history, and since this history is not finished and not a cyclical repetition, how would you be able to know the true nature of man? Does it not depend on a multiplicity of factors which are still unknown to us?

E. Voegelin: Precisely—every attempt to know the nature of man, which begins from his history, is doomed to failure. History is indefinite; it has no essence; and we never know but a limited portion of it. But in the interior of the horizon of our experience, we can discern no change in the nature of man.

L. Goldmann: Permit me to say that that is a mere convention of vocabulary. You admit that we have only a limited experience of history, which can, consequently, reveal to us only a limited view of that which you call human nature. In that case, I ask again my previous question: What authorizes you to decree that the recognition of transcendence more authentically expresses the essence of man? And I add, if you permit, a second question which refers to the exposé of Sebag. You reproached him for having used formulae which belonged to the domain of existential rhetoric, when he was relying on givens which were simply empirical. If you refuse these empirical givens, which seem to be of the same type as the formulae that you accept—when you speak, for example, of "Christian values" or of "experiences of transcendence," I find it hard to see how you distinguish, epistemologically, that which is for you analytic and that which remains at the level of the *topoi*.

E. Voegelin: If I give a privileged position to the recognition of transcendence, it is because it manifests a progress of reason in its effort to differentiate, to the maximum, the diverse regions of being.

L. Sebag: But is every differentiation in itself valid?

E. Voegelin: The differentiations that reason works appear at an established moment of history. It is accordingly, for example, that Plato distinguished philosophy from what was called *philodoxie*. Now, we are living today in a civilization where the confusion of ideas is such that everything that Plato had rejected as *philodoxie* is called philosophy. When you refuse to make that Platonic distinction—so precisely and so strongly substantiated in the work of Plato—it is for you to justify your position.

L. Goldmann: I am not a specialist in Platonism, but still it seems to me that Plato was unaware of the eschatological conception of history. It would be more appropriate here to refer to Hegel or to Marx.

R. Aron: I would wish that the discussion not take a too technically philosophical turn. It runs the risks, moreover, of ending in an impasse, for Professor Voegelin will certainly recognize that, if he himself makes a fundamental distinction between the domain of the analytic and that zone which he calls pre-analytic (and which is the zone of *Weltanschauungen,* of visions of the world), that which precisely characterizes the manner of thinking of his contradictors is that they reject that distinction. If these contradictors had dared tell you the essence of their thinking, I believe they would have said that what you take for a philosophical reality different from the existential *topoi* is, in its turn, only an existential *topos.* Perhaps they are wrong in thinking it, but the demonstration of your respective positions is evidently beyond the compass of our discussion. It would be more fruitful, I believe, to take another direction, which was touched on in your exposé and which concerns the relationship between the becoming—progression or regression—of analytic thought and the actual course of events. For, after all, you must have certain ideas on the significance of this becoming within the global development of society. If, when speaking here of the present fate of Western civilization, if you described the movement of analytical reason, it is because you see there something essential for the interpretation of civilization. Therefore, I would like you to explicate what has remained implicit in your exposé—that is to say, the connection that you establish between this movement of philosophy strictly speaking and the events which we are in the process of living.

E. Voegelin: If we consider civilization as a social reality, in the Toynbeean sense, we cannot speak of a decline of Western civilization. The development of physical science, of technologies, of productivity, etc., are incontestable progressions. But I hold, at the same time, on the strictly intellectual plane, they are evident regressions.

J. Madaule: But the problem would then perhaps be to know what is the relationship between these progressions and this regression.

Would it be a question of the mere coexistence of contrary movements within the bosom of the same civilization, or must we rather think that what you call regression within the intellectual order is structurally linked to the progress of science and technology?

E. Voegelin: I think there exists, in fact, a link between these two phenomena, but this link is anterior to industrial development.

J. Madaule: You mean to say that, without a doubt, the advancement in industrialization and the philosophical regression proceed from a common source. This source for you is probably the theme of the conquest of the world, such as it appears, for example, in the works of Bacon and Descartes. From there, great successes are going to be acquired on the road to the domination of nature; but at the same time, many other fundamental questions, touching on social organization, development of personhood, the nature of reason, are going to be neglected: all of which leads to the present crisis—to man who acts more and more, but who knows less and less why he acts.

K. von Fritz: I would like to say a few words about a problem which seems to me essential—that is, the relationship between human nature and historical conditioning. One of the characteristics relating to human nature is, obviously, to be always in a historical setting, to actualize itself only within determined historical conditions. Now, among these historical conditions, we must include that change of which we spoke when dealing with value judgments. But what remains constant is not less important, and perhaps even more important. It will be found paradoxical that I take Professor Voegelin to task precisely for having made, in his exposé, too great a place for change. Has he not perhaps by doing that provided weapons to his contradictors? From my point of view, I would object, for example, to what he said about the limitation of man, in Aristotle, on the level of the polis. According to Aristotle, it belongs to the essence of man to live in a "city"; to escape this necessity, man would have to raise himself above the human condition. But although man always lives in cities that change, although this change in historical conditions is able to create the illusion of a radical diversity, man remains always man. Usually opposed to each other, for example, are the Marxist and the capitalist value systems. But it seems to me that it is not by accident that the adherents of the two systems use the same terms in a common fashion—that they both speak of justice and freedom. If these terms did not resonate in all human beings, they could not be used in the two camps for pure purpose of propaganda.

O. Anderle: The discussion has been raised to such a level of abstraction that it will not be surprising that a mere specialist of cultures, or of the comparative morphology of cultures, would wish to see the problem which we have to debate posed in a more concrete and relevant fashion—and the problem concerns the future prospects of Western civilization.

Practically speaking, the question is as follows: Is it possible to foresee the future of a culture, is it possible to formulate demonstrable scientific propositions about this future? In physics, prediction works as a function of rigorously established causal laws. Can we determine, in the field of cultures, structural laws relating to a becoming which, as such, would itself be structured? Of course, such predictions would not in any case reach to the detail of events, but are they possible in that which concerns the general sense of the evolution; and can we, for example, herald—as Professor Toynbee seems to do—the probable advent of a universal state?

In that which concerns the West, prediction is particularly difficult, because our future depends perhaps less on the internal structure of our own civilization than on its relations with the rest of the world. Consequently, in order to predict what will result from the conflict between East and West, it would be necessary first to formulate predictions on the internal future of the East—all of which is not impossible to the extent that this other cultural world has, as does ours, a certain internal structure. But then remaining would be the measuring of the consequences of the meeting and the interference between these two dynamic structures. That is a difficult task—a task which can only be that of the specialist of world history or of the specialist of the comparative morphology of cultures.

If we admit Professor Toynbee's conception, according to which the Eastern world is only a branch detached from the Western whole, it is necessary to suppose that this branch will one day return to the whole of which it is only a part. But from another perspective, the East may be seen as the progressive outcrop, the emergence, the flowering of a new superior culture; in this case, the descending curve of the West will somewhere meet the ascending curve of the East. But what would then be decisive would be, I think, less the crossing of these two curves than the fact that the Western world has not yet arrived at the stage necessary for universal empire—if one admits, of course, with Spengler that every superior culture begins and ends in a state of universality; whereas the Eastern world is still under the action of the first phase of the becoming of its own civilization—that is to say, under the universality of the Byzantine type. This asymmetry can make us pessimists as regards the future of the West; I believe, however, that our superiority is precisely in understanding our situation and, I believe, our decline is not inevitable.

J. Taubes: I would like to pose two questions—one to Mr. Voegelin, the other to his socialist adversaries. As to the exposé of Mr. Voegelin, it seems to me that there is a problem which has its source in his attempt to attach the Christian vision of the world to a Greco-pagan vision—by admitting that the expression "nature of man" retains, for Saint Paul, for example, the meaning that it was able to have for Plato and for Aristotle. It seems to me that the fundamental lived experience of Christianity is that of conversion, of the *metanoia*, the passing from the old to the new Adam. And that was not always understood by the thinkers of the Middle Ages, who wanted to retain Greco-pagan concepts while giving them a Christian content. Therefore, I would be in agreement with Goldmann, who thinks reference to Plato is not very enlightening for our purposes and that the discussion would be taken up in a more fruitful fashion between Saint Paul and Hegel—that is to say, within a perspective which gives a new meaning to the idea of nature, such as the ancient philosophers did. Saint Paul and the socialists are in fact in agreement in denying the existence of a human nature in the Greek sense, and they are in agreement in admitting that man can change in a profound way. The only difference is that, for the Christians, grace alone works this transformation, while for the modern revolutionaries, it is man himself who transforms himself by transforming nature.

As to the socialist critics of Mr. Voegelin—and among them, if he will, I include Mr. Aron—I am surprised only that they have appeared to accept so easily on behalf of modern industrial society the eschatological status which had been at issue within a totally

different perspective. That there might be a certain American messianism, a certain Russian millenarianism—that is possible in one
sense, and even probable—but the rationalism of industrialized
society seems to me a totally different type.

J. Madaule: Before giving the floor to Mr. Voegelin, who will certainly want to respond to those remarks and some others, we would
like to know Professor Toynbee's reactions to today's discussion.

A. Toynbee: I would like first to emphasize, along with Mr. Aron,
this totally new fact, which is material power, physical power
without precedent which today is conferred on man by the progress
of science and technology. It is a factor of such importance that it
makes, I believe, all prediction of the future almost impossible—
which prediction would have to be founded on past experience. Let's
take, for example, the case of war. War has always been, up to now,
an instrument, highly uncertain without a doubt, but nonetheless
an instrument of politics. Now, today, a third world war would
perhaps not be ended as preceding wars by the triumph of a victor
or by a reasonable compromise. The new forces that technology
places at the disposition of man are so disproportionate to the
human faculties of reflection and foresight that they can no longer
be considered as means in the service of certain ends; these forces,
by their very nature, elude those who claim to be using them.

Faced with this extraordinary growth in his power, a moderation
would be required of man—a discipline, a spiritual maturity equally
extraordinary. And that is not a question that concerns only the
West, for, as Mr. Sebag has noted, today it is the entire world
that wants to possess modern science and technology, that wants
to make the ambiguous heritage of our Western civilization bear
fruit. This need—universal—of a moral discipline takes us back to
the problem of change, which cropped up in our system of values
at the end of the seventeenth century. Mr. Voegelin appeared to
suggest that we would be able, in brief, to return to the conception
which was ours, let's say, at the time of Bossuet. But that is a
too provincially Western point of view. I believe that in this new
debate—philosophical and religious—each of the other civilizations
can and must bring their own positive elements. I predict, speaking
for myself, a return to man's traditional interest in religion and
philosophy; but not a return to the traditional philosophy and
religion of the West: because, on the one hand, the West, after the

experience of the last three or four centuries, would in no way be able to return to its traditions without radical change; and on the other hand, because other traditions, in a universe which is less and less compartmentalized, will bring their important contribution to a spiritual debate which this time will be truly universal.

L. Goldmann: I would like, not to take up all the questions already posed—which would raise many diverse problems—but I would like to recall to mind, however, in a word, that the socialist conception—which I wish to call eschatological, but which is founded, when all is said and done, on a wager—is not philosophically so distant from the true Christian position. The Christian, like the socialist, lives, in fact, in the world, a world which contains mystery and the irrational; but their action in this world is oriented toward something beyond their present state, and this effort at actualizing a better future gives, when all is said and done, a meaning to their lives. The essential thing is not to consider Christian transcendence or the better future of the socialist society as means of escape and evasion.

R. Aron: I was a little surprised to have been placed, a moment ago, in the socialist camp. Although I am, rather, a liberal, I do not consider being called a socialist a dishonor. I would, however, like to make it clear that the only socialism which I would accept being placed on me is in no way an eschatology, but a more or less rational conception of social organization.

J. Madaule: I will now give the floor to Mr. Voegelin—I will not say to close, but rather to conclude a debate which he so brilliantly opened.

E. Voegelin: My colleague von Fritz will pardon me for not returning to the question—a little too technical—of the polis and of the *politeia* in Aristotle. Moreover, I do not think that it is very important to our central problem.

To Mr. Anderle, who reproaches me, if I have understood correctly, for escaping into a too theoretical debate when the present world presents us with so many practical questions—to him I answer that theory is the necessary basis of every interpretation of reality—in its most immediate and most concrete. In order to be a veritable empiricist, it is not sufficient to refuse to place into question the premises that you use in a so-to-speak spontaneous way. Now, there were in Mr. Anderle's remarks many unanalyzed premises; for example, that cultures exist, that these cultures are structured, etc. I tried, in fact, in my initial exposé, to show that it is first necessary to resolve the problem of the object. Are the only units that present themselves to the scientific work of the historian these societies that we call civilizations? Must we not add to them the forms of units defined by Polybius or, moreover, those that have appeared in the modern world since the fifteenth or sixteenth century? Because of the lack of time I cannot return now to the previous question which appears to me of capital importance.

Mr. Taubes asked a question which is equally very important—that of the Judaeo-Christian eschatology. A serious historian is necessarily confronted, sooner or later, with this problem, and whether he likes it or not, he has to formulate a philosophy of eschatology. On this subject, I will simply note that, within Judaeo-Christian eschatology, the transformation of man, the change in the constitution of being, is the product of a divine act. Now, if the transcendent is eliminated, while retaining the idea of metastasis, it is to human action that we must attribute the change of nature. The perspective is totally different. In the first case, neither science nor philosophy can say anything of worth, because it is a question of a revealed mystery. But in the immanentist conception, science and philosophy have the right to interfere—they can introduce an analysis of notions which make evident the derivative, bastard, illegitimate character of that which is in reality only a modern form of ancient gnosis.

J. Madaule: In heartily thanking Professor Voegelin on behalf of all members of the audience for the significant themes for reflection that he suggested to us, I would like to say in conclusion that if he found himself facing a resolute opposition—and probably an unshakeable one—to aspects of his thought, he has at least fed a discussion which was often very thrilling. Tomorrow, we will take up again the problem of the prospects of Western civilization under another light, beginning with the preliminary reflections that Raymond Aron will wish—and I thank him for it—to present to us.

9

World-Empire and
the Unity of Mankind

An inquiry into the topic of world-empire and the unity of mankind sounds, at first hearing, like a dubious enterprise. One's imagination roams over the history of mankind; it evokes empires ancient, medieval, and modern; and it recalls their claim to dominion over the world. The subject seems to be boundless. Moreover, the theoretical implications of the term *world-empire*, although it is generally used in historiography and politics, are quite insufficiently explored, so that the difficulties caused by the boundlessness of materials are aggravated by the inadequacy of conceptual instruments. What can be sensibly said, in the course of a lecture, about so vast and unexplored a topic?

Nevertheless, these are precisely the reasons that justify the inquiry and even, considering the claims to world dominion that threaten us, endow it with urgency. What is doubtful is less the reason and urgency of the attempt than its wisdom in terms of results. Will the philosophy of politics, in its present state, allow of a result worth the effort? With regard to this question I am optimistic, I hope not unduly so—not that a topic of such complexity could be exhausted by a lecture, but it should be possible at least to draw the main lines of the problem.

Originally published in *International Affairs* 38, no. 2 (1962), this essay is reprinted here by kind permission of the Royal Institute of International Affairs and Cambridge University Press. As the headnote states, it was given as the "Stevenson Memorial Lecture No. 11, arranged under the joint auspices of the London School of Economics and the Royal Institute of International Affairs and delivered at the London School of Economics on 3 March, 1961. Sir Sydney Caine, K.C.M.G., presided." Ibid., 170.

Before entering into the analysis, however, we must have a preliminary understanding about the meaning of world-empire; and as the conceptual core of the term, as I have suggested, is too uncertain to be useful for the purpose, the subject-matter will be best circumscribed if we briefly recall the historical phenomenon of empire and its relation to the unity of mankind.

I

There is agreement among historians that a certain period of ancient history has eminently the character of an age of world empires. It is the period beginning roughly in the sixth century B.C. with the Iranian expansion over Mesopotamia, to the Indus in the east, and to the Anatolian littoral and Egypt in the west. In its own geographical area the Iranian establishment of a multi-civilizational empire was followed by the conquests of Alexander, by the Diadochic, and ultimately by the Roman and Sassanian empires. In the wake of the Iranian and Macedonian conquests, then, the new model of large-scale dominion was imitated in India by the Maurya empire. And without any causal connection with the events farther west as far as we know, although at the same time, classical China went through the troubles of the Chou period, culminating in the creation of the first Chinese empire through Ch'in Shi Huang Ti and the Han dynasty.

Parallel in time with the creation of empires spanning the ecumene from the Atlantic to the Pacific, there occurred the famous outbreak on the spiritual level that has fascinated historians, and especially philosophers of history, ever since the data and dates became known with some accuracy early in the nineteenth century. As much as the empires, the appearances of Confucius and Laotse in China, of the Buddha in India, of Zoroaster in Iran, of the prophets in Israel, of the philosophers in Hellas have marked an epoch in the history of mankind. In recent times its cardinal importance has been illuminated by the discussions of Bergson, Toynbee, and Jaspers. With impeccable caution it has been characterized by Bergson as the "opening of the soul"; and less impeccably, with an anti-Christian prejudice, by Jaspers as the *axis-time* of mankind. The outbreak of imperial expansion was thus accompanied by an opening of spiritual and intellectual horizons that raised humanity to a new level of consciousness.

The parallelism of the two phenomena suggests a connection between them. Not, to be sure, a connection on the level of causality, for assertions that the spiritual openings were caused by imperial expansion or that the founders of empire were inspired by the prophets and philosophers would be simplistic generalizations to be quickly falsified by references to historical facts. It is rather an ontological connection, inasmuch as the parallel phenomena in the areas of power and organization and of spiritual penetration of human existence display a parallelism of meaning. For the empires were world-empires, not by arbitrary declaration of the moderns, but by their self-interpretation as attested by the literary texts; and the outbursts of the spirit were accompanied by the consciousness of achieving a new truth of human existence. An affinity of meaning subtly connects a creation of empire that claims to represent mankind with a spiritual efflorescence that claims representative humanity. The parallel phenomena, while not causing one another, are parts of a configuration of history by virtue of the adumbrated connection. Moreover, the *dramatis personae* of history were well aware of the affinity and acted upon their knowledge. Within the meaningful configuration, which as a whole is beyond causality, there run the motivations of pragmatic history, resulting in associations between imperial order and spiritual movements, such as the association of the Achaemenid empire with Zoroastrianism or of the Asoka empire with Buddhism. Especially symptomatic for this awareness of affinity on the ontological level are the Chinese and Roman cases, in which the governments conducted something like a series of experiments with imperial theologies: in China the experiments with Taoism, Confucianism, Buddhism; in Rome a first attempt, at the beginning of the principate, with the *theoi eleutherioi* of the polis who were supposed to endow the empire with the character of a "free world," followed by the later experiments with the Baal of Emesa, the Sol Invictus, and finally with the God of the Christians. These tentative and experimental associations among the parallel phenomena, based on the recognition of their affinity, should be included in the type concept of the configuration. We gain thereby a definition of the first tier of world-empires beyond the strictly cosmological empires of the Mesopotamian and Egyptian type.

A power organization, informed by the pathos of representative humanity, and therefore representative of mankind—that would be the core, as it emerges from the historical phenomena, of a definition of world-empire. With the conceptional core laid bare, the specific differences of various types of empire will, for the present purpose, need no more than a word. The first period of empire just considered is characterized by the parallelism of imperial creation and spiritual efflorescence, by the awareness of affinity between the phenomena, and by their tentative and experimental associations. In the second period the affinity of meaning as well as the necessity of association is taken for granted; and perhaps for that reason the association becomes so stable that one can speak of an orthodoxy of empire. It is the age of emergent new societies to which we accord the rank of civilizations: the Western Latin and the Eastern Greek Christian empires, the Islamic empire, and the Neo-Confucian empire in the Far East. The case of India displays certain peculiarities— a Hinduist orthodoxy without formal power organization—that cannot be dealt with in this context. Roughly around A.D. 1500 begins a third period, which reveals the stability of the orthodox empires as deceptive. Global movability opens new perspectives of imperial expansion, with the Western national states as power centers; it is the age of the Spanish and British empires on which the sun never sets; moreover in America and Russia further centers of large-scale organizations are formed. From the spiritual side, at the same time, the formative force of the orthodoxies begin to wane and the gnostic movements arise as rivals for the rank of representative humanity. At present, the dissociation of the orthodoxies has not yet given way to new associations that one would dare to characterize as definite. New worlds are in formation—a new "free world," a Communist world, and a *troisième monde;* new civil theologies are in the making; and the association of empire and spirit has again become tentative and experimental.

These reflections will be sufficient for a preliminary understanding of the subject matter, preparatory to analysis proper. It is only fair to state, however, that even these preliminaries involve major theoretical problems, such as the distinction between historical causation and the meaning of configurations beyond causality, which cannot be more fully developed on this occasion.

II

An analysis should start from the meaning of words accepted at the time by the general public. Since we are living in an age bent on increase of power through the advancement of science and control over nature, I shall start from the meaning of *world-empire* as dominion over a sizable part of the globe and a correspondingly sizable part of its inhabitants. In the combinatory term the world, whether in the sense of territory or of people, is an object of dominion; it signifies a datum, a given thing. What becomes manifest in this meaning is an intellectual climate in which the instrumentalist attitude toward things is extended to man and ultimately to the world at large.

The meaning of an object of dominion beloved by the age is a theoretically useful starting point, because in the very act of extending the instrumentalist attitude beyond the realm of things, there open the fissures into which one can drive the wedge of analysis. For things inanimate may pass as objects to be used and managed—although even in this case there is lurking in the background the issue of the cosmos as the habitat of man but not the unconditional means for his purposes, the issue of a nature liable to be defiled. But men as objects of dominion certainly raise the ethical problem that, in the eighteenth century, provoked Kant to postulate man as a purpose in itself, never to be used only as a means to an end. Not that the postulate was well reasoned—for the man who is a purpose in itself has lost his status as *imago Dei*, the true source of his untouchable dignity; he is on the way toward becoming a contemporary "existence" that takes charge of itself (to use the existentialist jargon)—but precisely because of its secularist distortion the postulate in its Kantian form should be recalled as an act of resistance, however ambiguous, against the theories and techniques of psychological management that, in the spirit of ascendant instrumentalism, the French *philosophes* had already developed after the middle of the eighteenth century.

With the extension of the instrumentalist attitude to the world itself we come to the heart of the problem, namely, the maltreatment of symbols of transcendence as things at hand. For if by *world* is meant an expanse of territory as the object of dominion—in the sense in which Roman legal language used to speak of the *orbis terrarum* as the area of imperial jurisdiction—we run into the discrepancy of unbounded space and the territorial finiteness of empires. It is a discrepancy, to be sure, that the theoreticians of empire can overcome, at least to their own satisfaction. In the case of the Mongol empire, for instance, the chancellery assumed all lands under heaven to be *de jure* part of the empire; the actual limitations were to be considered only a de facto situation. As a consequence, the Mongol empire never expanded by war; the territorial expansion was cast into the legal form of imperial execution against rebellious subjects. A construction of the same type causes the difficulties in so-called peaceful coexistence between the Western powers and expanding Communism. The Communist assumption became articulate in the famous concept of *status quo* developed by Mr. Khrushchev in an interview; *status quo* means recognition of the revolutionary character of Communism, of its inevitable expansion into areas not yet engulfed by it, and of the irreversibility of the process in the sense that non-Communist areas can become Communist but Communist areas cannot become non-Communist. The construction is spiritually a little more sophisticated than the Mongol, inasmuch as the acts of imperial expansion are wars of liberation rather than a submission of subjects (although at least the governments of non-Communist countries are "war criminals" in the Mongol manner), but in substance it is the Mongol assumption of a de facto situation that in due course will be brought into conformity with the situation *de jure*. It is part of an imperial development already envisaged by Marx as inherent in a Russian revolution, a development to which Lenin has affixed the term *Asiachina*.

Even the best construction, however, does not abolish the spatial limitations of so-called world-empires. Still, the continuing discrepancy can be obscured in the concrete situation by the prevalent conception of the world. In the case of the Persian Wars against Hellas, for instance, one of the motives of the attack, if we can trust Herodotus, was the idea of uniting the whole world through the addition of the last unconquered segment. The idea made sense, if by *world* was understood the ecumene, the inhabited surface of the earth, as far as it was known to the Persian government. The idea had to clash with reality, however, when an actual course of expansion proved the ecumene to be much larger than had been expected. That is what happened to Alexander when he penetrated into India, driving toward the edge of a world bounded by *Okeanos*. On the Indus, with a teeming subcontinent still extending indefinitely ahead, his army mutinied because it cared less than Alexander to find out how much world there was left to conquer. In a reverse of this kind there comes to the surface the theoretical issue that is our present concern. For the instrumentalist attitude operates within the category of things, although the world is not a thing; hence, the instrumentalist is philosophically a literalist who transforms a symbol of transcendence into a datum that, if it is not at the moment to hand, can be brought to hand. The adumbrated literalism in the building of world-empires makes sense, as I have suggested, only as long as the unboundedness of space is experientially held below the level of consciousness and, within that general unconsciousness, as long as the actual extent of the inhabited land masses on the earth is sufficiently unknown. By the time of the Roman empire, literalism of this type had lost much of its force. The Roman *orbis terrarum* could, without emotional disturbance, coexist with the neighboring world-empire of the Sassanians as well as with the knowledge of a further expanse of ecumene in India and China. This acceptance, without surrendering the idea of world-empire, indicates that other factors besides dominion in the instrumental sense go into the making of a world, factors that will occupy us presently.

First, however, we must dwell for a moment on the recrudescence of literalism in the modern period. The picture of the universe created by modern science, one would think, would put a damper on the idea of world-empire in the literal sense of dominion over territorial expanse. Nevertheless, the idea can still be discerned, first in the period of global control, and secondly in the so-called space age.

True, the plurality of imperial creations from a metropolitan base in one of the Western national states precluded a monopoly of global control for any of them. Still, one can speak of a Western control of the globe inasmuch as the Western powers, in spite of their rivalries and wars, achieved a unity of purpose manifesting itself in the principle of a balance of power, as established by the Peace of Utrecht in 1713 and by the Concert of Europe after the Congress of Vienna in 1815. The nineteenth century witnessed indeed a Western *imperium mundi*—although we today are perhaps more conscious of it than the empire builders engrossed in the immediate tasks before them, because we today are suffering the aftermath of their activity in the form of a *mundus* in revolt against the West.

More intricate is the literalism of the space age. There is a foreground of rational interest, scientific and military, in the exploration of space through rocketry; but there is also a background of emotional dynamism that makes men dream of the conquest of space. But, we must ask, what can one conquer about space? The globe of the earth is exhausted; it has been known as such on principle since the age of discovery and has become a finite ecumene; it has no "beyond" on Earth as had the ecumene of antiquity. In what sense can space be a conquerable "beyond" of the earth? To this question we find curious answers on the level of dreams. Our globe has acquired an imaginative "beyond" in fantasies of a spatial ecumene, spilling over from the literary genus of science fiction and the comic strip into speculations about life on other planets, and precipitating itself into literalist concreteness in such phenomena as the mass panic on the occasion of Orson Welles's *Invasion from Mars* (two instructors at a great university hurried to the supposed scene in order to observe the event), or experiments actually conducted by physicists to send signals to, or receive them from, other inhabited celestial bodies, or in the flying saucer craze. The pathology of these phenomena is not yet sufficiently explored; but even at this stage one can say that they project the image of a conquerable ecumene into unbounded space.

The problem to be solved by such fancies will become clearer if we recall an intermediate situation at the beginning of the modern period, when the global expanse of the earth occupied man's imagination. In Sir Thomas More's *Utopia* we hear the wanderer over the globe explain to his friend that he is at home at one place as much as at another, because every place is the same distance from heaven. The Christian *viator* toward eternity is about to become the wanderer through space; he has not yet completely lost the awareness that journey's end lies beyond this world; but he has become sufficiently restless not to draw the conclusion that one might just stay where one is, if wandering through this world does not lead to Somewhere but only to Utopia, that is, to Nowhere. We can estimate the enormous change in the spiritual climate if we consider that More could still distinguish the Somewhere and the Nowhere when faced with the minor expanse of the globe, while today the great mass of people seem to have lost this sense even when faced with unbounded space in which one can travel wherever one wants and still be as far away from a periphery as before. When unbounded space has been raised to the level of consciousness as the potential expanse of dominion, the literalist attitude reveals its essential senselessness.

III

Instrumentalism is a spiritual fall, literalism an intellectual derailment. They both are possible, in various historical contexts, at any time. If both characteristics occur at the same time strongly enough to become the signature of a period and to form its language, a philosophical analysis that starts from the accepted usage operates under a heavy disadvantage, because the corruptive nature of the starting point prevents the analysis from reaching its goal in either the theoretical or the historical respect.

The analysis is forced to remain theoretically incomplete, as by its means we could not extract more from the unpromising materials than they contained. If the initial conception of empire is instrumentalist, a good deal of the meaning of world-empire is distorted, if not lost. As I said, other factors than dominion in the instrumental sense go into the making of a world.

Nevertheless, the instrumentalist conception of empire, defective as it may be, is a historical phenomenon in its own right. While the intent of our analysis was primarily theoretical, it incidentally described a historical phase in the conception of empire. Even this historical description, however, could not achieve its goal. For the spiritual fall entails a comparatively low level of consciousness and, as a consequence, the instrumentalist conception does not contain explicit reflections on its own motivations. Hence, the analysis could not go beyond the demonstration of essential senselessness, leaving the pathological background of the phenomenon obscure.

By these observations the lines are drawn along which the inquiry must proceed further. In the first place, the missing components of the meaning of world-empire must be introduced; we must find out what sense of *world* is required to make sense of a *world-empire*. And second, the incomplete historical description must be supplemented by sources that will make intelligible the pathology of contemporary instrumentalism.

First, the meaning of the term *world*. It presents extraordinary difficulties to philosophical analysis. But I shall not bother you with technicalities. One can penetrate to the heart of the matter by having recourse to the dictionaries. They will circumscribe for us the two great areas of Western Christian and ancient-pagan usage.

It may come as a surprise to learn that the first meaning of *world* given by the *Oxford Dictionary* is that of "human existence," and further of a state, or phase, or mode of existence. The meaning obviously originates in the Christian ambience in which we speak of this world and the world beyond, of worldly and saintly existence, of going into or retreating from the world, of an old and a new world. It can then expand into modes of existence characteristic of historical ages such as the ancient, medieval, and modern world; of areas of civilization such as the Western, the Free, the Communist world, and the *troisième monde;* or of artistic creations such as the worlds of Shakespeare or Balzac. Only in the second and third place does the *Dictionary* list the meanings more readily associated with *world,* that is, of the earth or the universe, of the human race, the whole of mankind or part of it, of the world of fashion, the great world, and so forth.

I used Liddell and Scott and Georges for information on the meaning of the word in classical times. In Greek, *kosmos* primarily signifies a kind of order. *Kosmos* is the order in which people sit or lie, behave or do not behave, the order in which things are or no longer are; it can be good behavior, discipline, a natural or established order; moreover, it can mean an order as well as its regulator or artificer, and consequently a beautifully designed artifact such as an ornament or decoration; and finally it can mean order in the "cosmic" sense—the universe and its order, the order of the earth, of the heavens, and of the underworld. In later Greek, *kosmos* became synonymous with ecumene, the inhabited world, as when Nero was styled the lord of the whole *kosmos;* and at the same time it blends into the Christian meaning of "this world" which in the *Oxford Dictionary* is listed first. The Latin *mundus* displays a similar chain of meanings, extending from ornament and decoration to the harmonious order of the universe, the heavens, the *orbis terrarum,* the world of man, mankind, and world opinion.

Both the ancient and modern sets of meaning include the elements of territory and people that become predominant in the instrumentalist conception of world-empire; but they contain a good deal more. There seems to be alive in them a desire to express linguistically a substantive order pervading all levels of being as well as being as a whole. Furthermore, while they have in common the desire to pervade all realms of being, they achieve their purpose not in the same manner—there seems to be more than one way to conceive the world. The difference can more easily be sensed than described. One might say perhaps that the two sets overlap more clearly with regard to certain areas—the universe, the heavens, the earth, the whole of mankind—than with regard to others; and that the areas that they do not have in common are precisely the ones that determine the tonality of meaning for their respective set. In the ancient set, the accent lies on the visible and external, on the cosmic order in a preeminent sense; in the Christian set, it lies on the internal order of man. The differences of meaning apparently reflect the actual historical process in which the experience of human existence under a world-transcendent God has differentiated from the primary, more compact experience of existence in a cosmos that includes both gods and men. We are returning, on the linguistic side, to the phenomena of the spiritual outbursts that occur parallel with the great imperial creations beyond the level of cosmological empires, to the parallel phenomena of representative humanity and imperial representation of mankind.

With these materials in mind, one can attempt more precisely to formulate the issue specifically relevant to our inquiry.

There are to be distinguished a primary experience of the cosmos, of a cosmos "full of gods," and a historically secondary experience of a universe under a world-transcendent God. For the adequate expression of these experiences certain symbolic forms have been created. The experience of the cosmos expresses itself through Myth, the experience of the universe through the forms of Philosophy and Revelation. In the first experience the accent lies on the visible-divine order into which man must integrate his existence; in the second one it lies on the transcendent-divine order to which man must attune his existence. Although they distribute the accents differently, however, they still are experiences of the same total structure of being: In the compact experience of the cosmos ritual attunement to divine order is required as much as pragmatic adjustment to its visible order; in differentiated experience of the universe under God, pragmatic adjustment to the visible order is necessary as much as the attunement of existence to the "unseen measure." What is at stake in both cases is the truth of human existence, truth in the sense of a willingness both to understand and to accept the *condicio humana*—although it requires the advance toward the differentiated experience of transcendent Being in order to establish explicitly the insight that the order of the world is not of "this world" alone but also of the "world beyond."

A "world" is thus more than a visible order, and a "world-empire" more than a dominion over territory and people. To establish an empire is an essay in world creation, reaching through all the levels of the hierarchy of being. This essay is always related to the invisible order through the attunement of existence to transcendent Being; it is an evocation of true existence within this world, through participation in the order of the world beyond. The character of an evocation attuned to the "unseen measure" makes a human imperial creation analogically commensurate with the world, endows it with the sense of a "world"—a sense that it could never gain on the level of material expansion however vast, since material vastness, being finite, must always remain incommensurate with the unboundedness of the visible universe.

IV

The initial analysis had to remain incomplete in both the theoretical and historical respects. The first defect, although I could do no more than draw the outline of an intricate issue, has now been repaired: The language of world-empire makes sense, if its establishment is understood as the creation of a cosmic analogue or, as it has occasionally been called, a *cosmion*. The imperial order is an epitome of the constitution of being, reaching through all the realms of being from the material to the transcendental.

The pathological background of the contemporary conception of world-empire was the second issue left in suspense. In order to isolate the decisive factor we must briefly reflect on the stratification of meaning which the symbol "world" acquired in our time.

When we speak of "world wars," we mean a historical situation in which wars involve the peoples and resources of the whole earth, or in which the theater of war has become global. The usage harks back to the classical meaning of the ecumene as the inhabited world; it means no more than the growth of a tightly textured field of power in which disturbances at any point may have global repercussions. We encounter a second stratum of meaning in such phrases as a Western and a Communist "world." Now the term signifies two "worlds" in the sense of manifestations of two different conceptions of existence, each trying to incarnate itself in visible dominion over territory and people. Hence, the world wars in the global sense are at the same time wars among worlds, each trying to establish and preserve itself and, if possible, to overcome the other one. The power struggle, when it becomes a war among worlds, acquires a new deadliness beyond the worst fratricidal strife within one world under the principles of *raison d'état* or national interest, because the issues of spiritual existence are involved. The third stratum of meaning is already indicated by the rivalry of several worlds to become the one world whose dominion is coterminous with the global ecumene. There is a clear consciousness in existence today that under modern technological conditions the economic interdependence of societies and the destructiveness of wars require an organization of sufficient effectiveness to reduce conflicts to the scale of domestic quarrels within a global society, to be settled with the least possible violence. Far from being a world, as is so often assumed without much thought, the global ecumene is in search of a world. Whether it will become a world, or whether the existing worlds will achieve its destruction to the point that only limited societies, separated by areas of practically uninhabited wasteland, will remain—that is the sinister question of our epoch.

The three strata of meaning must not be separated from one another; it is their constellation that reveals the pathological character of the situation: (1) the existence of an ecumene; (2) the feeling that the ecumene, although it is not a world, should be one; (3) the "coexistence" of rival worlds within the ecumene; (4) the absence of symptoms to show that one of the rival worlds was persuasive enough to capture the ecumene and become its only world without violence; (5) the absence of symptoms that a new world was in the making that could capture the ecumene and replace the present manifold of worlds; (6) the apparently insoluble bond between the conception of a world and dominion in the instrumentalist sense; and (7) the consequent threat of a destructive conflict of arms. Moreover, this complex of characteristics is more than historically contingent (although elements of contingency enter into the concrete situation, too); it is a meaningful constellation indeed, since the dangerous impasse on the ecumenic scale is the result of originating in Western civilization. Whether we consider the geographical explorations and discoveries, the development of science and technology, industry and systems of transport, colonialism, political expansion, or the creation of new military potentials; or whether we consider the dominant ideas of nationalism and democracy, of liberal progressivism, positivism, or Communism; the factors entering into the situation have been meaningfully connected by their common origin in the Western revolutionary explosion since roughly the middle of the fifteenth century.

The Western process has produced and engulfed the global ecumene. Within this process there is a critical juncture, in the middle of the eighteenth century, when its pathological character becomes evident and the syndrome of the disease discernible. I shall briefly relate the symptoms as they appear in Turgot's *Discourses* at the Sorbonne of July and December 1750, supplemented by the later fragments of his project of a *Universal History*.

Turgot places the ecumene, as he sees it emerging, in the context of an evolution of mankind. He assumes a unity of mankind in history, a society engaged in a process governed by three principles. The first principle is the historical individuality of every man, as the substance from which the whole of the *humanitas* is built; the second is the continuity of cause and effect linking the generations; the third is the accumulation of substance through collective memory in language and script. A *trésor commun* accumulates, is transmitted from one generation to the next, and passed further on to future generations. Moreover, the accumulation has progressive character—a *fil des progrès* runs through the history of mankind— and the criteria of progress can be identified as (1) the softening of the *mores*, (2) the enlightenment of the mind, and (3) the intensified commerce between formerly isolated nations to the point of global intercourse. While this process suffers interruptions and delays, the net result is an increasing perfection of mankind.

The pathological character of the assumptions is obvious, but the dogmas of Turgot have become so thoroughly an accepted part of the intellectual climate that it will be not only apposite but necessary to point out what is wrong.

The dogma of an evolution of mankind is dubious because it projects the emerging ecumene of the eighteenth century into the past. There never was a mankind in evolution, its generations connected by cause and effect, a collective memory. Empirically, as far as we know, there were only concrete societies, geographically widely dispersed, with insufficient communications or none at all, their members blissfully ignorant of the supposed fact that they formed a unity of mankind accumulating a collective memory. Hence, it requires a good deal of imaginative construction to transform a multiplicity of societies in history, which even today range from neolithic tribal communities to Anglo-Saxon democracies, into a unity of mankind with an evolution common to all. To these difficulties, of which Turgot was fully aware, he found a remarkable answer. He admits that the line of progress does not run an even course through history but suffers interruptions and setbacks; he admits that the process is distributed over a multitude of civilizations and nations that do not all move at the same speed, while some do not move at all; but he insists that nevertheless *la masse totale* of mankind marches toward an ever-increasing perfection. The *masse totale* is the symbol by which he tries to beat down the obstreperous facts. To my knowledge it is the first time that the word *total* makes its appearance in modern political thought; and it is fraught, even on this first occasion, with the atrocious implications it was later to unfold. For the *masse totale* is nothing less than the sum total of all human beings past, present, and future, lumped together as a society to be represented by the enlightened intellectual of the Encyclopaedist type. The issue of representative humanity thus reappears on the scale of the global ecumene—but Confucius and the Buddha, the philosophers, the prophets, and Christ have been replaced by the representative humanity of a gentleman with soft mores, an enlightened mind, and a ticket for a trip around the world.

Thus far the affair is no more than funny. At best it could afford the temptation to write the *Pickwick Papers* of a club of representative gentlemen. But enlightened intellectuals are not a harmless curiosity; they are dangerous maniacs. They take themselves seriously, they really believe they represent mankind, and if a recalcitrant *masse totale* insists on being formed in the image of God, they will use force to correct the mistake and remold man in their own image. They are not satisfied with making the best of this world, but want to make a world of the worst. For mankind may not be aware of the progress it has achieved through its representatives unless properly informed; it may never become a *masse totale* at all, unless made into one by suitable treatment; and the treatment requires an instrument. Hence, in the generation after Turgot we find Condorcet positing, as the instrument, a new class of men "who are less interested in the discovery of truth than in its propagation." And with relish he describes their procedure: They will employ

> all the charms which erudition, philosophy, brilliance, and literary talent can put at the disposition of reason; they assume all the tones,

use all the forms, from pleasantry to the touching, from a vast and scholarly compilation to the novel or pamphlet; they cover truth with a veil in order not to frighten the weak, and to have the pleasure of surmise; they are skillful in catering to prejudices in order to deal even more effective blows; they neither attack them all at the same time, nor one quite thoroughly; sometimes they give comfort to the enemies of reason by pretending that in religion they do not want more than semi-tolerance, or in politics more than semi-liberty; they are moderate toward despotism when they fight the absurdities of religion, and toward the cult when they rise against tyranny; they attack the two scourges on principle when they seem to castigate only some revolting or ridiculous abuses; and they strike the tree at the roots, when they seem to trim only some rank branches.[1]

By these methods there will be produced the *opinion générale* or *publique* of the ecumenic type. (One easily recognizes the methods that have been brought to perfection in our time by National Socialism and Communism, the methods that ever since Marx are called the "tactics" of the revolution.) And again, a generation later, the *masse totale* of Turgot has grown into Comte's *Grand-Être* of mankind under the directorate of positivist intellectuals, into the brotherhood of men to whom *la recherche de la paternité est interdite.*

Empirically, as we have said, mankind is not a *masse totale.* The ideal was projected into the past in order to construe history as an intramundane process that will lead with inevitability to a global ecumene under the directorate of intellectual sectarians of the intramundane gnostic persuasion. This aggregate of ideas— the intramundane process, its inevitability, its culmination in the global empire directed by gnostic sectarians—is the constant factor from Turgot and Condorcet, through Comte and Marx, to the gnostic empire-builders of the twentieth century. The aggregate was successful to the point of having become the dominant political force in our time. And its success had good psychological reasons. The intramundane tribalism of mankind implied in the *masse totale* holds a powerful appeal to spiritually and intellectually immature men who can reap the emotional benefits of being members of the tribe in good standing without submitting to the unpleasant discipline of spirit and intellect; when the truth of existence as an obligation for everyman is abolished, one can participate in

---

1. *Esquisse d'un Tableau Historique des Progrès de l'Esprit Humain. Ouvrage posthume de Condorcet* (n.p., 1795), 243 ff.

representative humanity without effort. And equally powerful is the appeal to forceful personalities who can indulge their *libido dominandi* as the leaders of mankind. They can even, as Comte did, establish themselves as the *Fondateurs de la religion de l'humanité* and replace the Era of Christ by the Era of Comte.

V

Nobody can predict at this juncture how the attempts at transforming the ecumene into a world, while destroying the truth of existence that alone could make it one, will end. It is only certain that they cannot succeed. This, however, is not the last word to be said in the matter, for behind the certainty that a "world" cannot be created when the orientation toward transcendent Being is excluded from its order, there lurks the question whether it can be created even when the truth of existence is included. At first hearing the question may sound absurd, as historically such worlds have existed in fact. Nevertheless, it cannot be simply dismissed, as it has been raised once before in history, on the occasion of the Roman conquest, and the answer, although not completely thought through, tended to be negative. In conclusion, therefore, I shall recall this earlier preoccupation with the problem, as it may shed some light on the future into which our present situation will issue.

The question became acute, as we said, on the occasion of the Roman drive to conquer the ecumene. The term *ecumene* originally signified the civilized, inhabited world as it is known. Polybius was the first historian to use it in the technical sense, when he defined the rule over the ecumene as the *telos* of the Roman conquest. Since Polybius, however, although not a philosopher of the first rank, was a man of philosophical culture (thereby distinguishing himself from his enlightened *confrères* of the eighteenth century and after), he had to ask himself the question what sense ecumenic rule could have. When the Roman rule over the ecumene was established, what then? Some day, would Rome herself not suffer the fate she had prepared for Carthage? Such reflections hark back to the rhythms of the cosmos with their fatality of rise and fall, but at the same time they convey a disillusionment with cosmic order, a sense of senselessness that will no longer accept a rhythm for a *telos*. Their suspense reveals the disconcerting character that the question had assumed by the time of Polybius. Moreover, the experience of senselessness was not assuaged by the Roman success; on the contrary, by the time of Christ it had gripped the population of the Roman empire with sufficient strength to make both intelligible and acceptable the solution offered by Christianity. In Matt. 24:14 we find the missionary order that sounds like a deliberate literary answer (although it hardly can be one) to Polybius: "And this gospel of the kingdom shall be preached over the whole ecumene, as a testimony to all nations; and then the *telos* (the end, or fulfilment) shall come." Polybius thus questions the *telos*, the sense of imperial expansion, while the Gospel roundly transfers the sense of order to the expansion of Christianity and the apocalypse of the Kingdom. Polybius understands ecumenic dominion as an inconclusive enterprise, while Saint Matthew demands that the ecumene be filled with the Gospel in order to gain its *telos*. Between them they have gained the insight that the end of human action does not lie within this world but beyond it; this insight, which had been secured for personal existence by Plato in his Judgment of the Dead, has now expanded to include the *telos* of society in history. The fulfilment of mankind is an *eschaton*; the great theme of history and eschatology has opened.

I have taken pains to isolate the philosophical meaning of eschatology imbedded in the Gospel, for only that part of the symbolism is of relevance to political science as a permanent gain. For the rest, the conception of the *telos* beyond this world is still wrapped up in the apocalyptic speculation on the new aeon, on the new world that is supposed to replace the old one. In its context the *telos* of Matt. 24:14 signifies a transformation of the world, a metastasis, a new disposition in which there will be no problems of world-empires—a meaning that is confirmed by the immediately following reference to the Danielic apocalypse.

Nevertheless, the passage is of absorbing interest to our inquiry precisely because of its apocalyptic content, for the Enlightenment conception of the perfect ecumene to come (continued in the Communist conception of the final realm of freedom) is an apocalyptic speculation, too, although of the intramundane variety; and in the Christian case, the implications of the apocalyptic *telos*, as well as of "ecumene to come" (Heb. 2:5), were explored at least to a degree. The difficulties of the conception became obvious by reflections on the date of the apocalyptic event. If the *telos* of the future ecumene was not reached soon, what profit was its coming to those who had died before the event? Was it a *telos* for them? Saint Paul had to assure the faithful, therefore, that the Second Coming would occur within the generation of those then living; and as death took its toll while the *Parousia* in fact did not occur, he had to keep down unrest by the assurance that those who had died in Christ would rise with Him when He returned in a not-too-distant future. Such consolations and concessions, however, could do no more than tear wide open the great problems of history and eschatology in a world that is going on without *Parousia*; for the structure of history is empirically nonapocalyptic, and any attempt to comprehend it by means of apocalyptic symbols, whatever form they may assume, will invariably force the awkward questions that in our totalitarian empires are suppressed by violence, while in our so-called free societies they are prevented from becoming too uncomfortably apparent by the social terrorism of the intellectuals— the questions: What profit is the perfect realm to those who do not live to see it? What happens to the generations of mankind who lived before the world became enlightened? Is it really the function of man to "contribute" to a Progress of which the profits will be reaped by future generations—to be a stepping stone for a rational world to come? Is it really his purpose to live in a theological or metaphysical "phase of history" in order to elevate Comte to the pinnacle of Positivism? Is it really his purpose to be a class-struggler through history in order to make final Communism prevail in 1980? In apocalyptic attitudes that compel such questioning we sense a profound unconcern about everybody except those present; it is a primitive brutality, which breaks through in Turgot's conception of the *masse totale.* "Mankind" seems to be reduced to the generation of those living at present, or perhaps even more narrowly to the group living in the fervor of the respective apocalypse.

Metastatic faith, although it is a historical force, will inevitably run afoul of the nonapocalyptic structure of history. If a genuine eschatological insight is imbedded in apocalyptic symbolism, it must come to terms with the reality extending in space and time beyond its point of origin, if it wants to survive effectively. Christian compromise with reality has assumed the form of the Church that is neither an empire nor a community living in expectation of the imminent end of the world, but an institution representing the eschatological *telos* within the world. The Christian answer to the question of "world-empire" was thus the separation and balance of spiritual and temporal powers within the order of a society. Whatever the shortcomings of the solution proved to be in practice, the construction at least held fast to the insight that the end of society in history is a question of eschatology. If the solution proved unstable nevertheless, the fundamental reason must be sought in the inadequacy of the compromise. For the Church never quite disengaged itself from its apocalyptic origin—its apocalyptic unconcern about mankind in history narrowed its intellectual horizon so badly that it never developed an adequate philosophy of history. By the eighteenth century, finally, the gulf between our knowledge of historical reality and the limited understanding provided by the Church had become so wide that the gnostic movements could pour into the vacuum with a vengeance. The long-neglected reality of mankind in historical existence came into more than its own when the new movements, while taking their stand firmly within this world, denied the reality of the world beyond and consequently replaced the eschatological by an intramundane *telos*. If the church in possession of the *eschaton* had neglected to explore the structure of history, as well as its own place in it, the new movements threw out the *eschaton* altogether. What they preserved from the Jewish-Christian tradition was its most dubious element, i.e., its metastatic faith in the new aeon. This preservation, one may say, was theoretically and historically ineluctable. For, on the one hand, after Christianity one cannot go back to cosmology but only forward to a more differentiated understanding of the unity of mankind in history under the mystery of the *eschaton*; while on the other hand this advance was precluded by the anti-Christian character of the revolt that had removed the *eschaton* together with the remnants of an apocalypse that had the ghastly farce of an apocalypse without an *eschaton*. In its wake have appeared, under the title of "philosophies," the apocalyptic deformations of history, changing with the changes of pragmatic positions and circumstances; the question of empire has been reduced to an ecumenic dominion that never can become a world; and "mankind" has become a synonym for the inmates of an apocalyptic concentration camp.

In the light of these last reflections it will be possible to formulate the results of our inquiry into the question of world-empire and the unity of mankind.

The attempts at representing mankind through imperial organizations have a long history beginning with Mesopotamian and

Egyptian establishments. Confining the enumeration to the types that belong to the past, one can distinguish within this history the cosmological, the ecumenic, and the orthodox empires. While they all intend to incorporate the universal order of human existence in the particular order of a finite society, they are more than individuals of the species "world-empire." For the types do not follow one another at random; they form a meaningful sequence, each presupposing the preceding one, so that the sequence becomes an irreversible whole of experiments with the problem of order. The first type is still compact, incorporating the universal order by means of the myth of the cosmos; the problems that become troublesome later have not yet emerged. The second type gains a differentiated experience of the truth of human existence, while imperial order develops a tendency to become ecumenically expansive; the two diverging movements that would result in the loss of "world" for the empire are brought together again by tentative associations between imperial order and representative humanity. In the orthodox empires, finally, this association is understood as a necessity and becomes stabilized over long periods. So far the sequence makes sense, and the sense is irreversible.

Can one say that the modern sequel to the series is intelligibly continuing this line of meaning? The answer to this question must take into account that the global revolution of modernity has its origin in the West. Two factors stand out in the West as responses to the Christian *contemptus mundi*, to the neglect of the structure of this world: (1) the revolt of the individual and the release of its forces—which has derailed into the *libido dominandi* of the Gnostics; and (2) the revolt of society and the release of its forces in history—which has derailed into the intramundane apocalypse. The combination of these factors determines the issue of empire in our time.

We have seen that an empire, in order to be a world, requires participation of its order in transcendent Being. As such participation is precluded by the intramundane character of the revolutionary movements, their attempts at transforming the ecumene into a "world" are doomed to failure; what can be achieved is only the apocalyptic concentration camp. One should furthermore note as a parallel development the intellectual breakdown that has depressed the discussion of such questions in our time below the level that had been attained even by Polybius. Nevertheless, neither intellectual breakdowns nor political catastrophes must blind us to the fact that every revolution has its reasons. As an advance of meaning we must acknowledge the breakthrough to the structure of the world, both in nature and history. The modern release of individual and social forces is not reversible and, in particular, we shall never return to the limited historical horizon of early and medieval Christianity. One might even consider the deadly antics of our apocalyptic movements to have a cathartic function in the historical process. For the question of apocalypse has never been satisfactorily disposed of, either experientially or theoretically; hence, the apocalyptic movements of the intramundane variety, as they seem to move with acceleration toward a climax of lethal stupidity, may turn out to be the painful but inevitable process by which the problem of the apocalypse will be relegated to the past.

The *reductio ad absurdum* performed by apocalypse on itself also extends to the ecumenic empire it wants to create. If an apocalyptic concentration camp is not a world, by the same token it is not an empire representing mankind, even though no man living should escape the reach of its power. For the apocalypse of Turgot and his successors has made abundantly clear to everybody what was not unclear to philosophers even before, that mankind is more than the global collective of human beings living at the same time. Mankind is the society of man in history, extending in time from its unknown origin toward its unknown future. Moreover, no crosscut at any time represents mankind by virtue of a common power organization. For the living can represent mankind universally only by their representative humanity; and their humanity is representative only when it is oriented toward the eschatological *telos.* Organization, to be sure, is necessary to the existence of man and society in this world, but no organization can organize mankind—even global ecumenicity of organization is not universality. The dream of representing universal order through the world of empire has come to its end when the meaning of universal order as the order of history under God has come into view.

These propositions can be summarized in the thesis that the age of empire is coming to its end in our time. A period of five thousand years, characterized by the attempts to represent mankind by means of a finite organization in the present, has run its course and reached an epoch in the original sense of suspense. In this suspense we know that old forms are dying, but of the new forms we know no more than the prefigurations I have tried to sketch.

10

History and Gnosis

A debate with Professor Rudolf Bultmann is an intellectual adventure to be enjoyed. In his essay on the relevance of the Old Testament to Christian faith there is no less at stake than the meaning of theology, philosophy, and history. Moreover, the essay is joined with related studies in a volume to which its author has given the title *Glauben und Verstehen* ("Faith and Understanding"), indicating thereby his conception of theology as the enterprise of *fides quaerens intellectum*. The inquiry, therefore, is linked to the great problem of faith and reason. Philosophically, furthermore, he is not content to leave the conflict of the two truths in the form given to it by the scholastics, but transfers that of Martin Heidegger, to whom the volume of essays is dedicated. And finally, the inquiry receives its tone from Bultmann's work of demythologizing, a work motivated by the responsibility of making the Gospel in its purity accessible to men of our time to whom its symbolism has become strange. The problems raised by Bultmann thus are presented with the authority of both spiritual concern and intellectual penetration; they cannot be evaded, they must be answered.

A critical examination of the principles that have induced Bultmann to deny theological relevance to the Old Testament is forced into definite form by certain characteristics of his work, the decisive one being the vein of gnosticism running through it. Under the aspect that concerns us presently, gnosis is a mode of existence

Originally published in *The Old Testament and Christian Faith*, ed. Bernhard W. Anderson (New York: Harper & Row, 1965), this essay is reprinted here by kind permission of Bernhard W. Anderson.

that distorts the order of being by placing negative accents on world and history and correspondingly positive accents on the means of escaping from them. The thinker who interprets human existence in this mode need not necessarily indulge in wrong propositions with regard to reality; his purposes may be served as well by focusing attention on the means of escape into world-transcendent reality to the neglect of large sectors of mundane reality. A gnostic thinker, therefore, can exert a peculiar fascination, especially in troubled times. He deals with the all-absorbing mystery of human existence, and provided he is a competent scholar, his voice will carry conviction because what he has to say positively is true. If, then, he is careful enough not to draw attention to the sectors of reality omitted (sometimes the construction of a system is helpful for the purpose), the inexpert reader will be overpowered by what impresses him as the light of truth. A good deal of the fascination Heidegger's work holds for the unwary is due to the subtle blending of truth presented with conviction and untruth through omission. In Bultmann's work, although it is fundamentally Christian, the gnostic strand is still effective enough to place important areas of reality beyond the horizon of his inquiry. Under the circumstances adumbrated, a critical examination of his essay would run against a blank wall if it were to extend only to the positive propositions, for Bultmann's scholarship, as is well known, is excellent. Hence I shall proceed, first by presenting Bultmann's positive thesis as well as the modifying corollaries; then I shall submit the thesis to critical analysis until it becomes clear that the argument has a semblance of consistency only because an important sector of reality was omitted from consideration; and when the omitted sector is determined, finally, I shall explore the gnostic motivation of both the omission and the thesis.

I

Bultmann's essay on the theological irrelevance of the Old Testament to Christian faith is written in a discursive and persuasive style that makes it incumbent on the critic to disengage the theoretically relevant passages from their context.

Toward the beginning of the article Bultmann formulates the "theological" question: "Whether to the faith that sees in Jesus

Christ the revelation of God, the Old Testament still has relevance"; and toward the end he gives the succinct answer:

> To the Christian faith the Old Testament is no longer revelation as it
> has been, and still is, for the Jews. For the person who stands within
> the Church the history of Israel is a closed chapter. . . . Israel's history
> is not our history, and in so far as God has shown his grace in that
> history, such grace is not meant for us. . . . To us the history of Israel
> is not the history of revelation. (31)

Between the beginning and the end, Bultmann engages in a series
of reflections that admit the historical and ontological (sachliche)
relevance of the Old Testament to the Christian believer. We must
also present these qualifying reflections disengaged from their cir-
cumstantial context.

1. Since the Christian understanding of existence (Daseinsver-
ständnis) claims to be the only true one, it is burdened with the duty
of justifying its claim against all rival interpretations of existence.

2. While the rule, formulated in a general manner, appears to
apply to all other modes of existence, presumably also the Far
Eastern ones, Bultmann recognizes a special duty with regard to the
modes that, through the continuity of history, are constituent of our
own present, i.e., the Hellenic and Israelite. In particular with regard
to the Israelite he insists that only in a critical encounter with the
Old Testament shall we gain clarity concerning the interpretation
of existence that guides our own historical will and action. The
Old Testament cannot be simply abandoned; for our own historical
present, in order to be adequately understood, requires justification
before its tribunal.

3. The historical dialogue with the Old Testament is compulsory
for the Christian, because the Gospel, by its self-interpretation, is
the "end of the Law." If the Christian wants to understand precisely
the "end" or "fulfillment" that has come, with Christ, he must
understand what the "Law" means.

4. Up to this point the argument is historical in the same sense
that it requires the Christian to have an adequate knowledge of
the Old Testament in order to understand the language of the new
body of literature that has grown in its ambiance. From here onward, however, the argument seems to take an ontological turn.
For Bultmann considers that the pagans understood the message of
the Gospel quite as well as the Jews. The "Law," although it has

achieved in Israel an optimal clarity of meaning, expresses the generally human experience of existing under the divine "thou shalt." The Gospel, it is true, presupposes the Law. "But the Law that embodies itself in the Old Testament needs by no means to be the Old Testament concretely." The pre-apprehension (*Vorverständnis*) required for understanding the Gospel is given wherever man experiences himself in conscience bound by the general moral demands that grow from his existence in society. If the Christian churches prefer the Old Testament for inducing pre-apprehension, their reasons are primarily pedagogical; the Old Testament deserves preference because the Decalogue and the Prophets present the demands with incomparable power and clarity. (Bultmann, as far as I can see, makes no attempt to reconcile the present argument with the preceding one.)

5. In his essay on "The Problem of Natural Theology,"[1] Bultmann has further clarified the concept of *Vorverständnis*, which I have rendered as pre-apprehension. The clarifications contained in this essay must be added to the argument. From the position of theology, Bultmann asserts, unbelief (*Unglaube*) is the fundamental mental constitution of human existence. Philosophy interprets this constitution of unbelief as the original freedom in which existence constitutes itself. In the very act of interpreting existence as constituted in freedom, however, philosophy knows the questionableness of freedom; for in knowing about the free resolve to take charge of existence as one's own (*das Dasein übernimmt sich selbst*)[2] it knows the alternative of rejecting the decision and also the possibility of faith, although the possibility will appear "senseless" to the philosophical position in which "sense" is synonymous with existence in freedom. Nevertheless, in spite of the difference of opinion concerning "sense," Bultmann assumes the understanding

---

1. Rudolf Bultmann, "Das Problem der 'natürlichen Theologie,' " in *Glauben und Verstehen: Gesammelte Aufsätze,* 2d unchanged edition, 5 vols. (Tübingen: J. C. B. Mohr [P. Siebeck], 1954), 1:294–312: first published in 1933, as yet untranslated—EV. A one-volume edited version was published in 1969 in English as *Faith and Understanding,* ed. Robert W. Funk, trans. Louise P. Smith (reprint, Philadelphia: Fortress, 1987–); J. C. B. Mohr issued a "Uni-Taschenbücher" edition in four vols. ©1993.—Ed.

2. *Das Dasein übernimmt sich selbst* is a stock phrase of Heidegger's existentialism. The English reader should not be deprived of the joy of knowing that the phrase in German has a double meaning not intended by its author. It can be rendered either as "existence takes charge of itself" (the meaning intended) or as "existence overreaches itself" (what, indeed, it does when it takes charge of itself). Needless to say, no philosopher would play with the fire of "taking charge" of his existence.

of faith from the philosophical position to be identical with the self-understanding of faith. "For faith understands itself as the concrete resolve, the concrete decision in a concrete situation constituted by the word of the Gospel and by fellow man." Hence, inasmuch as philosophy elaborates the pre-apprehension Christian understanding of existence, it creates the pre-apprehension of faith—with the reservation, however, that the character of *Vorverständnis* accrues to unbelieving existence in retrospect from the position of faith.

6. Through the clarification of *Vorverständnis* the ontological intention of Bultmann's argument has been established beyond a doubt. "Law" and "philosophy" are coordinated as two variant expressions of the generally human pre-apprehension. Moreover, Bultmann accepts the philosophical interpretation of existence (or, as we should say more cautiously, what he considers a philosophical interpretation) as true, endows it with the character of "natural theology," and considers it the task of theology to elaborate the meaning of faith "in constant debate [*Auseinandersetzung*] with the natural understanding of unbelieving existence."

When the argument is presented in this rigorous form, its gnostic character becomes visible. Above all, we can recognize the technique of identification, familiar from Hegel's gnosis, by which historical phenomena are transformed into states of consciousness. We start from the Law, which in historical concreteness is the Torah. Through identification, not formal but in substance, the Torah changes into the "thou shalt" that is alive in every-man's conscience. And the "thou shalt" as pre-apprehension of faith becomes identical with unbelieving existence in freedom as interpreted by the philosopher. The historical relation between the Law and the Gospel, between the Old and the New Testament, is thus transformed into the ontological tension between the natural existence of man and the Christian existence in faith. History in the sense of the *progressus* of mankind in time, shrouded in the mystery of a meaning incompletely revealed—the history we have in mind as long as we are not existentialists—has somehow disappeared. Moreover, with the transformation of history into ontology the relation between Bultmann's theology and Heidegger's existentialism comes into better view. For Bultmann's identifications, as they reduce history to existence, make sense as an enterprise of *fides quaerens intellectum* only under the assumption, first, that Heidegger's existentialism is philosophy at all (and not, as I have indicated on another occasion, a type of gnosis) and, second, that it is the true philosophy of existence. In Bultmann's work Heidegger has moved into the position that in scholasticism was held by the *Philosophus*.

II

The oscillation of things between the status of historical phenomena and of moments (in the Hegelian sense) in a gnostic speculation is possible only if the fundamental concepts of history, philosophy, and theology are sufficiently indeterminate to allow for such movement. Indeterminacy of terms as a gnostic symptom is correlative to the device of identifications. By indeterminacy is not meant equivocation of terms. It can be characterized rather as a disturbance of contact with the reality to which the terms refer. The terms are neither developed through adequate analysis from reality nor do they, when used, refer to the reality to which the reader would assume them to refer. This brief characterization must be sufficient for the present purpose. I shall now consider Bultmann's thesis—that the Old Testament is historically but not theologically relevant to Christian faith—under the aspect of its indeterminacy.

For this purpose we shall imagine a reader with a liberal education, a man who is conversant with the Western tradition of philosophy and theology, without being attached to a particular school. Such a man, when reading Bultmann's thesis, will be baffled by the intentions of the author. What fundamental opposition should exist between theological and historical relevance, he will ask himself. Is God's revelation not a revelation to man in society and history? Is the revelation from Sinai and the conclusion of the Covenant not a historical event? Is it not even an event that marks an epoch in history? Does not Bultmann himself speak of a history of revelation to Israel? And should not the history of mankind, in which this epochal revelation to the sector of mankind called Israel occurs, be a theologian's concern? And if these revelations reported in the Old Testament are historically but not theologically relevant, should not the same rule apply to Christ? Is the Incarnation of the Logos not a historical event, again marking an epoch? Will the Christian theologian say that the Incarnation is theologically irrelevant to Christian faith, too? The questions are pertinent, especially the last one.

At this point of his questioning it will be time to furnish the reader with the opening sentences of Bultmann's *Theology of the New Testament.*

> The message of Jesus belongs to the preconditions [*Voraussetzungen*] of a theology of the New Testament, but it is not part of it. For the theology of the New Testament consists in the unfolding of the thoughts in which Christian faith assures itself of its object, its ground, and its consequences. Christian faith, however, exists only from the time of a Christian kerygma, i.e., a kerygma that proclaims Jesus Christ as God's eschatological deed of salvation, Jesus Christ as the crucified and resurrected. And such proclamation is given only in the kerygma of the *Urgemeinde,* not in the message of the historical Jesus.[3]

The reader's reaction to this information will be a mixture of relief and new bewilderment. He will be relieved to find Bultmann consistent enough to let the message of Jesus fall under the theological ban just as much as the Old Testament, but he will wonder why only part of the New Testament falls under it. He will then be relieved, again, by the definition of "Christian faith" as the formal object of theology in relation to which everything else falls off to the level of mere history, because he may hope that the definition of theology will bring the answers to his questions. But as soon as he starts pondering the rather restrictive definition it will arouse new misgivings because he can find no reason for it. For Bultmann will accept as the unquestioned starting point of the theologian's work neither a body of dogma nor the *litterae sacrae,* embracing both the Old and the New Testaments, but wants to let his object emerge from the New Testament itself by applying historical and philological methods to the literary text. If theology, however, is identical with the critical exposition of a literary source by the methods of historical and philological science, for the purpose of making intelligible the message of Christian faith contained in it, there seems to be no reason why the term *theology* should apply only to the historian's work on the New Testament (or even only a part of it) and not equally to his work on the Old Testament. As a consequence, the thesis that the Old Testament is theologically irrelevant to Christian faith would mean no more than that Judaism

---

3. Voegelin's translation from the German original, now available in English: *Theology of the New Testament,* trans. Kendrick Grobel, 2 vols. (New York: Scribner, 1951), 1:3—B. Anderson.

is not Christianity—a proposition that the reader can accept, although he does not know why this truism should be advanced as a notable discovery. Clearly, however, in distinguishing between historical and theological relevance of the Old Testament Bultmann wants to do more than distinguish between the Israelite-Jewish and Christian modes of existence under God for the sole purpose of more carefully elaborating the specific character of the latter (although that is also one of his purposes). He rather wants to break the continuum of revelation between them: The revelation of the Old Testament has to be an event entirely apart from that of the New Testament. It seems to be impossible, however, to achieve this separation on the level of history and historical method in their conventional sense—for who can deny the continuous stream of history in which early Christianity emerges from its Israelite and Jewish antecedents? How can historical method furnish a reason why the work of the Christian theologian should be confined to the *evangelium de Christo* as its formal object, excluding the *evangelium Christi* and the Old Testament? And how can historical method justify the exclusion of history itself from theological exploration? Against such questions there still stands Bultmann's thesis: Although there are both a "history of Israel" and "our history"—a revelation both to Israel and through Christ, a theology of both Old and New Testaments—there can be no theology of the history of revelation that embraces them.

When the imaginary reader has arrived at this point in his reflections, he will conclude that Bultmann, since he cannot have derived his thesis through the use of historical method, must have introduced a selective principle from elsewhere so as to be able to select certain parts of the canonical text as specifically "Christian" while rejecting others as irrelevant to "Christian faith." And furthermore, although the reader may not be sure whence the principle of selection did come, he may wonder about the implications of its use. For if the "history of Israel" is not "our history," perhaps "our history" is not "Israel's"—and if not Israel's, is it anybody else's? If the reader thinks through the implications of the thesis, he may discover that Bultmann has come very close to the position of Jaspers that Christianity is of interest to Christians only, while the rest of mankind should rather be concerned about the vistas opened to human reason by the "axis time" between 800 and 300 B.C. in which the great philosophers and religious founders appeared in the major civilizations, a Confucius and Laotse, a Buddha and Zoroaster, the prophets of Israel and the philosophers of Hellas.

A piece of work in science is not a solipsistic outburst. It is socially bound to the past of predecessors who have once elaborated the problem now under revision, and to the future of readers who will accept the revision as legitimate and build their own work on the new basis. That is what is called cooperation in science. I have introduced the imaginary reader representing the tradition of problems because he has the duty to ask his questions and right to have them answered. If the answers are not forthcoming, something is wrong. By means of this device we have established, first, indeterminacy of terms as the nature of the trouble and, second, the restrictive definition of theology as the source of the disturbance.

It would be premature, however, to formulate the implications of the result, for Bultmann raises a further issue that must be clarified. His endeavor to break the theological link between the Old and New Testaments is motivated by his opposition to the methods of allegorical interpretation and scriptural proof that intend to supply the link in question. The point needs careful consideration, because in this concern Bultmann is on solid critical ground. It was Nietzsche who in Aphorism 84 of the *Mogenröthe* scoffed at Christianity as the religion

> which during the centuries since its foundation performed that unconscionable philological burlesque around the Old Testament; I mean the attempt to pull the Old Testament from under the body of the Jews with the assertion that it contains nothing but Christian doctrine and belongs to the Christians as the true Israel, while the Jews had only usurped it. One can indulge in a frenzy of interpretation and supposition which could not possibly have had a good conscience. However much Jewish scholars protested, everywhere the Old Testament was supposed to speak of Christ and nothing but Christ.

Every historian will share Nietzsche's disgust with the abuses of interpretation as well as with the doctored translations, even if he does not follow him in his conclusions. Bultmann shares it, too. He forcefully insists that although the Old Testament can be considered the Word of God at a remove (*in vermittelter Weise*) because it conveys an understanding of the relation between Law and Gospel, it must be so understood only on the condition that its original meaning (in the philological sense) be preserved and allegories be renounced. This is no more than a demand of intellectual honesty. Nevertheless, the demand, justified though it is, does not touch the issue itself. For however long the catalog of hermeneutic abuses be made, it remains a negative demonstration; it cannot prove, as Nietzsche assumes, that the link does not exist. Against the assumption stands the fact that the abuses are not a late development in Christianity but go back in continuity to the scriptural proof and allegorical interpretations used by the New Testament writers themselves, who sensed the link to exist even though they used inadequate instruments for expressing their conviction.

Bultmann is, of course, aware of this problem. He disposes of its several aspects by various methods. A first aspect is the strictly philological one of adequate interpretation. In Bultmann's opinion scriptural proof and allegories do not become any better if a New Testament writer uses them; a fanciful scriptural proof does not become true if it is to be found in Saint Matthew. Nothing can be said against this part of his position. Under a second aspect he recognizes frankly that the authors—in particular he mentions Saint Paul—interpret the Old Testament indeed from their new eschatological consciousness, in which the older Scripture only now reveals its true meaning. This interpretation, in his opinion, is justified as long as it brings to fuller understanding the creatureliness of man under the claims of God. "We, as the men called to believe, find ourselves mirrored in the Old Testament." That is to say that we, as natural men, are mirrored in the Old Testament. Bultmann suppresses the decisive point by switching from the historical to the ontological level; only ontologically, not in any theological respect, does the Old Testament become something like a secondary (*vermittelt*) Word of God. If in regard to the second aspect the ontological evasion could be used in order to suppress the issue, there seems to be no possibility of evasion in regard to the third point, that is, the theology of history explicitly contained in the New Testament, as for instance in Romans 9–11. To be sure, these chapters abound with scriptural proof, so that numerous philological exceptions could be taken; and since their interpretation of the Old Testament is inspired by Saint Paul's eschatological consciousness, one still could let them slide into the ontological rubric. Nevertheless, on this occasion the issue itself becomes thematic—no philological method or device of identification can dispose of the hard core of Saint Paul's theology of history, that is, his profound concern with the structure of history itself. We must consider the issue briefly.

The revelation of God to man occurs in concrete situations to concrete human beings who receive it representatively for all men. History has a structure inasmuch as it has representative centers of reception from which revelation is communicated to the rest of mankind. This structure of history is a "mystery" in the sense of Rom. 11:25. The mysterious structure had occupied even the prophets. As early as the eighth century one can notice the intensified experience of the "Word of Yahweh" as the ordering force of history, with its powerful expression in Is. 9:8 ff. In the sixth century, in Deutero-Isaiah, the experience of the "mystery" crystallized in the vision of an exodus of Israel from itself to penetrate with its revelation all mankind. The mystery then assumed a very disconcerting aspect in the time of Saint Paul when the revelation through Christ that had come to Israel seemed to penetrate pagan mankind but was not accepted at the center of its reception, among the Jews themselves. Saint Paul was so profoundly disconcerted by the extraordinary structure he saw in formation that he was driven to assume a special gift of wisdom, given to the *perfecti*, who by its virtue could penetrate the mystery and reveal the future course of history, and to act as a *perfectus* himself by predicting the future course in Rom. 11:25 ff.

Even if we discount the special sorrow of Saint Paul, the mystery remains as torturing today as it has ever been in the past. It can be summed up in the three questions, often asked in the age of the Enlightenment and since: (1) Why is there a history of revelation at all? Why is revelation not given to mankind from the beginning? (2) Why does revelation operate by the clumsy method of being given to representative men or communities, to be communicated by them to the rest of mankind? Why is revelation not given to all men equally? (3) Why do the centers of reception become only partially effective? Why do men engage in the resistance from which the structure of historical mankind as we know it results? The answer to these questions would define the meaning of history. But no answer can be given. And when we receive one nevertheless, as in the desperate attempt of Rom. 11:25 ff., we must agree with Bultmann's judgment, expressed in his *Theology of the New Testament,* that the answer is no more than a flight of speculative fancy. The mystery must remain intact as the core of every theology, or for that matter philosophy, of history. It must not be downgraded to a problem capable of resolution.[4]

We can resume the question of what Bultmann has to say concerning the Pauline theology of history—for the issue is real, even though we have little use for the apocalyptic fancy in which Saint Paul manifests his sorrow on the occasion. The information on the answer will not be surprising to those who are familiar with the existentialist technique of debate: Bultmann has nothing to say on the Pauline theology of history; he does not mention the subject. In an essay on the theological relevance of the Old Testament to Christian faith, the New Testament sources of its central theme are treated as if they did not exist. At the critical point, Bultmann uses the existentialist technique of annihilating reality by excluding it from the universe of discourse.

We can only state the negative result—nothing more can be said about an essay that evades every pertinent question. Nevertheless, we cannot leave the matter as it stands, for although we are not overly interested in the thesis itself (it hardly raises a meaningful issue, since empirically we have no knowledge of a Christianity to which the Old Testament is theologically irrelevant), the motivations of the peculiar construction merit our attention.

III

In 1954 Bultmann published an article on history and eschatology in the New Testament ("Geschichte und Eschatologie im Neuen Testament")[5] in which again the theology of history became thematic. Although the article enters into the substantive problem no more than the earlier one, at least the reasons for the peculiar reticence become visible. I shall first draw the main line of the argument, which concerns the changing conceptions of history.

1. The Greeks understood the historical process as part of cosmic movement, which, in spite of all surface changes, reproduces always the same constellations.

2. The Israelites understood history as the field of unlimited dominance of the God who had chosen Israel as his people. It is

4. Cf. Voegelin's later discussion of "Question and Mystery" in *Order and History*, vol. IV, *The Ecumenic Age*, chap. 7, §5 (1974; available Columbia: University of Missouri Press, 1999; also as *CW* 17).—Ed.

5. Reprinted in Bultmann, *Glauben und Verstehen*, 3:91 ff. See also *New Testament Studies*, vol. 1, trans. E. Kraft (1954), 5–16.

essentially the history of Israel according to the divine plan; and the future of salvation, even when it is painted in supernatural colors, is always understood as intramundane.

3. In the postexilic Jewish conception the expectation of an intramundane future of salvation is retained, but the new apocalyptic element of a "Son of Man" as the savior, as well as of the two aeons, enter and combine with a world-historic view of the empires in Daniel. While the older Israelite conception makes the process meaningful through insight into the justice of God that guides history toward its end, the later Jewish apocalypse illumines history through knowledge of the secret counsels of God. In the older view the individual as part of the community is responsible for the destiny of his people; in the later view the individual is responsible only for himself. The community of the nation has been replaced by a community of individuals.

4. In the message of Jesus, then, both conceptions are present, although the apocalyptic view distinctly preponderates.

5. In the early Christian community Bultmann observes a tension between the received Israelite conception and eschatological expectation, a tension that is resolved in the "decisive change" that the "secret of history" shifts from divine guidance of Israel's history to the eschatological events, be they the eschatological drama proper (as in 1 Cor. 15:51 ff.) or the events of Incarnation, Passion, and Resurrection.

6. The same "decisive change," only more marked, is to be noted in the theology of Saint Paul. The older Israelite conception is still present, but "history is swallowed up by eschatology." "Saint Paul's understanding of history does not originate in his reflection on the history of Israel, but in his anthropology." The course of history from Adam through the Law to Christ consequently can be cast in the form of the autobiographical "I" in Rom. 7:7–25a. Salvation has definitely shifted from fulfillment in the people's history to the individual as a member of mankind. With this shift, however, eschatology has lost its meaning as the end of history; it has become the end of individual human existence. The history of the past is transformed from this new position into the history of the individual who is freed from sin and death to life under grace (Rom. 6:14).

While the history of the people and the world loses in interest, another phenomenon is now discovered: the true historicity of human existence. The decisive history is neither world history, nor the history of Israel or other peoples, but the history experienced by every man himself. To this history the encounter with Christ is the decisive event, in fact it is the event by which individual man begins to exist historically, because he begins to exist eschatologically.[6]

To the believer in Christ the old aeon has indeed reached its end; he lives in the aeon of fulfillment under grace.

7. The further development of a theology of history in this direction was, in Bultmann's opinion, impaired by the nonoccurrence of the expected Second Coming. The generations after Paul did not have the force to live in his eschatological tension; and the time of waiting for the Parousia degenerated into a chronological category. The eschatological consciousness changed into sacramental piety, the church from a community of the saints to an institution of salvation (*Heilsanstalt*). Eschatology became partly a doctrine concerning the end of the world; partly it was replaced by sacramentalism. The interim period of expectation moved back into world history, because Christianity was viewed as a world phenomenon having a history.

8. The development just adumbrated seems to Bultmann to obscure "the understanding of the history of Jesus as an eschatological event." The true understanding is Saint Paul's and more particularly that of the Gospel of Saint John with its gnostic strand.

It is characteristic that gnosis abandoned the Old Testament and with it the faith in a God who as Creator is also the Lord of history, as well as traditional eschatology. In Saint John and the Johannine epistles the abandonment of traditional eschatology is accompanied by the renunciation of any appeal to the testimony of Old Testament history, though the faith in a Creator God is retained.[7]

9. This seems to Bultmann "the true resolution of the problem: the Now receives eschatological character through the encounter with Christ, because in this encounter the world and history come to their end and the believer as a new creature is *entweltlicht*." Nevertheless, some history seems to be left, for Bultmann insists on the reality of the "paradox" that the eschatological event has occurred in history and still occurs wherever the message of Christ is preached. This remnant of history, however, is no more than

6. Bultmann, *Glauben und Verstehen*, 3:102.
7. Ibid., 98.

"profane history"; it must not be understood as "history of salvation" (*Heilsgeschichte*). What has ultimately come to light is the dialectics of human as historical existence. "The history of man as a person can no longer be understood as a function of world history, it lies beyond world history." In these formulations Bultmann concentrates his own position.

I am not concerned with the correctness of Bultmann's description of the various conceptions of history in every detail. Only *en passant* be it noted that serious exceptions must be taken to his characterization of the Hellenic and older Israelite views. I am interested rather in the elusive premises that allow him to arrive at the odd thesis about the Old Testament. In the earlier article, with its burden of indeterminacy and identifications, the disturbing factor proved to be the restrictive definition of "theology." This crucial issue we shall now examine in the light of the second article just presented.

Disregarding all questions that would arise if the postulates of pre-Reformation theology were taken into consideration, and conceding to Bultmann the widest latitude of a Protestant freedom of inquiry, we still must say that he has radically broken the bond of tradition inasmuch as he does not accept the Bible integrally as the source of truth *in rebus divinis*—as the body of materials to be clarified and ordered by the Christian theologian. Moreover, since his definition of *theology*, which determines the selection as relevant, or rejection as irrelevant, of certain parts of the Bible, is not developed through the analysis from the source itself but imposed from the outside, it cannot for its justification plead the methodological principle that every interpretation of a source must be selective. Since, furthermore, the existentialist conception of man to which Bultmann's definition conforms does not even faintly approach the fullness of the Bible's understanding of man, the definition of "Christian faith" as the formal object of theology becomes both restrictive and destructive. As far as this procedure affects the autonomous status of theology, the debate must be left to the theologians—but I must note as one of the phenomena of the times that a Christian theologian of stature, succumbing to the *Zeitgeist*, surrenders the autonomy of his science to one of the intellectual eruptions of a diseased age. My own remarks will be confined to the philosophical implications of the surrender.

The definition is destructive because it is grafted on an existentialism that ironically takes its name from the denial of existence to everything but the moment of a man's flight from existence toward an eschatological future. In Bultmann's formulations the denial is manifest in the distinctions between a "decisive" or "true" and a presumably "indecisive" or "untrue" history. "Decisive" or "true" is the history experienced "by every man himself." Historicity becomes in fact a category of exclusively human existence; the encounter with Christ is the event by which man begins to exist historically "in reality," because his existence has become "eschatological." In this encounter "world and history come to their end"; the believer in Christ has been *entweltlicht,* i.e., the world has lost to him the index of reality. And by the same token history has lost its index of reality, a modification that Bultmann indicates by applying to history the title "profane." Since Bultmann, as a Christian theologian, has to force existentialism on the recalcitrant word of the Bible—which has a few things to say about such "indecisive" and "untrue" matters as God and man, the world and society, the history of peoples and of mankind—the formulations are inevitably awkward because the same vocabulary has to be applied to the "true" as to the "untrue" reality. The secularists among the existentialist thinkers are strategically better placed because, in elaborating the problems of "true" historical existence, they can ignore the "untrue" reality; they simply do not talk about God and the world, about the nature of things and man, ethics and history. In a sense, therefore, we have to be grateful to Bultmann for his attempt to square the biblical circle with existentialism, because only in such forced confrontation will the philosophical poverty of existentialism be convincingly demonstrated.

This judgment of philosophical poverty, however, must be qualified. To be sure, it is justified with regard to a movement that uses philosophical vocabulary and pretends to give a philosophy of existence; but one must also recognize that the "philosophy" in existentialism is a facade behind which an entirely different, a nonphilosophical intention is at work. Again, we must be grateful to Bultmann's survey of the conceptions of history for having pointed out the nonphilosophical motivation behind the annihilation of world and history. "It is characteristic that gnosis abandoned the Old Testament," he says rightly; and it is the gnostic element in the Johannine writings that leads to "the renunciation of any appeal to the testimony of Old Testament history." The hatred of world and history, the experience of man as a stranger thrown into the prison of the world, the hope of escape from the untrue to a true reality, the understanding of this situation as the means of escape, the consequent negative characterizations of world and history as a magic opus of destruction—this complex of experiences and actions is indeed gnosis. In the New Testament, of course, the complex is no more than a strand; and not even the Gospel of Saint John, as Bultmann points out, will go so far as to declare the God of the Old Testament to be the daemonic Creator of the world prison from which man is to be released by a messenger of the true God. But a strand it is without a doubt; and this strand is virulent enough in Bultmann to follow Saint John in his removal of Old Testament history from relevance to Christianity.

Gnostic thought must be treated with circumspection. From the fact that gnosis is not philosophy it does not follow that everything a gnostic thinker has to say is wrong. For at the core of gnostic analysis of existence in our time, or of gnostic speculations of antiquity, there is an immediate experience of man's situation in the world. And while the interpretation of reality based on the experience can go wildly astray if it takes a fragmentary truth for the whole truth, the immediate experience itself cannot be wrong. We have indeed experiences of alienation; of being strangers in a world that is not ours; of a true measure of existence that is not taken from existence in this world; of a true reality, not of this world, whence this measure comes to us; of a longing for that other world, for a new heaven and a new earth; of a diminution of reality attaching to life in this world, the Pauline tonality of the "as if not"; in brief, of "eschatological existence." There is an experience of history being swallowed up by eschatology, as Bultmann formulates it; and again we have to be grateful to him for having sketched in his survey the process in which this experience is differentiated from the more compact experiences in which it was formerly embedded. A new phenomenon "is now discovered: the true historicity of human existence." To this sentence of Bultmann we must take exception only as long as it arrogates the monopoly of history to human existence and relegates the history of mankind, especially the history of Israel, to a limbo of theological irrelevance. But we can accept it if it is understood to mean that in the encounter with Incarnation the individual human existence has come into view as the point of transcendental irruptions that constitute history. While in compact experiences of the imperial type the area in which history is divinely constituted was located in the empire, under its ruler, with individual man participating in history only through his membership in the empire; while in the Israelite experience of the covenant type the ruler and the empire receded and society existed in immediacy under the kingship of God; in the encounter with Incarnation, we may say, history has become articulated down to individual man, who through his faith participates in the constitution of history. If the meaning be restricted in this manner, as pertaining to a differentiation of experience, Bultmann's analysis has admirably clarified one of the most complicated problems that plagues the philosophy of history. Moreover, it should be stressed that his reliance on contemporary existentialism has substantially aided the success of his analysis.

The preceding paragraph opened with a warning against a non sequitur. From the fact that an interpretation of reality is wrong it does not follow that the experience at its core does not contain a truth. We must now warn against the inverse non sequitur. From the fact that a truth has been differentiated through a new experience it does not follow that everything else known as true in the more compact experience has now become untrue. From the fact that an experience of "eschatological existence" has been differentiated it does not follow that a Christian is an existentialist who believes in Christ. Bultmann says, "The history of man as a person can no longer be understood as a function of the world history, it lies beyond world history." This verdict seems to me hardly acceptable, either as a whole or in its parts, because throughout it uses unanalyzed concepts. In a debate with a theologian it will not be inapposite to appeal to the Bible, I hope, and to insist that the subject of history is neither the world nor the individual person but mankind as symbolized through Adam and his descendants. Further excluded from the discussion should be certain terms frequently used by Bultmann, such as *Heilsgeschichte* (the invention of a nineteenth-century theologian) and "profane history" (I have not been able to discover its origin). Let us speak simply of the history of mankind, articulated by concrete societies and the human beings who are members of them. This history is partly structured by such events as the Sinai Covenant and the Incarnation, commonly called revelations; partly by other irruptions of transcendent reality, such as the illumination of a Buddha or the *opsis* of a Plato; and to the largest extent by the compact experiences of divine reality in archaic and primitive societies that do not yet display a clear differentiation of a *theologia supranaturalis* from the *theologiae civiles* which dominate the contemporary scene. Among these structuring events the encounter with the Incarnation holds the dominant position because it has differentiated the "eschatological existence," as Bultmann calls it, of individual man and has correspondingly, with optimum clarity, established the comprehensive society of mankind as the subject of history. The event has affected history in several respects; more immediately pertaining to the present issue are the following:

1. The epiphany of Christ has occurred in history and is part of its structure.

2. In its wake Christian churches and Christian civilizations have developed, which, again, have become part of the structure of history.

3. Our knowledge of history has changed through the aforementioned differentiation of "eschatological existence" and the comprehensive society of mankind as the subject of history.

4. Our sense of history has changed through awareness of the tension between all history transacted on the level of human intentions and the mysterious drama of mankind enacted unknowingly by finite actions.

About the importance of these changes there can be no doubt. Nevertheless, none of them has affected the nature of man. As I have formulated it on another occasion: The leap in being is not a leap out of existence—and when I use the term *existence* I use it as a philosopher, not as an existentialist. Man still exists under God in the world, within the limits set by his nature, within society and history, with all the obligations and responsibilities such existence entails. Hence, the various formulations of Bultmann suggesting an annihilation of history must be considered fallacious. A partial truth newly differentiated has mistakenly been assumed to exhaust the truth contained in the formerly compact experience of history.

The fallacy inspires the style of Bultmann's survey of conceptions of history. The conceptions follow one another as a series of increasingly true propositions concerning history, culminating in the "true solution" formulated by Bultmann himself. This is, on principle, the method used by Auguste Comte when he lets the symbolic forms of theology, metaphysics, and positive science form a series of increasingly true propositions concerning reality, ignoring the fact that theology and metaphysics deal with areas of reality not covered by science. As a consequence of the fallacious assumption that the newly differentiated sciences of the external world are coextensive in scope with theology and metaphysics, the large sectors of being not accessible to the methods of natural science will be either neglected or even denied the status of reality. In contemporary gnostic movements the Comtean fallacy has become one of the most effective instruments for the purpose of annihilating reality. In the same manner as Comte, Bultmann assumes the reality covered by the differentiated truth of "eschatological existence" to be coextensive with the reality covered by earlier conceptions of history. The differentiated truth becomes the "true resolution" of a problem, the earlier conceptions correspondingly the "untrue resolutions" of the same problem. Under this assumption the earlier conceptions must indeed be considered irrelevant, since they are no more than obsolete and inadequate formulations, now to be superseded by a better understanding of history. In one respect, therefore, Bultmann's philosophy of history is a variant of Comte's; and this factor must be recognized as one of the determinants in Bultmann's thesis of the theological irrelevance of the Old Testament, as well as in his omission of the Pauline theology of history.

The relation to Comte has its general significance as an instance of the variegated roots that Bultmann's position has in the movement of modern gnosis. In addition, however, the application of Comte's method to conceptions of history has a specific importance for both the theologian and the philosopher inasmuch as it affects the problem of prefiguration. Earlier in this study, I have declared my sympathy with Nietzsche's and Bultmann's revulsion against the misuse of scriptural proof and allegories, but at the same time I cautioned that there is more to the issue than meets the philological eye. For prefiguration, as can now be said with more precision, has its solid basis in the historical process of differentiating experiences and symbols. Christ is indeed prefigured in the Old Testament, especially in Isaiah and Deutero-Isaiah, even though in specific cases zealous interpreters have found more in it than there is to be found. This ebullience of scriptural proof, as well as the controversies in its wake, are caused by the inadequacy of a method that does not distinguish between experience and symbolization.

Compact experiences will be expressed by compact symbols; and the full meaning of compact symbols cannot be understood without analysis of the motivating experiences—an analysis that obviously can be conducted only from the historically later position of experiences that have differentiated from the compact complex. The symbols created in the process of differentiation, however, will specifically express only the area of reality newly differentiated. Their creators, absorbed by the importance of their new insight, will rarely shoulder the burden of creating additional symbols for the areas of reality left behind in their passionate search for the specific truth. Hence, when reflection turns to the continuity of the historical process and when, in order to demonstrate the continuity, the later position is confronted with the earlier one on the level of symbols (and that is what scriptural proof does), the peculiar problems of prefiguration will arise. Symbolisms like the Isaianic Prince of Peace or the Deutero-Isaianic Suffering Servant can, according to the interpreter's preference, either be locked up in the history of Israel as an autonomous entity, if the reflection is addressed to their compact surface, or be drawn into the continuous history issuing in Christ and Christianity, if the reflection recognizes behind the compact surface the differentiated area of truth that they also embrace in their compactness. Bultmann's philological method, while deprecating scriptural proof and allegories, uses their very technique of relating successive positions in a continuum on the level of symbols, but since he recognizes only the compact surface of the earlier symbols and disregards the tensions of experience pointing to future differentiation, the result is a separation of the history of Israel from that of Christianity. This result, however, should not become an occasion for hasty criticism of Bultmann's method. On the contrary, it is the only result at which one can arrive if philological method is used conscientiously. The drastic result, even if we admit that Bultmann would not have arrived at it unless the gnostic factor in his work had supplied the motive power, should rather make us aware that the historical process in which experiences and symbols differentiate requires more than philological methods for an adequate exploration. Even though a spiritually sensitive reader of the Bible may be satisfied with scriptural proof, it is time that prefiguration should emerge from the twilight of benevolent acceptance into the full light of a science of experience and symbolization.

If we come to an end, it is not of problems barely outlined, but of an inquiry that purports to elucidate Bultmann's thesis. Its motivations proved to be rather complex. At their core we found the reliance on a gnostic existentialism that wills the annihilation of nature and history. Over long stretches, this existentialism could be successfully used as an instrument of interpretation because Christianity, in the encounter with Incarnation, has indeed differentiated "eschatological existence"—a mode of existence that, if taken as the integral existence of man, can blend into genuine gnosticism. Moreover, gnostic tendencies of this type are present in the New Testament, especially in its Johannine parts. Nevertheless, setting aside the personal factor of Bultmann's Christianity, which motivates his theological concern with the New Testament, the very text proved an insurmountable obstacle to a radical derailment into gnosis. For the reality of Scripture is much larger than the reality admitted by existentialism, and since in particular it includes history, Bultmann's gnosticism had to assume intermediate forms. Among them we have especially stressed the indeterminacy of terms with its attendant difficulties—difficulties that the existentialist theologian cannot escape, for his text forces him to deal with the problem of history, while the secular existentialist can easily dispose of them by excluding history from his universe of discourse. In spite of paying the debt of indeterminacy, however, Bultmann could not quite avoid resorting to existentialist technique, when at the crucial point he had to suppress the Pauline theology of history. We then had to dwell on his criticism of scriptural proof and allegoresis, as well as on the support it derives from the critical methods of both philology and Comteanism. This issue is, in my opinion, of primary importance for every philosophy of history, quite independent of Bultmann's existentialist theology. Within the limits of the present study I could no more than suggest it, stressing its implications for the problem of prefiguration. Within the context of Bultmann's articles, however, the positivistic arguments have only supporting rank; the center of motivation is the existentialist will to annihilate history.

What has to be critically said against Bultmann's thesis I have made plain. Against the existentialist will no argument is possible. I can only say that I prefer to be troubled, in the company of Saint Paul, by the mystery of history.

11

Industrial Society in Search of Reason

I. The Pragmatic Pressure of Industrial Society

1. The pressure toward pragmatic rationality of action derives basically from industrial technology. The pressure factors may be defined as follows: (a) Compared to earlier methods of production (in agriculture and manufacturing), the machine separates the worker from his tools. He can no longer produce by himself or in small groups. (b) The socialization of work, because production on a large scale is organized around a whole complex of machines and raw materials (this aspect of de facto socialization had already been noted by Marx). (c) The result is an increasing interdependence of the members of society. (d) The fact that everyone is dependent on the smooth functioning of the organization. (e) The assurance of an annual increase of productivity as soon as the organization has attained the sector of technical research.

Due to the pressure of the various factors, the following questions are, to an ever-increasing degree, reduced to a simple pragmatic status: (1) Ownership of the instruments of production. (2) Planning—whether carried out by private companies or government agencies. (3) Economic class status.

2. To these basic factors, which have a part in any national industrialized society, must be added those that apply specifically to Western Europe: (a) Industrial technology determines the optimum size of society as far as total exploitation is concerned. (b) The

Originally published as *Colloques de Rheinfelden*, ed. Raymond Aron (Paris: Calmann-Lévy, 1960), the English version herein is taken from *World Technology and Human Destiny*, ed. Raymond Aron, trans. Richard Seaver (Ann Arbor: University of Michigan Press, 1963) and is reprinted by kind permission of the University of Michigan Press.

American and Russian societies fulfill the requirements as to size. (c) European national states are too small. (d) For technological reasons, the European common organization is a pragmatic necessity. It is also a condition for survival in a situation of power politics.

3. On the international scale, the most important pressure factor is "the bomb" as a means of mutual and radical destruction. It imposes the necessity of avoiding wars that would lead to the use of atomic bombs.

4. Pragmatic pressures and ideologies. The pragmatic pressure of the factors listed has not affected the structure of ideologies, but it has seriously diminished their credibility and their influence as a social factor. As a result, we can clearly see a growing area of basic agreement on questions of social organization. This consolidation has not always taken place because of a positive agreement on principles, but because of the pragmatic pressure that has removed many types of problems from the arena of political discussion by raising the specter of the terrible material consequences that threaten everyone alike.

II. The Russian Problem

1. Any discussion of Russian affairs requires that a distinction be made for the three following problems: (a) The creation of an industrial society competing with the West. (b) The institutional method of its creation, taking the time factor into consideration. Governmental despotism will probably produce the desired result faster than a free evolution would. (c) The rule of the Communist Party with its immanentist eschatology.

2. Reality versus Ideology. The debate is vitiated by a lack of distinction between the ideological and scientific statements of the problem. According to the ideological declaration, as it appears in the Soviet constitution, the Russian problem must be thought of in the following terms: (a) The Soviet Union is a socialist society. (b) Its political regime is a temporary dictatorship of the proletariat. (c) Its goal is the establishment of a Communist society, of the realm of freedom in the Marxian sense.

Reversing the order would give the following scientific counter-declarations: (a) It is impossible to establish a Communist society in the Marxian sense, because this symbol is the immanentist hypostasis of a transcendent eschaton. (b) There is no dictatorship of the proletariat in the Soviet Union. A sectarian community imposes its despotic rule on a people who, by the contingencies of its history, has shown itself incapable of establishing a representative form of government in the Western sense of the term. (c) An industrial society, characterized by cooperative and state ownership of the instruments of production, is in the process of being developed.

3. Viewpoints to be taken into consideration:

(a) "The pragmatic pressure of industrial society will to a large extent reduce the sector of problems in which the ideological non-meaning can possibly influence or affect the rational functioning of the organization." This is certainly a tenable opinion, but it does not follow that pressure will affect either the institutional methods (despotic) or social ascendancy of the Communist eschatology.

(b) "Communist eschatology will die of an atrophy of faith if the Communist realm is not established after a certain length of time." In the long run, this opinion will also doubtless be valid, but the period of time may well be very long. The following arguments can be advanced in favor of this reservation: (1) Lenin anticipated criticism concerning the nonrealization of Communist society by suggesting that it might take a century or two. (2) The argument of a hostile imperialist world. (3) The limited success in building the industrial society. The West had been living the myth of "Progress" for two hundred years before realizing that it was really material progress and stopping to ask itself: "Is that all there is to it?"

(c) The imponderable factor: the spiritual and intellectual life of the Russian people: (1) How much longer can a young generation that has grown up under the system bear the weary annihilation of spiritual life? (2) How long can the irrationality of Communist ideology resist the growing pressures of rationality in the industrial sector of the society?

III. Reason and Society

1. The postulates of classical politics: (a) Man participates in the Logos or transcendent Nous. (b) The life of reason consists of actualizing this participation and making it sufficiently important so that it becomes an influence on the development of character. (c) In regard to the life of reason, men are potentially equal, but empirically (for whatever reason) they are unequal in the actualization of their potentiality. (d) Men capable of an optimum actualization

are a minority. (e) A society has a de facto hierarchical structure in terms of actualizing the life of reason. (f) The "quality" of society depends on the degree to which the life of reason, actively carried out by a minority of its members, becomes a creative force in that society.

2. Additional postulates: A number of other assumptions must be added to the classic postulates. These were of course implicit in the politics of Plato and Aristotle, but only became explicit at a later date. (a) The psychic tension of the life of reason is difficult for the majority of the members of a society to bear. (b) As a result, any society in which the life of reason has reached a high degree of differentiation has a tendency to develop, along with the life of reason, a "mass belief." By sheer social expansion, mass belief may reduce the life of reason to socially meaningless enclaves or even forcefully suppress it. (c) In the case of early Jewish society, Jeremiah diagnosed this tendency as the "fall" of the people away from the "true God" to "false gods." At the height of the spiritual flowering of the Middle Ages in the West, Joachim de Fiore conceived of a "Third Realm" in the framework of history, and this has, with a certain number of variations, become an element of mass beliefs in the West today. Plato was aware of the problem when, for reasons of political expediency, he made concessions to the "popular myth" and accepted it as a parallel to existence in philosophical form. Examples prove that mass beliefs can assume many different forms. When the situation is favorable, as in the cases of the Hebrews and Greeks, the people can retain, or revert to, a living polytheistic myth; when, as at the height of the Middle Ages in the West, no living myth exists, the search for a mass belief is directed toward immanentist symbols of the apocalyptic or secularist-ideological type. (d) The coexistence of mass beliefs and the life of reason in a society has, since the Stoics, been classified under the headings of *theologia civilis* and *theologia naturalis*. (e) The rise of ideologies to social and political power in modern society must be considered in the context of attempts to establish a civil theology.

IV. Western Civil Theology

Western society emerged from the Middle Ages without a civil theology for the masses of the growing national states; even less likely is there to be discovered in the heritage of the past a civil theology for the industrial society that has transcended the limits of the national state. The efforts to cope with this problem have brought to light certain systems:

1. The Gelasian System. Included among the varieties of the Gelasian system should be included all the attempts to adapt the division of temporal and spiritual powers to the changing demands of philosophy, the national states, and ideologies. The succession of representative examples is the following: (a) Gelasius: Emperor-Pope; (b) Dante: Emperor-Philosopher (Averroist); (c) Bodin: National Sovereign-Philosopher (Mystic); (d) Comte: Industrial Manager–Positivist Intellectual (Ideology).

2. The Minimum Dogma. In order to satisfy the masses and at the same time protect the life of reason, philosophers have tried to distill from the life of reason a series of dogmas that everyone is supposed to believe, leaving the masses free to adopt any other beliefs so long as they do not conflict with the minimum dogma. Spinoza wanted to have the minimum dogma instituted as a state cult, with the proviso that those people whose emotional life was not satisfied by the bare minimum be authorized to establish more elaborate private dogmas and cults. The precedent for Spinoza's construction is found in the Platonic attempt to outline an obligatory minimum dogma in the *Laws*.

3. The attempts of sectarian communities to impose by force their immanentist beliefs on a society as a state cult. The principal examples are: (a) the Puritan revolution; (b) the French Revolution; (c) the National Socialist revolution; (d) the Communist revolution.

4. The Civil Government in the Lockean sense. A "natural" political sphere should be separated from the life of reason and spirit. This "natural sphere" has the monopoly of being public. Hence there will be no state cult; churches and sects are reduced to the status of private associations. In order to make this construction valid, Locke had to establish a careful equilibrium between tolerance and intolerance. On the one hand, the civil government allows complete freedom to the life of reason and spirit, together with its social manifestations; on the other hand, sects and ideologies that insist on making a political issue of their faith cannot be tolerated (Catholics, Mohammedans, Antinomians, and Levelers were denied civil status). The civil government operates on the premise that the way of life of a liberal-Protestant community must and will become the way of life of the nation.

5. Constitutional Democracy. Based to a large extent on the Lockean concept of civil government (but less rigidly constructed, so that it could absorb the problems of industrial society), this system has been practiced in Western governments, and especially in the Anglo-Saxon countries. In order to operate, it presupposes that the constitution itself is in a way an article of faith, that "constitutional democracy" is the predominant mass creed, the civil theology of the society. If this condition is fulfilled, the society can be "pluralistic" to the extent that free rein is given the residues of intellectual and spiritual movements (churches, sects, ideologies, and, last but not least, philosophy), assuming that they will live side by side without subverting the constitutional structure. The strength of constitutional democracy, especially in the Anglo-Saxon countries, is the eschatological tension left over from the Puritan revolution, which endows the constitutional form with a character of "finality" as the successful experiment in organizing a society with a classical and Christian tradition.

V. The Good Society

The "good society" is a concept of classical politics that requires considerable refurbishing if we are to use it to analyze contemporary politics. According to the classical concept, the "good society" is one that: (1) is large enough and wealthy enough to make the life of reason possible, at least for the minority capable of putting this human potentiality to work; (2) is organized in such a way that the life of reason becomes a social force in a society's culture, including its political affairs.

The concept also bears the burden of two assumptions that have become debatable in our time: (a) that a society, in order to be good, should not be any larger than a polis; (b) the fact that a sizable percentage of men in every society are slaves by nature justifies the institution of slavery and, in general, the maltreatment of those who are scarcely capable of facing up to the responsibilities of citizenship. The second assumption can be dismissed out of hand, since it has been replaced by the Jewish-Christian concept of man as the image of God, of man's dignity and inviolability regardless of how society may judge his conduct or value. But the first assumption requires closer consideration.

1. First, we must clear up a point that in our ideological environment is too easily obscured. A good, or even an excellent, society in the classic sense by no means means an ideal society. The Platonic-Aristotelian paradigms take into consideration the fact that men are unequal in actualizing their equal natures; the structure of society is in fact, for unknown reasons, hierarchical and not equalitarian, and we know of no way of changing this situation. The classical political thinkers were realists. Most of their modern colleagues are not.

Two corollaries must be added: (a) The model of the good society is not an a priori datum. Its construction is extremely elastic and must vary with our empirical knowledge of human nature and society. One sure thing is that the social effectiveness of the life of reason, which is constantly developing, must be included. For the rest, the field of construction is wide open—as is proved by Plato's readiness to consider second, third, and fourth best paradigms, to none of which he would deny the title "good society." The problem of the "good society" evolves into that of setting up a scale of societies with varying degrees of goodness. (b) The title "good society" does not contain any eschatological overtones; its establishment is not a final achievement that brings imperfect history to an end. Even the best of the good societies follows, according to the classical concept, the cyclical law of decline and fall; and its corruption begins from the moment of its inception. Or, in noncyclical modern terms: The idea of a good society is incompatible with the ideological dreams of a terrestrial paradise that will last forever.

2. The question of size poses a delicate problem. According to the classical concept, modern societies are not good because they are too large and do not allow the citizens to participate fully in public affairs. This notion cannot be dismissed out of hand as preposterous; some excellent authorities today, Leo Strauss for one, think it is valid. At the other extreme from this radical view may be listed the factors that were nonexistent in antiquity and that today make possible the building of a good society on the vast scale required by industrial society. Among them are: better organization of transportation and communications, the development of representative government and federalism and, last but not least, Christianity, thanks to which the meaning of human existence is no longer circumscribed by its expression in political life. Nevertheless, anyone

who has had the opportunity of observing life in the provinces of a large country—with its accumulation of resentment and frustrations, the sense of being left out, neglected, of having failed, the attendant warping of the mind, and the development of a ghetto atmosphere—will have to admit that the very size of society creates problems that require a great deal of attention and adequate treatment.

The problems of size, which prejudice the "goodness" of any modern industrial society, have become of prime importance on the international level because the material standard of living of Western societies is universally accepted as the condition of a "good society." With the acceptance of these standards the underdeveloped countries have, from the psychological point of view, been transformed into provinces of a world society whose center is in the West and especially in the United States. The problems of Communism, for example, have in political practice assumed a very peculiar form, not at all inherent in the dogma, because the Soviets have concentrated all their efforts on building an industrial society whose efficiency and productivity will be comparable to those of the United States.

3. The problem of viability is closely connected with that of size. To be good, a society must first of all exist, and "goodness" is itself no guarantee. With the arrival of the era of empires the city-state was doomed. If we were to accept without qualification the classical concepts it would follow not only that industrial societies are worthless but that, in the age of industrial societies, "good societies" can survive only if they are tolerated by the major powers, which are not terribly "good." Therefore the question of "goodness" cannot be treated without reference to the historical conditions of social existence, and we must once again study the "pragmatic pressure" of industrial society from the viewpoint of its influence on the life of reason.

The development of modern science, technology, and industry is a historical process, and as such not at everyone's disposal. The romantic revolt and the dream of returning to the simple life make no sense at all; no one would think of advising the underdeveloped countries to remain in their happy state and be glad they had escaped the fate of industrialization. The general agreement on this point is more than a consensus on the level of materialism; it can be justified rationally by the results of industrialization in Western society as we have been able to observe them. It is evident that in its initial stage industrialization caused social evils that in turn engendered ideological revolts, so that Western progress seemed to be self-defeating. Moreover, the social nightmare of that period still weighs menacingly over the West, for it materialized in a monstrous way through Communism and its political consolidation in Russia. And yet in the internal development of Western society the later stages of industrialization have strengthened rather than weakened the Western experiment in constitutional democracy. Since Western society is in fact "good" to the extent that it has absorbed and preserved the classical and Christian traditions, it was exposed to the serious danger of destruction from within by the immanentist ideologies. The expansion of industrial society during the present century has, because of the pragmatic pressure previously mentioned, eliminated a large number of, if not all, irritations from the area of serious discussion on an emotional level. Therefore the chances of preserving a "good society" have substantially improved. We have been granted a sort of reprieve, and are obligated to use it to the utmost to repair the damage that the age of ideologies has inflicted on Western substance.

4. In the West, constitutional democracy as a constitutional form is so closely allied with the notion of the good society that we must note a strong tendency to forget, both in theory and practice, that "goodness" is the quality of a society and not of a governmental form. When society is good it can function under the form of a constitutional democracy; when it is not good, it cannot. Thus a society that is not qualified for this governmental form can easily start down the road to disaster if it adopts a Western-type constitution. Unconscionable damage to millions of people throughout the world has resulted from ill-considered constitutional experiments modeled after the West. It is imperative that we face the facts. Not all societies are good, and the attempt to imitate the Western type entails revolutionary changes that can perhaps only be brought about by dubious means. The problem, although it has become in our time particularly acute, is not a new one. The classics were well aware that "goodness" cannot be exported. In the nineteenth century, John Stuart Mill in his *Essay on Liberty* limited representative institutions to those societies in which the life of reason and rational debate were sufficiently developed, while for "barbarian" societies he recommended "despotism" as the form best suited to

improving them. It is only in the twentieth century that we have developed that fateful blindness to the fact that a good society is something that must grow historically and that this growth is painful. If we take into account historical dynamics (a problem that was not taken into account by the classics), and especially contemporary dynamics, the question of "goodness" will require a certain amount of revision and refinement. We must admit that constitutional democracy may be a terrible form of government for an Asian or African country, whereas some form of enlightened despotism, autocracy, or military dictatorship can be the best if we believe that the rulers are using this means to try to create a good society. It will not be an easy matter to judge or give concrete advice. At one extreme, the sanguinary dictatorship of a Stalin is no longer deemed good even by the Russians. But if the mild rule of a Nehru results in the fantastic and irremediable disaster that, if we are to believe the Ford Foundation report, will overtake India in a few years, that will scarcely be considered "good" either.

These thoughts give rise to some unpleasant questions. Will the impact of the West on an Asiatic civilization such as India result in disaster and terrible suffering over a long period of time before the situation can be brought under control? Is rapid industrialization, copied from the West, always the best means of achieving a good society? Is it ever the best means? For, historically, industrial society has evolved in the West within the framework of rationalism. Can the historical order of cause and effect be reversed—as a certain Marxist precept holds—and the good society be expected to rise as the superstructure above industrialization? Should not the process of industrialization in societies where it is not indigenous be accompanied by profound changes if certain unexpected and perhaps undesirable results are to be avoided? For the moment we shall have to leave these questions unanswered.

5. The essential nucleus of a good society—without which it is worthless no matter what its accomplishments may be in other areas—is the life of reason. In order to make this notion useful for political analysis we must make a distinction between rational action in areas peripheral to the human psyche and action that affects the central order of the psyche itself. I shall therefore distinguish between pragmatic and noetic reason, pragmatic reason being understood as all rational action in the sciences of the external world, the development of technology, and the coordination of means and

ends as they apply to the external world, whereas noetic reason includes all rational action in the sciences of man, society, and history, both in the formation of the order of the psyche and of society. These two areas of rational action are relatively independent of each other. Any society, even the most primitive, includes an area of pragmatic rationality, since without the rational action that provides the means of existence there would be no society. The development of pragmatic rationality is, in any event, quite compatible with a high degree of irrationality in the sphere of noetic reason—*homo faber* corresponds perfectly well with Levy-Bruhl's "prelogical" mentality of the primitive—and ideological governments can build industrial societies. Conversely, a highly developed life of reason in the noetic sense—in the Athens of Aeschylus or Plato—does not necessarily lead to the expansion of the sciences of the external world.

6. Before the notion of the life of reason in the noetic sense can be applied a further distinction must be made. The difficulties of rational debate on an international scale arise from two different types of irrationality [among those who] are supposed to become our partners in a debate of this kind: (a) In some civilizations, such as India and China, the life of reason has never extricated itself completely from the cosmological myth. Even if there is a small group of leaders capable of carrying on a rational discussion in the Western sense of the term, the masses are still living at a less differentiated cultural level. (b) In the West a very different type of irrationality— that of ideologies—has developed. They all have in common the denial of the *participation*, the *methexis*, in transcendent Reason as the source of the life of reason; all of them have these derivative characteristics to the extent that they are immanentist perversions of a life of reason that is already historically differentiated.

7. The application of the concept to our problem of rational debate would require a complicated and careful casuistry. A few typical examples are:

(a) In Western society, our first difficulty concerns the intellectuals and the ideologies they represent. Debate in the true sense of the term is impossible, because they refuse to discuss the basic problems of the life of reason; the immanentist position must be accepted without question. The only result of any attempt to draw the ideological intellectual into a debate will be the use of techniques that consist of skirting the issue or reiterating the premises as if they had never been questioned, and apologetic rhetoric (although the long-term results of such attempts are of course incalculable). The difficulties of debate are still widely prevalent in Western society, although there has been some change in the course of the last generation; the hard core of resistance can be found today on the level of the mass media of communications, especially in the United States, while the academic sphere shows a notable improvement. It seems that the age of ideologies is drawing to a close—for reasons inherent in the structure of these ideologies, which cannot be discussed here in detail. This process of exhaustion is accelerated by the "pragmatic pressure" already mentioned.

(b) In the debate with Russia there do not seem to be any obstacles on the level of pragmatic reason, that is, in the mathematical sciences and in power politics: The argument of the "bomb" is fully understood. Difficulties arise in sciences where Marxist ideology has been able to make itself felt: The Lysenko affair is sufficient proof. In philosophical matters there seems no possibility of discussion. In its interpretation of man, society, and history, Communist ideology remains an untouchable, inaccessible block that is not open to question.

(c) As for those civilizations that have not completely emerged from the culture of the myth, serious difficulties arise on the pragmatic level. It would appear that the techniques have not yet been found that will convince the Indian masses in a short period of time that cattle should be eaten rather than allowed to run rampant through the fields, that the caste system should be eliminated, and that habits of diet should be modified—not to mention the difficulties encountered in trying to inculcate rational habits of organization and administration.

(d) A special problem has grown up during the height of the age of ideology through the education in Western universities of the elite of the underdeveloped countries. Besides out-and-out Communism, we should also mention that strange cocktail of Rousseau-Marx–John Dewey, with a dash of neo-positivism and British analysis, which was given to non-European students as the very essence of Western culture. Just as our corruption of the nineteenth century now comes home to us with a vengeance in the form of Russian Communism, so in the course of the past two generations we have studiously built up centers of intellectual resistance to the life of reason in China and India, in the Arab countries, and in Africa.

The effects of this unfortunate period of Western "education" will plague us for a long time to come.

(e) These last remarks lead us back of the position of the West in the present conflict. What do we have to offer by way of guidance or leadership in this worldwide transformation of society? The answer is: everything and nothing. We know what the life of reason and the good society are; we can cultivate the former and try, by our actions, to bring about the latter. We can restate the problem: the formation of the psyche by encouraging participation in transcendent reason—which is what I have done, in however brief and imperfect way, in this paper. And that is all one can do; whether or not this offer is accepted depends on the Spirit that blows where It pleases. Collectively, as a society, there is at the moment little, if anything, we can do. For the dissemination of knowledge on a massive scale is the province of institutions, and what we disseminate by institutional means, be they the media of mass communications or academic organizations, may perhaps do more harm than good. To be sure, the ideologies have not been able to destroy the life of reason in the West, but the damage is serious—even though we hide it under the euphemism of "pluralistic society." If everything goes well, it will take at least a generation before the Western stables are clean enough to make the power of the West, which rests on its life of reason, institutionally visible and persuasive once again.

12

Man in Society and History

The organizer of our colloquium has asked me to take the first lecture. It is supposed to be something like an introduction to the theory of institutions. Yet it was not easy to determine its object more exactly and, as the general character of my title shows, basically the effort has been unsuccessful. Why?

Institutions are not objects with an essence about which a theory could be developed. The expression "institution" is a topical concept. We all operate freely with it; we even hold lecture series about institutions of the most diverse kinds such as, for example, parliaments and interest groups. But this linguistic usage is nothing more than a convention for designating complexes of relatively constant modes of conduct that are especially noticeable to us in society or appear to be especially important. In terms of theory, these complexes would have to be resolved into types of action for the realization of order in society; this resolution would lead us to further questions about the order to be realized; and these in turn to questions about human nature and its right ordering. If seriously undertaken, any attempt at a theory of institutions would lead back to the basic issues of that political science that Aristotle summarized as *philosophia peri ta anthropina*. Institutional regulations in the sense of prescriptions for rightly ordered behavior in determinate situations would have to involve the entire realm of the realization of human nature. And this realm is quite large. It encompasses not only the noetic nature of human beings in their personal, social, and historical realization. It encompasses also what Aristotle termed its

Translated for this edition from the German by Frederick Lawrence, this essay originally appeared as "Der Mensch in Gesellschaft und Geschichte," in *Österreichische Zeitschrift für öffentliches Recht* 14, nos. 1–2 (1964), and is reprinted here by kind permission of Springer Verlag, Vienna.

synthetic nature, i.e., the participation of human being in several realms of being, its character as psychological, animal, vegetative, and physical nature. Its realization spanning every reality of being from the physical to the spiritual, and every one of these further differentiated according to the personal, the social, and the historical aspects, reaches at every place and every time into the problematic of institutions.

One cannot give a lecture about an object with such a boundless scope—but when the question is formulated as it has been in the previous paragraphs, then what is most fundamental is actually thereby stated as well. In terms of theory, we cannot get away from the fact that institutions are complexes of modes and rules of conduct that we can distinguish as relatively permanent and which we are interested in for one reason or another.

Once this has been established, the questions cast up by our use of the expression "institution" are not yet taken care of. Conventions have their reasons, even if we are not clearly aware of them. If we examine the conventional use we make of the expression, then perhaps one insight or another of political science will result along this path.

In the context of civil law we speak of the institutions of property, family, marriage, contract, inheritance law, and many more of the same sort. Common to all these complexes is their character as institutions of order. On the contrary, we are less inclined to speak of other, equally constant and interesting, complexes such, for example, as murder, robbery, fraud, divorce, juvenile delinquency, and so forth, as included among the institutions of a society—we gladly yield complexes of this type to sociology. But once again we surely are inclined to name those arrangements that serve to do away with or to penalize such complexes of disorder institutionally, for example, the institutions of criminal law. In accord with the consensus of linguistic usage, then, complexes that order conduct are designated as institutions, whereas we just as clearly deny this name to various and interesting complexes of disordered behavior. Linguistic usage implies an idea of order, and therefore of norms of order. This leads us back again to the theoretical questions, but it engages them at a far more concrete level than do the basic propositions about human nature and its realization stated above.

At this more concrete level it is still sometimes more difficult to decide whether a complex is to be classified as an order or a disorder. As long as we remain with the great institutions of civil and criminal law, we are fairly much in agreement about what order and disorder is—although also in these questions such differences of opinion may arise as can only be settled by a revolution. But there are cases that seem to be limiting cases in principle.

For example, what about war? Is it a disruption of institutional order, or is it one of its complexes? There are cultures and historical situations in which war is an institution. In the Israelite conception of kingship, for instance, it is a part of his aura that early each year the king wages a war; if he neglects waging his war, this becomes disadvantageous to his respect and to the institution of kingship. Or what do we make of Clausewitz's formula that war is the continuation of politics by other means? There, too, it seems as if politics is "normally" conducted in the formation of the constitution and in diplomacy, so that one still has to make use of the institution of war if the normal institutions are not sufficient for executing the political aims—just as the institutions of criminal law subsidiarily serve the restoration of normal order. Or what is to be made of the idea of the *bellum justum*? Doesn't it turn war into an institution by which a disturbed order is restored? Further, how about wars for carrying out revolution? Above all, what about revolution itself? Is a revolution a disruption of institutional order, or is it one of those processes by which historically institutions submerged in disorder are changed or abolished, so that it would itself be an institution of order? Especially, what about cases of revolution where we have a philosophy of history according to which certain phases must be passed through? Do actions that serve the coming about of a dictatorship of the proletariat have an institutional nature, since they are obviously undertaken in accord with an idea of the order of humanity in history? From our standpoint a dictatorship of the proletariat may be a highly disordered arrangement; but from the standpoint of persons who believe in Marx's apocalypse it is a necessary phase on the way to a condition of order, and so is itself once again an institution of historical order.

This brief overview of linguistic usage and limiting cases justifies the following consideration. As long as we move within relatively "ordered relationships," as long as society is relatively stable, we can talk about its distinguishable complexes of modes and rules of conduct as institutions—without getting into too great difficulties. But when society enters the swamp of historical process we cannot make do simply with the *topos* "institution." A science of institutions in the sense of the conventional *topos* can be based on the established institutions of a relatively stable society. It can study the appropriateness of institutions for the realization of any given conception of order; and it can make practical suggestions for their improvement. But beyond this lies the infinitely differentiated field of social and historical processes, the field of the foundation, maturation, and decline, of the reform and revolution, and of the collapse of institutions. The class of phenomena in motion and change is not covered by a doctrine of established institutions and their purposiveness. As the reference to apocalyptic revolutions makes clear, it reaches out into the sphere of the noetic and pneumatic order of humanity, and that means: into the spheres of theory on the supreme level of generality.

How then have theoreticians dealt with this tension between established institutions and the phenomena of motion or change? I will treat first a modern case, the theory of Maurice Hauriou, which is understood to be a theory of institutions. It was developed in the 1920s. In my analysis I refer especially to Hauriou's *Précis de droit constitutionnel* (2d ed., 1929) as well as to his *Théorie de la fondation* (1925).

Above all: Under *institution* Hauriou understands the state—an entity about which one does not think primarily when one approaches the issue from the perspective of the institutions of civil and criminal law. He takes his stand on the history of the French national state, handles its creation through dynasties and its further evolution through revolutionary regimes since 1789, and then speaks of the power of the ruler who is legitimated by his function as representative of the institution, namely, of the state. Now what is this institution? Its core is the idea of organizing a still diffuse group of people into a stable society. Hauriou calls this idea the *idée directrice.* To state the matter simply but clearly, whoever emerges as the entrepreneur and tries to realize the idea is the representative of the institution that at first was only real in the form of an idea. The representatives of the institution can be dynasties, but they can also be republican regimes. The authority of the ruler stems from his subordination to the idea in accord with which the institution was conceived; and the institution only becomes a complete reality when the exercise of rule is formalized for the purpose of the realization of the idea by rules of law; when a constitutional law has been developed that regulates organization, spheres of competence, and procedures of the representatives; and when the regular position of the representatives has gained the *consentement coutumier,* the consent of the people organized under the rule. Hauriou's theory thus derives certain basic concepts like the organization of society, representation, rule, authority, and law from the process of the creation of institutions. At the beginning of this process, from which the concepts introduced are derived, stands the *idée directrice* and the people who, as entrepreneurs, realize the idea in history.

From this construction there results the unique problematic of Hauriou's theory of law. First of all, its positive side: Law has the purpose of regulating the realization and maintenance of the idea. It has no [inherent] authority of its own. The ruler does not legitimate his position by the constitution, but the constitution derives its legal validity from the function of regulating the implementation of the idea. This point Hauriou especially enjoins; and it is a matter of an insight that is unfortunately misunderstood all too often when any board of directors that itself has no political or executive qualities issues a written constitution and expects that the piece of writing will function as the constitution of the society. A constitution can in fact only function if there are persons who are recognized as representatives of the society and as rulers in the sense of the constitution. If the social reality presupposed by the constitution exists, then the written constitution functions; if it does not exist, then de facto modes of conduct will result that deviate very strikingly from what is foreseen in the written project.

This insight is quite valuable in an age in which there is no lack of infantile attempts to organize a new society in accord with constitutional models that have no relationship to the factual representational situation in the society to be organized. So this construction is worth taking very seriously when we inquire about the rightness of an order and about the standards of rightness. The problem comes up in Hauriou when he speaks of ordered power, and indeed in almost the same sense in which Machiavelli had spoken of *virtù ordinata* (without there having to be any literary dependence) in opposition to the usual *virtù,* which, to be sure, can produce extraordinary political and historical fireworks but not a rightly ordered institution. By the salutary expression "ordered power" Hauriou acknowledges the existence of the problem, but he has nothing to say about the question of the contents and criteria of right order. So significant is his emphasis on representation and the executive or entrepreneurial factor that his doctrine of institutions does not go beyond the field here characterized as established institutions. The French state is the object of Hauriou's investigation just as it has emerged from history and as it functions as an already achieved enterprise of social organization. About the more comprehensive processes of the formation of the Western nation states in the territory of the empire; about the relationships to the churches and the transnational ideological movements that also pertain to a political investigation one finds nothing at all in Hauriou.

Now let us compare the classical theory of Aristotle with the modern one of Hauriou. Nothing could be more beside my point than to play one off against the other. Instead you will see that different areas of the problem of institutions are handled, all of which pertain as equally essential to the subject. Aristotle elaborated three such areas.

As a first I mention the subject matter of order, which was neglected by Hauriou. Aristotle dealt with this circle of questions programmatically in the last book of the *Nicomachean Ethics*. The purpose of human life is the good life, the *eu zen*. One has to be educated to the good life and to educate oneself; and therefore the institutions of education are the central problem of the theory of institutions. If a person knows furthermore what the good life is, then certain consequences result for the establishment of society beyond the educational institutions as they are unfolded in Books VII and VIII of the *Politics*. This area, insofar as it includes the content of order and the criteria of its rightness, thus enlarges Hauriou's theory. I do not raise now the question whether the rules of Aristotle are correct or false, whether they were right for their age but today need to be revised, or not; but I only contend that this area pertains to the subject and ought not simply be passed over by an investigation of established institutions.

More relevant for the tension between established institutions and the phenomena of motion or change is the second area, the theory of *stasis*, which Aristotle handles in *Politics* V. The theory of *stasis* has remained an established staple of political theory through the centuries; one runs across it in different variations in unexpected places. For example, most of the political recipes in the name of which Machiavelli is moralistically devalued and condemned the Italian thinker actually borrowed from Aristotle. Or, to name a more recent work, Harold Lasswell's *What Is Politics? Who Gets What, When, How?* is written in the spirit of *Politics* V. By this I do not mean to say that every author who deals with this area copies Aristotle; because materially it is a perduring experience that resides on the *commonsense* level, and so is originally accessible to any person who has eyes and ears for his political environment. Only the care and precision in the elaboration of this field is specifically characteristic of Aristotle.

Let us examine the basic concepts. Aristotle speaks of a *metabole* or *kinesis* of society, that is, of movements and overthrows of a relatively permanent established order. He inquires why a relatively stable, balanced order enters into disorder; because when one knows the causes of disruption, then one can possibly work out institutional recipes for avoiding disorder. His posing of the problem is thus primarily pragmatic. In general, disorder arises on account of *stasis*. The concept is usually translated as *revolution*. This is not only wrong but also obscures a quite important process, because *stasis* means "to fix" or "become rigid." When someone becomes hardened in a position and offers resistance to the smooth interplay of society, then order enters into disorder. Because in reaction to the hardening of one position others become rigidified into counterpositions; there arise conflicts that lead to upheavals. The problem of rigidification is at the center of the theory of revolution: Institutions start to decline when for one reason or another the process of rigidification sets in.

Before going further into the question of rigidification and giving examples, I want still to underline that it is remarkable that Aristotle confines his object in treating *stasis* as much as Hauriou does in his theory of institutions. As Hauriou, when he develops his theory of the *idée directrice* and its entrepreneurial realization, limits himself to the case of the French state, so Aristotle confines his investigation of *stasis* to the case of the *politeia*. Whereas, indeed, the expression *politeia* in other parts of the *Politics* is a lead concept for all types of regimes, good and bad, its meaning gets narrowed down in Book V to that of a republican regime (*politeia*). Polity is set over against monarchy in its two forms of *basileia* (king) and *tyrannis* (tyrant). Monarchy in turn get excluded even more from the discussion because it is either the civilizationally primitive pre-form of *politeia* or one of its extremely derailed forms:

basileia as an extreme derailment of aristocracy; *tyrannis* as an extreme derailment of the democratic republic. The polity whose *stasis* and upheaval are investigated is thus a republican society that has to keep the eventual tensions among its citizens in balance. The comprehensive historical field that goes beyond the form of polity is excluded from examination.

For the case of polity Aristotle classed the great interest groups [or factions] that get rigidified and so can cause revolutions according to types. This set of types has remained fundamental until our day, although it has to be enlarged, broadened, and modified in the most diverse directions. The critical points at which *stasis* sets in are for Aristotle the rich, the poor, and the virtuous. The position of great wealth opens up possibilities of manifold abuses; and when abuses become rigidified and get defended as privileges, they provoke violent reactions. Correlatively, the position of the poor can get so rigidified through exploitation, neglect, and underprivilege of various kinds that resentment becomes revolutionary. And when ethical character in the socially relevant mass declines and rigidifies into the defense of a corrupt condition, then the possibilities of virtuous indignation and reactionary revolution are given.

Stasis at one of these points can cause a politics aimed not at the restoration of balance but at the radical suppression of rigidified groups. Aristotle devoted an investigation to this problem that has quite a modern ring to it. He raises the question: Should one, when rigidifications enter, make concessions to the demands for their dismantling? And he responds to the query with the consideration: The beginning is half of the whole. Once one starts making concessions, then one is moving along a course of ever-mounting claims. In conjunction with the sophistic syllogistic form of *sorites*, he casts light on the problem referred to today as "salami tactics": Demands for the abolition of an unjust condition are modest; but one modest demand follows another (without one's being able to say that any single one is unfair) until the political equilibrium has been so shifted as a result of the concessions granted that huge institutional transformations such as the swing from oligarchy to democracy or vice versa can be brought about.

Political actions of this kind, however, can only be perpetrated and head toward the goal of a political overthrow because they factually or in pre-given ways occur in dealing with problems having to do with material justice; and questions of material justice, in turn, are inspired by equality and inequality among people. All people are equal according to their potential nature; and when this essential equality is violated in the organization of a society, then there result the opportunities for indignation, rigidification, and revolutionary upheaval. Yet people are unequal in actuating their [potentially] equal essences—an inequality that is expressed in achievement and the consequent economic, social, and political station. Hence, when a society is organized in an egalitarian way, the "unequals" furnish resistance, and it can come to political upheavals because the principle of inequality has been violated. Now people are inclined to push either the principle of equality exaggeratedly in an egalitarian direction or the principle of inequality in an elitist direction. Therefore a constitution needs to be constructed so that it keeps tensions between egalitarian and elitist extremes in balance.

Aristotle goes much further into detail in his classification by types of the concrete occasions that have the effect of *stasis* or counter-*stasis*. His list, although capable of being expanded and in need of it as well, has not yet become outdated. On the top of the list stands insolence, either on the side of the rulers or on that of the ruled. Then follows fear, and indeed not just fear before the ruler, but specifically fear in the face of the consequences of a transgression that consistently leads to further transgression and to the rigidifyinq of a position of injustice. Next, he names too high a degree of outstanding qualities, which provokes the envy and awareness of guilt of others and is to be controlled by the institution of ostracism. Then follows despicable conduct by the ruler (affairs with women and other excesses) that makes his authority shaky and calls for his removal. After that are named election plots, filling offices with unqualified persons, and other expressions of behavioral negligence and pettiness that excite ill will. And finally there will be shifts in the balance of power through the disproportionate growth of one or another sector of the populace.

The third area with which Aristotle is concerned is the historical one of *politikon anakyklosis*, the cycle of political forms. His investigations of *stasis*, as mentioned, are confined to the republican polity. In the realm of historical memory, however, there also reside the older phases of monarchy and aristocracy as well as the institutions of tyranny. For Aristotle, therefore, the question arises whether there is one historical process with certain determinants of the direction in which the various types of regimes succeed one another according to a rule. He believes he can recognize such a rule of seriation and discovers its cause in the process of civilizational saturation. Under primitive conditions, monarchy is the most just regime, because a qualified person is rare; once the society has reached a certain level of culture, the personal qualifications stand out less in relation to the trained capacities of greater numbers of people. The monarch cannot hold onto his position against the claims to rule of equally capable persons, and so there follow aristocratic, oligarchic, and democratic regimes. The phenomenon of saturation is called forth by transformations in the structure of the economy. To be sure, there was not an industrial revolution in Aristotle's time. But the progress from agrarian economy to the production of goods for market, the development of trade relationships, of wealth through the business of import and export, is effective enough to elicit that degree of saturation that forces changes of regime. Especially impressive were the shifts in the proportions of population groups in Athens due to the empire and the development of a fleet, just as in our industrial revolution there developed new groups of trade, shipping personnel, boat-construction and harbor laborers who quantitatively distorted the balance of the older polity forever and drove the political process forward in the direction of democracy.

Thus far the areas of the theory of institutions that Aristotle handled.

Fully as much as Hauriou's theory of institutions, that of Aristotle, too, has its characteristic limitations. Hauriou was primarily interested in the institution as an enterprise, while the issues of order, of the criteria of their rightness, and the historical succession of regimes became unimportant. For Aristotle the issue of the form, of the *eidos*, of the polis is central. Let us examine this problematic, which still plays a notable role today in the theory of institutions under the heading of "the forms of government."

Aristotle develops the teaching of the *eidos*, of the form, of the polis in *Politics* III. If he places the polis in the context of the metaphysical categories of form and matter, then only its constitution (*politeuma*) can be understood as the form of the polis, whereas the citizens have to play the role of matter. But Aristotle was a philosopher who understood his business; and so an insoluble aporia resulted for him from his application of the form-matter scheme, which does not bother modern institutionalists at all. Because form and matter together determine a thing, with every change in the constitution that brings forth a new form, a new thing would arise that would not be identical with the preceding one. Thus the construction conflicts with the commonsense experience that the polis of Athens does not cease to be the same polis when the democrats replace the oligarchs as rulers. The conflict between historical identity and newly constituted constitutional law has since antiquity occasioned repeated attempts of revolutionary regimes not to hold their predecessors accountable for their faults of state. And since there are ideological regimes, this conflict sets the conditions for a new type insofar as revolutionary-apocalyptic sects fundamentally dispute the continuity of history when they come into power, only to discover sooner or later that a Soviet Union still is always Russia, or a socialist concentration camp still always consists of the bodies of a historical people. And so we arrive at the important theoretical conclusion that institutions cannot be adequately placed under the form-matter scheme.

Not exactly a limitation, but rather a remarkable feature in Aristotle's theory when one compares it with Hauriou's is the utter lack of importance assigned to the moment of enterprise. This becomes all the more noteworthy inasmuch as enterprises have a quite significant function precisely in Greek politics—from the enterprise of the war against Troy (that dominated the notion of political activity throughout the epics), through the enterprise of the fleet and of the empire by Themistocles and Pericles, down to Alexander's enterprise against Asia in Aristotle's own time. In the *Constitution of Athens* Aristotle further describes quite exactly in concrete analyses the enterprising achievement of Prostasia in the politics of Athens. Nonetheless, this complex of enterprise is neither theorized by Aristotle nor taken up into the theory of institutions. Why not?

What is remarkable for us today might have its basis in Aristotle's still intact experience of God and in the principle that action is to be oriented in the love of God. No activity, not even political action, stands outside the law of having to be guided by *phronesis*. Specific achievements brought into the world by human action such as great political undertakings, the leadership of affairs of state, the establishment of new institutions, and so forth, are not "creations" of human beings, because the divine cosmos and its order are pregiven; but they are just human achievements that emerge at the intersection of substantive tasks and personal capacities. Precisely the "creation" of the polis is shrouded in the darkness of *synoik-ismos*. In Hellenic civilization human beings are not "creators" of history. They do not possess the Promethean-revolutionary "con-sciousness" of being able to create the society in which they live—a type of consciousness that appears to me to inspire Hauriou's idea of representatives who realize the *idée directrice*; and it does so to such an extent that the underlying question of "right action" is emptied out and only manages to slip in by means of the traditional carryover of "ordered power." Aristotle's God, in contrast, moves history, society, and personal activity of human beings by the fact that human action drawn by him is related to him and thereby generates just order in society and history.

The lack of this modern "creative" element in Aristotle very seriously limits the applicability of his theory of *stasis* to modern societies. Let us consider the interest groups once again among which his polity has to maintain a balance. They are the rich, the poor, and the virtuous. At another passage in *Politics* VI the catalog is expanded to include earners of daily wages, large and small trades-men, magistrates, and so on. What is nevertheless lacking—and it is a political factor of the first order precisely in modern societies— are the possessors of truth in the sense of prophets, apocalyptic seers, Gnostics, theologians, and ideologues. The whole world of pneumatic experiences, of the varieties of their expressions, and the demand for political dominance and institutionalization is missing in the Aristotelian conception of politics. His theory of *stasis* and of revolutions therefore has to be understood as the political theory of a pre-pneumatic civilization. Everything stated in *Politics* V about *stasis* and revolution is correct and can be accepted—but it ceases to be applicable as soon as pneumatic people emerge in a society as socially relevant groups. Because the rigidification of a pneumatic sectarian, especially of an ideologue, cannot be dissolved by the rational arguments or the standards of rational politics, the pneumatic *stasis* can only be dissolved by the dying out of its membership or by the violent suppression of the sect—unless the society chooses the alternative of subjecting itself to the demands of the pneumatics. The minute elaboration of a theory of *stasis* is conditioned by the fact that in the Aristotelian model there are no pneumatics. Furthermore, one would have to add that in Hel-lenic antiquity in general there were no revolutions in the modern sense; and that therefore rendering the expressions *metabole* and *kinesis* as "revolution" and "movement" is unreliable. One ought to be more careful in speaking of political upheavals, because the phenomenon of modern revolution first arises as a result of pneumatic experiences and community-formations as well as of their derailments.

Both modern and classical political theories represented by Hauriou and Aristotle contribute essential insights for understanding institutions, but neither one supplies the foundations for a satisfactory theory in that regard. The idea occurs of looking for the adequate foundations in a theory based on experiences of revelation. But we will also be disappointed in this quarter because the revelations of neither the Old nor the New Testament have to do with the organization of society. Think of the Decalogue: It gives rules for conduct toward God and toward human beings, but it says nothing about political institutions. Just as little can we derive advice for the establishment of a constitution from the Sermon on the Mount or the Letters of Paul. Since even the Chosen People had to live under the conditions of temporality we can distinguish two great phases in its history: the first one of immediate existence under God that Martin Buber called *theopolity*; and the second one, of the organization of a kingdom in accord with the model of "other nations," in order to do justice to the necessities of political existence in an inimical environment. As soon, however, as the kingdom is established there result the problems of temporal organization and of conflicts with the word of revelation; king and prophet are set over against each other as the representatives of social order in time and of the truth of revelation, respectively. The tension between king and prophet, between the organizer of the mundane existence of the people and of their spiritual life, runs from Israel through Christianity as a constant problem of institutions until the present. Even the Russian-Chinese tensions of our days are still tensions between temporal societies; and at the same time they are tensions between pneumatics who differ about the interpretation of the Word. Since, therefore, the Word of God has become constitutive for a community, the problems of social order become complicated by the tension between the institutions of eternal and temporal order, without this complication having so far led to a satisfactory theory of institutions, or even simply of societies in the line of Israelite-Christian tradition—not to mention a general theory that would also encompass classical society and the societies of the Middle and Far East. A comprehensive theory is today thoroughly in the realm of the possible, but I have no intention of entering into an issue of such a higher order in an incidental fashion.

In conclusion, therefore, permit me to refer to a few of the derailments of the experience of transcendence that are not helpful for the development of such a theory. By the experience of divine-eternal Being, whether it be the noetic experience of the philosophers or the pneumatic experience of the prophets, man is placed in the tension between time and eternity. Neither the tension itself, nor its poles, nor the order of human existence that results from the tension are objects. And yet these non-objects can be objectified and symbols can be developed to express these objectifications. These objectifications and their symbolic expressions can be understood under the heading of "derailments."

The first type of derailment is developed in classical Israel itself as the idea of the Chosen People in temporal existence. The tension of life in presence under God gets understood not personally but collectively and so can pass over into the idea of a politically organized status as Chosen; and the universality of the constitution of human beings in virtue of this tension toward God gets transformed into the idea of a human society in which the Chosen are assigned a function of leadership. This idea shattered in the factual course of history. The political organization of the Chosen People was destroyed by the ecumenical empires. Yet that does not mean that the idea of a Chosen People is dead. Still today it dominates the political scene in which more than one people feels itself chosen to enter into leadership of world society.

In the transition from Israel to Judaism, the idea of chosenness releases a new conception of history from itself that in turn has become one of the constants in world history: the idea of apocalypse. In apocalyptic thought the entire realm of history, in which the Chosen People sees its idea shatter, is objectified into a history of empire wielding power, which one can escape by a divine intervention. The intervention will abolish "all history up until now" and install a new history of the Kingdom of God. In the idea of the Fifth Monarchy, history becomes a history of the kingdom beyond the history in which we live. The contradictory structure of history in time is transformed into a history that has the structure of eternity. On another occasion I have called this idea of the transformation of temporal structure into an eternal one "metastasis." The metastatic ideas that determine politics until our day, for example, in the idea of a final Communist empire, move in the tradition of apocalyptic thought.

The idea of apocalypse shatters on the fact that the expected divine intervention does not occur. When the expectation of a metastatic transformation of historical structure from time into eternity is disappointed, there remains as a further dodge the idea that the world of temporality in its structure is not altered because it is the domain of an evil God, a prison; thus, the change into eternity that is experienced as real in the tension of the experience of transcendence is only possible through flight from the prison. The apocalyptic expectation under the pressure of disappointment makes the transition into faith in a knowledge that enables redemption from prison. The apocalypse becomes a gnosis. In the disappointment of apocalyptic expectation lies the starting point for the idea of the world as the creation of an evil demon, and the idea of a good God beyond the world, in whose realm indeed not human beings but their *pneuma* can escape the objectified tension of the experience of transcendence.

The fourth derailment is modern gnosis, in which the will to redemption of ancient gnosis is joined with the metastatic expectation of apocalypse and faith in the possibility of bringing about the metastasis through human action to form the remarkable complex of revolutionary consciousness. By *revolutionary consciousness* we are to understand faith in the gnostic recipes for redemption according to which humankind is to be displaced out of the structure of temporal history and into the structure of eternal history by revolutionary action. These recipes are handed down through Progressive, Positivist, or Marxist ideologies under the names of science or philosophy.

These negative statements are to be set over against the enumerated derailments:

1. History does not have the structure of ruling Chosenness;
2. history does not have an apocalyptic structure;
3. time and eternity are experienced as poles of the tension of existence in history itself. Its gnostic objectification into an evil history in time and a good eternity beyond history is meaningless; and
4. history does not have the structure believed in by "revolutionary consciousness."

Although these derailments do not agree with our experience of historical reality, they are today socially dominant ideas, and their symbolism determines the language of political discussion. The spiritual difficulty of achieving resistance to the social pressure of the dominant symbolism might be the greatest obstacle to the development of a satisfactory theory of institutions today.

I will end my overview of this problematic with this observation and open it up for discussion.

13

Democracy and Industrial Society

It surprises me as a newcomer to this circle that entrepreneurs have been apparently forced onto the defensive by an image of the entrepreneur whose characteristics come from attacks of labor and clichés of the intellectuals. I am surprised because instead I had expected offensive anger, which arises as a reaction out of self-awareness of entrepreneurial achievement. I would have expected this as the immediately obvious reaction, because the achievement that allowed the now-burgeoning economy to grow out of the ruins of the war's end is remarkable in any case, even if we do not wish to romanticize it as a miracle. But then I would have also expected it because the traditional image of the entrepreneur, which is undesirable and painful to you, emerged from past situations that are outdated today. In light of the trends we can observe in Western economy and society, and above all in the American world, that image is obsolete. Consequently, it would make sense, if, by way of introduction, I mention particular phenomena with which the outdated image would be contrasted. By making this kind of contrast, this image would of course not disappear from today's social practice tomorrow, since images of this kind have a social momentum that maintains them for a long time beyond the situation that once favored them; but perhaps the confrontation will cast a friendlier light on the difficulties that appear to bring pressure to bear on entrepreneurs today.

Translated for this edition from the German by Manuel Brieske, this essay originally appeared as "Demokratie und Industriegesellschaft," in *Die Unternehmerische Verantwortung in Unserer Gesellschaftsordung*, publications of the Walter-Raymond-Stiftung, vol. 4 (Cologne: Westdeutscher Verlag, 1964), and is published here by kind permission of Westdeutscher Verlag GmbH, Wiesbaden.

The debates we have followed concerning the entrepreneurial image get their peculiar characteristics from the identification, taken for granted, of the entrepreneur with the industrial entrepreneur. The tendency to enact and accept this identification stems from a relatively natural worldview commonly accepted today according to which there is an industrial society whose great social problem is the conflict of interests and consequent power struggle between entrepreneurs and workers.

An industrial society of this kind never existed. At the time the notion of it was fashioned, especially by Karl Marx, the industrial sector of society was relatively modest. This notion could only become socially dominant because the new industrial sector along with its social problems was projected speculatively into the future, as if it would absorb the future, as if it would absorb society in its entirety. The notion could be maintained, furthermore, because in fact the industrial sector grew at the cost of the older agrarian economy and, in relation to agrarian economy, it is still growing today. Yet around the turn of the century it became noticeable, and in the development of the American economy in the last three decades it has become clear beyond any doubt, that what is growing there may indeed be called industrial society; but it is only in part the industrial sector in the old sense of the production of goods by industrial methods of production. What is growing more strongly today are services, in the broadest sense of the term, including public services. If the notion of an industrial society defined by the social conflict between workers and entrepreneurs was not empirically applicable at the time it was created because the society was still predominantly an agrarian economy, it also becomes ever less applicable as each day passes, because we observe the service sector to be growing. This is not to say that we have to abandon the term *industrial society*. On the contrary, it is thoroughly justified, since the powerful transformations in the structure of Western society are based on the foundation of wealth created by technological productivity and the rationalization of forms of production. Without industry in the narrower sense of the production of material goods, there would be no growth in services. But we have to be clear about the fact that the structure of industrial society, which is growing here, has outgrown in unexpected directions the notion of a society of entrepreneurs and workers. Think of the fact that in America almost half the total wage income of labor comes not from the industrial sector of society but from the service sector.

If we apply our current terms with their old connotations to the new social realities, defective assessments of the situation result. Think, for instance, about the comparisons constantly drawn between the Soviet Union's Gross National Product and that of America. They are undertaken without consideration of the fact that the indices are incomparable because they express qualitatively diverse structures of economy and society. It has practically become a sport to draw comparisons that have to be misleading if they focus on old-style industrial production. This holds true especially for steel production, whose standing in the structure of the American economy is completely different from what it is in the Russian economy. It can be even more misleading to focus on the comparative figures of increased productivity, which are supposed to show that the Russian economy has caught up with American production in a short period. With the help of such comparisons, the differences in the structure of the economy and in the basis for wealth can only be obscured. One might not be reminded by these comparisons that in the Soviet Union as a whole there are not so many motor vehicles in use as America manufactures in one year.

But now for the issue of the entrepreneur. The industrial entrepreneur obviously remains a basic figure in economy and society also in those places where the qualitative transformation has advanced furthest, as in America. But precisely in the American case we can observe how other figures, to whom an entrepreneurial function—in the sense of creative initiatives for the order of society —has to be ascribed, emerge ever more prominently. Industrial society in the new style promotes entrepreneurial functions among which that of the industrial entrepreneur becomes merely one among many. Besides the capitalists in the old style and the managers of the new, there emerge the statesmanlike labor leaders of the John L. Lewis type; and besides both of these, there arise politicians and their intellectual advisers, with their initiatives. Finally, not to be omitted from this list, there are the "wealthy man" types—Kennedy, Rockefeller, Harriman—whose inherited wealth frees him for initiatives of a political and social nature. It is remarkable that in public debates this new type of politically active millionaire is not appraised as a capitalist, but as psychologically approaching more the worker or intellectual type who bears no business responsibility. Not so much the wealth of this type is objected to in critical remarks, but their lack of experience in money matters—never in their lives would they have had the responsibility of meeting employees' payroll on payday—and so they have no understanding of the problem of a genuine economic entrepreneur. These are only supposed to be examples of the broad scope of the new phenomenon of the entrepreneurial function, in the sense of a social initiative that has expanded in an industrial society far beyond the original industrial sector. To the degree that a society becomes an industrial society in the new style, in the measure, then, that its members are drawn with their whole existence into the web of mutual dependencies, new centers of initiative evolve that are responsible for the functioning of the whole. There results a division of responsible conduct in society that has as yet found no generally acceptable linguistic expression.

We can trace in all its detail the kind of practical importance this new division of entrepreneurial function, and the kinds of conflicts its presence manifests, with the clichés of the older entrepreneur/worker image on the occasion of President Kennedy's collision with the steel industry in 1962. The steel workers had so moderated their wage demands under White House pressure that they were kept within the framework of increases in productivity. Shortly after the conclusion of the tariff pact, the steel industry raised its prices against the president's wishes. The White House reacted with the heavy pressure of state power and forced a rollback of the price hikes. The economy reacted to this with the great stock market crash. Public discussion of these dramatic events articulated in a very basic way the various aspects that are of interest to us.

Above all there was posed the basic issue as to what right labor could have to claim a proportionally equal share of yearly profits from the increases in productivity. This is because the production increases in single industries depend on the society's overall state of technology—and quite diverse persons and groups contribute to this state: physicists, chemists, technicians, engineers, managers, market analysts, and others. Why the profits from these entrepreneurial achievements should accrue to labor in this or that firm, or why they should not be translated into price decreases (which would benefit all consumers) is not altogether clear. We could adopt the pungent dictum of a German leader who not long ago observed:

A worker has a claim on yearly wage increases, and therefore the entrepreneur has to take care that the productivity of the year increases enough to satisfy the claims for wage increases. Now this dictum should not be misconstrued as expressing an unusually reactionary attitude. On the contrary, it is a powerful advance in economic thinking that contrasts with the situation at about the turn of the century when a German economist drew upon himself the mistaken contempt of his socialist colleagues for asserting that labor's wage increases owe less to the valiant class warfare of the unions than to the circumstance that mounting productivity makes the payment of higher wages possible. If today even labor leaders already have understood that wage hikes derive not from the surplus value that needs to be pried from the hands of exploiting capitalists through the struggle for power but from production increases that result from entrepreneurial achievement, it is the happiest of gains in realism.

As the American case of the conflict with the steel industry shows, the realistic understanding has nevertheless not advanced so far that the workers' claim upon profits from increased productivity was challenged. An understanding of the diffusion of the entrepreneurial achievement in a fully developed industrial society is still lacking. In virtue of this diffusion, increased production in one specific branch of industry is a function of the general state of technology, which in turn is again a function of science, of technology, of organizational initiatives, of the constitutional and economically organized freedom for its unfolding, of the general condition of national education, and of many other factors. We also lack precise knowledge of why the absorption by wage raises of profits from increases in production endangers the capital formation from which there can flow the additional production increases among whose effects are wage hikes. Running counter to the American president's agreement to wage hikes as long as they are kept within the framework of productivity increases, the critical press also used the above-mentioned argument that millionaires who live off inherited wealth understand as little about economic processes as their intellectual advisers or the workers. This objection might be invalid, since competent national economists belong among the advisers to the president and they do not exactly keep their opinions to themselves. The questionable reasonableness of labor's demands might well be better explained politically, that is to say, by the social dominance of obsolete clichés about greedy entrepreneurs who in any case are in the right against the poor exploited workers.

It should have become clear that the president's collision with the steel industry is of interest less for the event itself than for the public reaction. The immediately ensuing stock market crash, the withholding of capital funds from investment, the sudden rise in savings and funds in bonds, as the government clearly grasped, were warning signals that time for political fumbling under the aegis of obsolete clichés about entrepreneurs and workers had begun to run out, because too large a portion of the populace understands too much about the functioning of industrial society. People grasp that at some point irrational interventions have shattering consequences for the whole of society. Furthermore, the critical press again sharpened issues that already have been debated for a long time. There was no dearth of pointed references to the fact that only a third of employed labor is organized into unions, which want to establish a monopoly for themselves relative to production increases. Comparisons between the unions and capitalist robber-barons of the nineteenth century were to be heard once again. More urgently, the notion that the power of the unions would have to be broken was brought into discussion, just as surely as capitalist excesses were reined in earlier by antitrust legislation. No doubt remained about the fact that the establishment of a profit monopoly in favor of labor in any branch of industry costs other sectors of industrial society that have an equal claim to a share in the increased social product. The revolutionary assertion was even made that there exists claims to a higher dividend.

As confusing as the situation in detail still is, we can state by way of summary: The unions that pursue their politics under the obsolete cliché of class warfare have, in Western industrial society, gone a long way toward being maneuvered, at least in the American phase of its evolution, into the position of parasites who want to appropriate unethical profit-shares at the expense of their social partners. While the nineteenth-century image of exploitative entrepreneurship has faded, the twentieth-century image of the exploitative worker has gained color. We can, moreover, observe as certain that the monopoly claim of industrial labor to the term *social* in industrial society has become obsolete as a matter of fact. The great social issue is no longer the class opposition between industrial labor and employers, but the objectively reasonable organization and politics of an industrial society in which industrial labor in the old style provides an ever-decreasing minority. Beyond this, the factual interdependence of industrial society undermines labor's claim to be the preeminently valued representative of morality, since the customary old-style means of warfare, especially the strike, under some circumstances harms the workers in other sectors of society much more grievously than the entrepreneurs against whom the strike is directly aimed—as the New York newspaper strike demonstrates so brilliantly. Therefore, the industrial entrepreneur no longer stands alone in opposition to labor, as in the old-style disputes, but can sometimes find surprising support in a public opinion fed by the dissatisfaction of a great number of persons who are by no means industrial entrepreneurs in the strict sense of the term.

At this point a word of admonition is in order. This analysis could awaken the impression that the worker is being put down as the villain in the piece. Nothing could be further from my intention. The illusion of a negative estimation of the worker could easily arise today by the fact that, in the contemporary phase of the process in which Western industrial society has to overcome old clichés and come to a proper self-understanding of its order, the worker appears quite frequently in the role of the profiteer—and the profiteers are always unloved because the all-too-human paranoid complex (for which the profiteers in a situation bear a responsibility to which guilt could be ascribed) works against them, even though they have contributed no more to the situation by their conduct than have those accusing them in such loaded terms. Be that as it may, profiteers probably will be less zealously concerned to conquer by reforms the elements of injustice in a situation so profitable to them than those undergoing suffering. But it would be catastrophic to demonize this humanness, as Marx did to the entrepreneurs and to the bourgeoisie in general in the nineteenth century.

We have to be clear about the fact that an interdependent industrial society can only function as a democratic society when the manifold tendencies toward a gnostic psychology of demonization of partners are radically suppressed. Whenever the psychology of demonization becomes socially dominant, no matter whether it springs from Marxist or positivist, from liberal or conservative backgrounds and subcultures, an industrial society becomes unable to function as a democracy. Since industrial methods of production cannot be jettisoned, there arises as an inevitable alternative the danger of a dictatorship of the right or the left. Clearly, we are dealing with a central problematic I unfortunately cannot go into here. However, in order to avoid all misunderstandings I would like to remark expressly that in the example of the conflict of the steel industry, the worker appears on the scene in the role of the profiteer; but that besides the entrepreneur/worker clichés there are yet other obsolete clichés out of whose dominance other groups live quite comfortably at the expense of foreign labor. Reflecting on the German situation, I recall well-known clichés about the spiritual healthfulness in soul and body of agrarian economic life (on which even the spiritual life of the entire nation is supposed to depend), in the name of which agricultural firms or forms of trade that had become unprofitable are kept alive by subsidy methods of various kinds at the taxpayers' expense. Whenever we undergo the coercive division of the federal budget into subsidies, we could assemble lists of profiteers and parasitic existences on which probably every sizable group in German industrial society would have its own representatives.

These more general observations nevertheless should also be interpreted less as a critique of evil conditions than as pointers to a fundamental problem in the organization of industrial society. Its material dynamism, which can be summarized under the title of increased productivity, is based on technological progress and the rationalization of production processes. The more strongly these sources of wealth flow, the more swiftly the structure of the economy is transformed. This tempo of change is the problem facing our Western industrial society, which so far has been satisfactorily solved neither individually by the development of habits of adaptation, nor socially by means of organization. The structural transformations in the course of which forms of business become unprofitable, and expert knowledge and professional experience lose their value, obviously demand a willingness on the part of people to shift into new professions and to acquire the requisite knowledge and the experience for its implementation. Shifts of this kind are labor achievements of an immensely higher order than those required by professional routines, and they meet a corresponding resistance on the part of those stunned by such demands. Hence the temptation is always great, with the help of state power, to maintain unprofitable methods of production, businesses, and positions whose raison d'être no longer exists. When the number of those affected is large enough, and they are sufficiently organized to exert political pressure, their efforts will also be successful. In regard to no other problematic will it be so clear that government in an industrial society has explicit entrepreneurial functions, inasmuch as primarily it is called on to maintain the rationality of economic processes for the common interest, by organizing and financing the needed adaptations and retraining programs. It should by no means be excluded that in concrete cases large enterprises, entrepreneurial associations, and unions participate in this entrepreneurial function.

From this digression, which is supposed to clarify further the problem of society, let us return to the case of the conflict with the steel industry. How does the most broadly developed region of Western industrial society cope with mastering the tasks indicated above? Quite clearly not in the best way, as this case shows. The unions' politics of wages is formulated in terms of the old clichés and threatens to monopolize the profits resulting from increased productivity for labor, and thereby to endanger the formation of investment capital from whose stock of funds future increases in production are supposed to result. For reasons of elective politics, the government takes the side of the unions, even though it perhaps does not have the clearest conscience in doing so. The entrepreneurs make serious tactical mistakes and provoke the government's antagonism by bad public relations. The pressure of obsolete clichés is quite heavy. Nevertheless, in relation to the passive positions in the situation there are to be reckoned the active ones the occasion has brought to light. The discussion of the case in the press proves that wide circles of those who define public opinion are thoroughly knowledgeable about the conditions under which industrial society operates. They understand exactly that these conditions get disrupted most seriously by union and government politics on the basis of outdated notions. Moreover, it was brought out clearly that misunderstanding the conditions endangers the functioning of democracy and has to lead to a socialist-dirigiste constitution of society. Finally, the stock market crash, which went far beyond a shake-out of overvalued corporations and in its price drops also discounted more solid stocks with good returns—the end, so to speak, of the free economy—injected a salutary terror into all concerned. The entrepreneurs gained an insight into their lack of facility in handling the situation. The government understood that it went too far. The president in the following months took the trouble in meetings with industrialists to speak in a tone one would have expected instead of a representative of an entrepreneurial association. Meetings took place for the sake of reconciliation; and whenever distrust of the government resurfaced, at least the immediate bitterness dissipated. As for the attitudes of the industrial entrepreneurs, the case demonstrated that there are limits that could not be transgressed without endangering their function (the importance of which function is clear) to the detriment of society as a whole.

On the basis of this analysis and its résumé we can pose the question: Why, in spite of all these difficulties and the survival of the obsolete clichés, does the overall process of industrial society function better in America than it does with us in Germany? In so inquiring, I would make *clarity of awareness* the criterion concerning the conditions under which industrial society operates for discerning the qualitative difference at stake in the question. This clarity of awareness has to be sufficiently widespread socially to react sensitively and with social effectiveness whenever these conditions appear to be seriously threatened. To answer this question, I need to go into points not adequately articulated in the previous discussion, namely, the economic order's function in the framework of spiritual order; and that the spiritual order of Anglo-Saxon and especially American society is different from that of the Germans.

Issues of spiritual order and their national differences are extraordinarily complex; I can provide no more than a hint here or there. Even these suggestions can amount to no more than appeals to historical knowledge out of which the bare necessities need to be enlarged. In order to discuss issues of spiritual order reasonably, we need fixed concepts to serve as coordinates for the judgment about any actually given order. So we must inquire: What are the sources from which the order of Western and American society are nourished? What are the disruptive forces that are at work throughout the West but operate much more devastatingly with us than they do in America? Because the external victory over the organizational power of National Socialism did not eliminate the widely pervasive destruction of spiritual order that became manifest to anyone: After the defeat it continues to last, and it generates the feeling of a spiritual vacuum even though the economic and social order functions after a fashion. In a recently published book, *Das deutsche Risko* (Stuttgart, 1962), Ruediger Altmann wrote of the "grotesque triviality" of the Federal Republic, and by this he meant the lack of any conception of political order. In what does such a conception consist? Thus we pose the issue of the source of Western order.

Order in the Western world goes back to antiquity. On the occasion of Justinian's great work on law, its sources were explicitly established as power, reason, and revelation. The ruler has to fulfill three functions: He must be *imperator* and so be able to defend and preserve the empire by military power; he must be *religiosissimus juris* and so administrator of the philosophical-rational order of law; and he has to be the *defensor fidei*, the defender of the revealed truth. These three sources are alive throughout the Middle Ages as *imperium, studium,* and *sacerdotium*. In his historical treatment of the nineteenth century, Ernest Renan could say that the foundation of Western culture are Hellenistic philosophy, the Jewish-Christian religion, and Roman legal and administrative order. Power, reason, and revelation have remained the primary sources of order until our day. Nevertheless, science has entered in as a secondary source, which is to be characterized as specifically Western, for only in the West have reason and revelation so de-divinized and de-demonized the world that the relatively independent structure of things could become visible and be objects of investigation.

And now about the sources of disturbances. They too have a long prehistory, which nonetheless ought not to preoccupy us here. They start to flow more clearly since the beginning of modernity, even if their destructive power only becomes fully effective in the eighteenth century. I shall call them the "anti-" complexes because they are aimed against one or another of the sources of order. Four of these can be clearly distinguished: the anti-philosophical, the anti-church, the anti-Christian, and the anti-world complexes.

The anti-philosophical complex begins to be influential with the Reformation, since the anti-Aristotelian animus of the reformers, directed against the intellectual armature of Catholic theology, was in principle anti-philosophical. For outside of the philosophy that emerged with the Greeks as the discovery of the order of reason and of being, philosophizing of any kind does not exist. Along with Aristotelian philosophy, philosophy itself as the use of reason for thinking through the order of man, society, and the world was thrown overboard. Down to our own day, this was a blow from which philosophizing has not recovered. Especially since the eighteenth century the anti-philosophical complex has gotten rigidly institutionalized and becomes socially dominant in ideologies of the following types: progressivism, positivism, and Marxism.

The second complex is the anti-church one. It is quite understandable as soon as one considers the wars of religion of the sixteenth century in France, and of the seventeenth century in England and Germany. The aftermath of these catastrophes was the demand for the separation of church and state, so that the public life of nations might never again be able to be rocked by the scandal of warring churches. This demand, which moves at the level of institutions, would not in itself have had to lead to anything but a more precise securing of the temporal realm of social order over against the spiritual, as was already arranged in the Gelasian distinction of temporal and spiritual powers, with their mutual delimitation. Nevertheless, it had other by no means intended consequences, because the renunciation of the churches' role in relation to intellectual and social problems of the age permitted, in the realm of spiritual order, a vacuum to arise into which there could stream the intellectual and social mass movements of the ideological type. As a result of this tension between the churches—the traditional staunch defenders of spiritual order—and the movements outside the churches that had to be ready for the burning problems of the time, the anti-church complex fatefully strengthened not only the anti-philosophical complex of the ideologies mentioned above, but also the anti-Christian complex closely connected with the anti-philosophical one.

The fourth, anti-world, complex is the one that is peculiarly characteristic of Germany. While it, along with the others, is also to be found throughout the entire Western world, it has unfolded in an especially intense way and been effective in destroying order in Germany. In the eighteenth century it becomes virulent as the attitude of Pietist subjects toward a regime understood as an authoritative ruling body. The formula of the "sacredness" of the ruling body comes from Kant through appeal to Rom. 13:1. For these Pietist subjects the governing body appears in the ambiguous light of a power imposed by God, which has to set limits to the evil in the world and which at the same time shares so intensely in this evil that by the nineteenth century the sentence "Power is evil [die Macht ist böse]" could become the credo in every bourgeois home. There are many concrete attitudes in which this anti-world orientation gets expressed. They start with the Pietist one of existence in expectation of redemption, which requires one to withdraw from the filth of the world and especially of politics. They extend to the contemporary one of ideological indifferentism that may be formulated: "If I shouldn't get into stupid politics, then I won't get into it [Wenn ich keine dumme Politik machen darf, dann mache ich gar keine]."

Common to all cases of this kind is lack of responsibility in relation to the duty to shape a life in this world—an irresponsibility that should be seen, not in the rosey light of an ennobling inwardness and the domain of "beautiful souls," but in the harsher light of laziness when it comes to thinking and fear when it comes to work. For responsible living in the world, work is inescapable.

I would point in particular to the institutionalization of the anti-world complex in the system of the German university that goes back to Wilhelm von Humboldt's idea of cultural formation (Bildung). Whatever the differing opinions about the merits and achievements of this system in the past, we want to place them out of dispute. Even so, however, Humboldt expressly expounded the antithesis between the political citizen of the ancient polis and the apolitical citizens of the constitutional government of his times. In his educational ideal he decided for the second type. Only if the citizen is not politically active can he fully unfold his personality through cultural formation; and this liberal Bildungsideal has been implemented in the organization of the university, in its business of research and teaching. This remarkable idea, according to which cultural formation swims like a kind of cream—some today would say scum—on the surface of the nation, and by its swimming on the surface in a mysterious way engenders order in the interiority of the nation, is also supposed to ground its claim to validity externally at the same time. In this special idea there is scarcely a trace of the Platonic conception of education as the art of *periagoge* toward the goal of the spiritual order of man and of society. In contrast, if you draw out the lines of this idea there is sketched out for us in its results the political-spiritual vacuum of a nation in which unfortunate things like National Socialism could be spawned. It presages the concentration camp's commandant who, after his loyal fulfillment of his duty as a subject in his day's work, goes home in the evening and, since he is an educated person, enjoys Mozart. Of course Humboldt was not responsible for the consequences he could not foresee; instead those who defend themselves against the reform of an obsolete system after its effects have not merely been suggested, but become gruesome reality, are to be blamed. No politics is as perilous as that of apolitical educational idealists.

Let us examine the English-American order. In England and America, too, everything is not rosy. There too the "anti-" complexes have engaged in their work of destruction. But the substantive order, which was more deeply ingrained in the institutions, was maintained much better than it was under German circumstances. Once again only brief points, especially regarding the early connection of the idea of national existence with the idea of a Christian community, are possible. Already in the fifteenth century, while the wars surrounding the consolidation of the dynasty were being waged in England, Sir John Fortescue was concerned in his *De Laudibus* and *Governance of England* about the puzzling nature of the emergent nation, and he qualified it as a regional *corpus mysticum*. Thanks to Henry VIII's politics of supremacy, the Reformation of the sixteenth century took on more of a schismatic character than a theological reformation, so that the antiphilosophical complex could not develop fully. The great political work of Richard Hooker in the Elizabethan Age could thus still be conceived in terms of the *Laws of Ecclesiastical Polity* in which each person is simultaneously a member of both the civil and the ecclesiastical organization. Again, the Puritans injected into English politics a strong dose of Hebraism in which the nation was imagined on the model of the Chosen People. At the end of the wars of religion and the beginning of the Settlement, therefore, stands Locke's *Two Treatises of Civil Government*, which, to be sure, explodes the *Ecclesiastical Polity* but still conceives the nation as the community whose political business has to concentrate on the *temporalia* of existence. Finally, the disruption of the nation in the eighteenth century was met by John Wesley's Second Reformation, the after-effects of which are still discernible both in England and in America in the fact that, in spite of their monstrous power, the ideologies have remained on the periphery that surrounds a core of Christian and rational moral knowledge.

These hints may have clarified the importance of spiritual order for the functioning of industrial society. The relationships are more favorable in America than elsewhere because its rational knowledge of order is less prone to disturbance by the "anti-" complexes and the ideologies, even though these disruptive factors play a role that is not to be underestimated. As a result, a more lucid public awareness of the conditions under which an industrial society can work in a democratic form can be brought about through rational discussion. I would like to conclude by summarizing and underlining the chief points among these conditions.

At the heart of the problem stands the increased prosperity for all of society's members through increased technological productivity and the rationalization of the labor process. For technical business reasons, these increases are necessarily connected with the growth in the mutual dependency of all sectors of society upon labor with rationalized expertise in other relevant sectors. The phenomenon that so aroused Karl Marx, namely, the dependence of the industrial worker in his material existence upon the functioning of a business in which he possesses no ownership rights and over which he has no control, has turned into the general phenomenon of interdependence without the particular problems of business being thereby resolved. Modern industrial society is a total enterprise that disperses entrepreneurial initiatives among persons and associations, industrial entrepreneurship in the stricter sense and unions, public and private bureaucracies, managers, services for recruiting, information and communication, commercial organizations, school systems, the organization of research by universities, economic enterprises and also government, laws governing social and economic orders, and many similar institutions. In this sense we have been speaking about a democratization of the entrepreneurial function.

The total enterprise called industrial society, precisely because of this diffusion of the entrepreneurial function, has the property of being, as a whole, an enterprise without entrepreneurs. This could exist only if all entrepreneurial initiatives required for the material capacity to perform were brought about freely and cooperatively. Moreover, this is only possible if the institutions required for cooperation—information, communication, consultation, and the balance of interests—are organized adequately. It is also possible only if no one seriously rejects cooperation, even in cases of great differences in opinion. Above all, it is possible only if fundamental mutual trust based on common spiritual order is not radically destroyed by ideologies and the gnostic psychology of demonization. It is completely obvious that to function in a democratic form industrial society demands a very high measure not just of entrepreneurial initiative but of disciplined cooperation. It is not a social milieu in which strident ideas, eccentrics, and "masters in their own houses" can be tolerated in positions of responsibility.

If cooperation in a democratic form is rejected, and it comes to serious disturbances of the enterprise, in the wake of which larger sectors of society are threatened in their material existence, or feel themselves threatened, the danger arises that the enterprise gets surrendered to one entrepreneur—whether this entrepreneur is set up by gnostic sectarians of the Communist type, or by the preemptive movements of the authoritarian right. Both the problematic and the danger are something of which America is lucidly aware, as I have said. This awareness perdures, not on the intellectual level of sheer knowledge, but as a living pathos of responsibility for the achievement of the experiment of a democratic industrial society in America. Allow me to close with an expression of such pathos— with a statement from a speech by David E. Lilienthal, former chairman of the Tennessee Valley Authority and, later, director of the Atomic Energy Commission, a man about whom no one would dispute the rank of a great entrepreneur:

> We are overspending our emotional energy on binges about Russia, India, China, the moon—everything except what happens here where we live. . . . The hopes of the world for the protection and the continuation of human culture, in short, of a civilized world, will not be determined by what happens in India, or China, or Russia, or Africa, nor indeed in Western Europe. It will be determined by what happens in our country.

Summary

There issues from the clichés current among us, such as that of the opposition between entrepreneurs and workers, that the emergence of new forms of society is not yet grasped. This knowledge is already further advanced in America because modern industrial society is more developed there. Its service sector has gained in importance at a relative loss to the producing sector. It has been recognized that the economy does not arise just from industry. Whoever seizes social initiative in any form—in the economy, as labor leader, as intellectual, as politician—is to be accounted an entrepreneur.

The practical importance of this new division of the entrepreneurial function in America allows the actual social problematic of our day to emerge with some clarity already. There it can be acknowledged, say, that the social problem no longer consists of the adaptation of wages to a firm's increases in production. Instead it resides in the issue of how the result of the total economy's productivity can be deployed in the most useful possible way for the future of the entire society. Inexhaustible union demands can meet with the same resistance on the part of all socially responsible people, just as did eighty years ago the unrestrained striving for profits. A strike gets condemned because of its consequences for the whole society, not just in relation to its effects on those involved. Labor's monopolizing of the word *social* thereby disappears. Be that as it may, shifts in the agricultural, industrial, and service sectors are not yet adequately grasped.

The process of industrial society is understood better in America than in Germany because the consciousness of the conditions under which this kind of society operates in a democratic form is clearer there. The criterion for the difference lies in questions of spiritual order, especially their distinctive historical origins. The original spiritual order of the West proceeds through separate developments, of which the important ones for us here are the Anglo-Saxon and the German. In the end, the different presuppositions in the particular countries for the new appearance of industrial society arise from these separate developments.

Corresponding to the differing spiritual presuppositions, agency in the industrial society of each country is different—in English countries, doubtless, more from the society; in Germany, more from the state.

In Germany the indispensable participation of the citizen of the state in important political and economic processes is thereby made more difficult. Yet a highly developed industrial society can only function if all its members understand how to cooperate, remain disciplined, and if each person tolerates and develops entrepreneurial initiative for the welfare of the democratic state in accordance with his own capacities.

14

In Search of the Ground

It is a great relief for a lecturer—you perhaps don't know how much so—if he can talk to people who know something about him. It is difficult, sometimes, to deliver a lecture in a foreign city and not know to whom one is talking, or what these people will think of every sentence, or whether they will misunderstand; but I feel very much at home, especially since I have been given a grand tour of this beautiful city, and now have had a perfect introduction in a friendly atmosphere.

I have selected as title for this lecture "In Search of the Ground." That should be explained or there might be a misunderstanding that it is a lecture on finding good spots in real estate! That it is not.

In recent years I have tried to find general categories that would make it possible to compare orders in various civilizations and find common denominators for their treatment, because, normally speaking, all the categories in which we talk about politics in the West have arisen either in antiquity, or through the Middle Ages, or are oriented by the modern national state and its problems, and therefore do not apply to political phenomena in India, or even in Russia, to say nothing of China. In consequence of this inapplicability we sometimes make ghastly mistakes in politics when dealing with Asiatic or African civilizations because we just don't know what those are. We have no ready-made political vocabulary to handle such matters.

One of the simpler categories that turns out to be of importance is the category of the ground. This is why it is suitable for a lecture

---

Originally a lecture delivered in 1965 in Montreal, taped and transcribed, this text was published in *Conversations with Eric Voegelin*, ed. with an intro. by R. Eric O'Connor (Montreal: Thomas More Institute, 1980).

of this kind; others are much more complicated and would require much more preliminary explanation. So let me talk about the ground.

The quest of the ground, or "search for the ground" as I formulate it, is a constant in all civilizations, as also in all subdivisions of civilizations in all societies. That is not to say that the search for the ground, or the expressions of it, always have the same form. As you will see, they sometimes have widely differing forms. But at least we can express them clearly in the form that they assumed in the eighteenth century, especially with Leibniz. There the quest of the ground has been formulated in two principal questions of metaphysics. The first question is, "Why is there something; why not nothing?" And the second is, "Why is that something as it is, and not different?" If you translate those into conventional philosophical vocabulary, the first question, "Why is there something; why not nothing?" becomes the great question of the *existence* of anything; and "Why is it as it is, and not different?" becomes the question of *essence*.

To the double-pronged question "Why are things at all, and why are they as they are?" there is of course no answer, because the ground from which things are what they are, and are at all, is a transcendent divine Ground; there is no answer except in the symbolisms of theology or of a myth or of a metaphysics of transcendent divine Being or something like that—which does not render any simple propositions for knowing about the matter. The question itself, you might say, implies its answer; because in raising this question the very nature of man who is in search of his ground expresses itself in questioning to the last point, or to the last resort, what is the ground of everything with regard to existence and essence. In this questioning one keeps open one's human condition and is not tempted to find cheap answers. There are various types of cheap answers, to which I shall refer later.

The whole problem is, of course, clear even in modern philosophy. Quests of the ground were made in the eighteenth century, and the problem of the quest of the ground is a much-discussed one in contemporary philosophy: You find it, for instance, in Heidegger. I want to enlarge this treatment a bit and speak generally of the problem of etiology, meaning by *etiology* the examination of the quest of the ground. *Aition* is the Greek word for "the ground," and in this sense it was used already in classic philosophy. Hence the classic etiology will be my topic, and then I shall give some subvariants of this quest of the ground.

The term for ground, *aition*, occurs in the philosophy of Plato and in the philosophy of Aristotle. It has there three meanings, which must be distinguished or one gets into trouble right from the beginning. One sense in which the term *aition* is used in philosophy is that which in physics we call "cause": recognizable regularity between phenomena in time and space. We had better call that "the cause" in order to distinguish it.

There is a second meaning of the term *aition* in Aristotle especially. *Aition* was translated into Latin and preserved through scholasticism and into neo-Thomism as the doctrine of the four *causae:* the *causa materialis*, the *causa formalis*, the *causa efficiens*, and *causa finalis*. These four *causae*—material, formal, efficient, and final—are something different, of course, from "the cause" in physics. They have as their model artifacts or organisms, but we are interested at the moment neither in artifacts nor in organisms.

There was a third meaning of *aition* in classic philosophy: the ground of existence of man first of all, then also of other things. The ground of existence in Platonic and Aristotelian philosophy, but especially in Aristotelian, is the *Nous:* Reason or Spirit or Intellect, whichever of these translations you prefer. Let's call it Intellect, or use the Greek word *Nous*. Here the model is man and his experience of such a ground; hence reason is the ground of existence for man, and especially the ground for everything rational in his action. I shall give further explanations, but just now only the distinctions among the three meanings of *aition:* the cause, the scholastic *causae*, and finally the Ground of existence that is divine.

The importance of this preliminary discussion of meanings appears immediately when you look at the analysis of rationality of action in Aristotelian ethics and politics. In our rather secularized civilization—an "enlightened" civilization since the eighteenth century—we mean primarily by "rationality of action" rationality in coordinating means to an end. If we have an end in view (building a building), we then coordinate means to that end, and if that is done adequately we say we have proceeded rationally.

In ordinary everyday life we leave it at that; we expect that a man acts rationally in coordinating means to an end. But in a theoretical examination of the problem we cannot be satisfied with the simple coordination of means to end because every end can be converted into a means by asking, for instance, "For what purpose have we built this building?" And when we have ascertained that purpose we can further ask, "And for what purpose do we do what we do in this building?" Thus we are led into an indefinite regression in which the supposed end from which we started always becomes a means in another means-end relation, and that end a means for the next means-end relation. We have rational adequacy in the pragmatic sense within any one relation, but the whole chain hangs in the air and we do not know whether the whole chain is rational.

Aristotle argued the impermissibility of letting the quest of the end drop off into indefinite regression, because that leaves the question of rationality of action up in the air. If we want to know whether we act rationally, and what it means to act rationally, we must consider whether we have an ultimate purpose, that is, an end to the chain, which can no longer be converted into a means for a further purpose. This leads sometimes to semantic paradoxes because all really ultimate purposes in our life have no purpose; they are the last ones and have to be taken for granted: we *start* from there. To have an ultimate purpose in life, as unifier for all single rationalities of action, is a condition of rationality for the whole life.

Now don't take that as dogma but simply as formulating a problem for the moment, because finding an ultimate ground that gives the answer to rationality in action depends on what Aristotle calls *episteme politike*, political science. Political science is thus the science of the rationality of our actions, including the ultimate good from which rationality radiates over the whole chain of action. The formulation up to this point is, you might say, hypothetical. In Aristotle's view, if there is only an indefinite chain there is no ultimate rationality. Therefore if you want to have ultimate rationality there must be an ultimate purpose but . . . *is there an ultimate purpose?* And if there is an ultimate purpose, do we know about it? Is it knowable at all? These questions are not yet answered, but a condition is formulated: We have no ultimate science of action unless we know something about an ultimate ground.

How does Aristotle proceed? What is the detailed argument in such matters? He starts from commonsense observations as all good philosophers do, especially the classic philosophers. One should be aware that we always act as if we had an ultimate purpose in fact, as if our life made some sort of sense. I find students frequently are flabbergasted, especially those who are agnostics, when I tell them that they all act, whether agnostics or not, as if they were immortal! Only under the assumption of immortality, of a fulfillment beyond life, is the seriousness of action intelligible that they actually put into their work and that has a fulfillment nowhere in this life however long they may live. They all act as if their lives made sense immortally, even if they deny immortality, deny the existence of a psyche, deny the existence of a Divinity—in brief, if they are just the sort of fairly corrupt average agnostics that you find among college students today. One shouldn't take their agnosticism too seriously, because in fact they act as if they were not agnostics!

The observation was made by Aristotle also: Everybody acts as if he had an ultimate purpose, whether articulate or not, whether denied or not, whether articulated wrongly or rightly. The question of an analysis is only to bring, if possible, into articulate consciousness what everybody takes to be true anyway, because he acts as if it were true.

Raising the level of consciousness means that we have to investigate first, on the commonsense level, the opinions that people hold about such matters, and then try to see whether we can find criteria for the rightness or wrongness of the various opinions expressed. That is, in fact, what Aristotle did and what one always must do. He had around him, as one always has, a pluralistic society—it is not a modern privilege to have a pluralistic society. One can observe that some people believe that the highest good is to live a life of pleasure. Others want to lead a life of politics and become, if possible, prime ministers of their communities. Others believe that a contemplative life is the most important thing for a man to achieve. Such types, such opinions, are what Aristotle gives. In every society there are such opinions. The next question is: Can we find criteria for deciding between these subjective opinions, and can we find out whether, objectively, some of these preferences are more justified than others? Is it justified to lead a life of pleasure? Is it justified to lead a life only of politics? Should every life contain also a touch of the contemplative?

We have now two levels: always the empirical observation of the pluralism of opinions, and then the scientific analysis of criteria to decide between these preferences, i.e., whether they are objective criteria. That is science. How does one find criteria? It is very simple. It is done by having recourse to the hierarchy of being in which man stands.

Man belongs to inorganic being; with a part of his existence he belongs also to the existence of the psyche; man has also a life of the spirit, a life of reason. The question then simply is: By what is man distinguished from animals, from plants, from inorganic matter? The answer is: by his life of reason. Therefore, conformity to the life of reason is what is best for man in order to live out his nature. It is the life of reason, in the sense of a differentiated criterion of man, that gives the guide for preferences. All preferences on the merely biological level of instincts and urges, or on the merely psychological level of hedonism or satisfactions or pleasures, or on the merely metabolic level of having good food, are on a lower level, which is not worth being considered as the ultimate purpose. The ultimate purpose is the life of reason itself, whatever that is. We have to talk about that presently.

In this way one can find out that the contemplative life, which is the life of reason, must be an important ingredient in everybody's personal life whether contemplative or active, even if one leads a political life or even, to a large extent, a hedonistic life. From this classification in the hierarchy of *being* also follows the hierarchy of *goods:* External goods are important because you can't live without them, for you have to have the means of subsistence; goods of the body also are important, like health, beauty and so on; but most important are, of course, the goods of the soul: the various virtues, the constellation of virtues, and the character—that is the highest level of goods. We have objective criteria and everybody acts, in fact, according to this scale of objective criteria even if he denies that there are objective criteria. One always acts along these lines. All this is comparatively easy.

But now comes a question: What is this nature of man that is briefly formulated as "the life of reason"? For expressing the life of reason we have quite a vocabulary already developed by the classic philosophers, which in part is identical with the Christian vocabulary and has remained a constant throughout the history of mankind. Here comes now that question of the Ground.

The Ground of existence is an experienced reality of a transcendent nature toward which one lives in a tension. So, the experience of the tension toward transcendent Being is the experiential basis for all analysis in such matters. For the expression of this tension, a vocabulary has been developed. Already Heraclitus knew three variants or nuances of the tension: love, hope, and faith [cf. *OH* II:228 f.]. Where love toward Divine Being is experienced; where hope for fulfillment in relation to such a Being is experienced as the point of orientation in life; where these experiences are present, there is that openness of the soul in existence that is an orienting center in the life of man.

The vocabulary of love, hope, and faith has remained in Saint Paul: the Letter to Romans, for example, has those three names for the tension experienced.[1] They are summarized in that openness of the soul that Saint Augustine has called *amor Dei* (the love of God) or that Bergson in his *Les deux sources de la morale et de la religion* has called the openness of the soul toward transcendence—which means openness toward the Ground of existence, because we all experience our own existence as not existing out of itself but as coming from somewhere even if we don't know from where. That is the vocabulary with regard to the tension itself.

However, such a tension means a participation in divine Being because you are engaged in tension toward It. And by what are you engaged toward It? (Please excuse me if I analyze these things in comparatively simple terms, but they are simple; I cannot make them more complicated than they are.) If there is such desire in existence, it must emanate from somewhere in man. In analogy to organs of perception—the ear for hearing, the eye for seeing, and so on—one calls *this* organ the *psyche*.

Philosophers have introduced the term *psyche* for that sensorium of transcendence, that organ of man, by which he experiences or in which he experiences the various tensions of which I have spoken. And insofar as it is engaged in such experiences, the psyche can be called the "noetic" self, "noetic" being derived from *nous*, the Greek term for the intellectual self. The first rule therefore in the self-esteem, the self-treatment of man, is to have some respect for the organ in himself by which he is aware of and desires a life toward the ground. And self-love, that is, love of *that* self and cultivation of *that* self, is therefore in Aristotle the first existential virtue.

Self-love in the sense not of a satisfaction of passions but of having due respect for the cultivation of the noetic self—that is, the divineness, the divine part, in man. Beyond this, since every

1. Cf. Rom. 13:8–10; 1 Cor. 13:13.—Ed.

man participates in love of the transcendent Being and is aware of such a ground—Ground, Reason, or *Nous*—out of which he exists, every man can, by virtue of this noetic self, have love for other men. In theory, this is the secondary phenomenon—in theory, not in practice. In practice we love others right away without having a theory for it. But in theory that is secondary because there is no particular reason—*reason*, I say now—to love other men unless they also participate in that same divine *Nous* and have such a noetic self. If a philosopher drops out that problem of the psyche, of the noetic self, and if he is moderately intelligent, he makes very curious remarks. Nietzsche, for instance, on one occasion said, "If I did not love other men because they also are an image of God, I would have no particular reason to love them because they are just horrible." So you see why differentiation of that point is of considerable importance.

Community in the *nous*, carried by that noetic self, is for Aristotle the basic political virtue, the *philia politike* [political friendship], because only if the community is based on that love in the noetic self will it have order. A common interest in a profitable business at the expense of other people will not be a particularly sound basis for a government or for a political community. What must always rule is that ultimate reasonableness for which we sometimes use the term *the common good*: It is common insofar as it is the common reason that we have to control our passions. *Philia politike* is the noetic love; and if there is, as in inner society, a factor that controls passions and keeps them under control (because passions are always there), then one can speak, in regard to outer society, of a *homonoia*, a common *nous*. Now *homonoia*, which was developed by Aristotle, is also Saint Paul's term for the Christian community: Instead of the transcendent *nous* as reason, the *Logos* of Christ has now entered as that community substance that constitutes *homonoia*. But the term is the same. In the King James Version of the Bible, it is translated "like-mindedness." At the beginning of this century, when we had not quite as progressive a sociology as we have today, "like-mindedness" was still used as the basic category in sociology—by John Dewey, for instance. Even in Dewey's time, secularists like Franklin Henry Giddings would replace "like-mindedness" by "consciousness of kind," but after all it was still the tradition. All had read the Bible and knew what they meant: *homonoia* in the classic and Christian sense.

I have given you a general picture for the moment, of what form that whole quest of the ground assumed in classic vocabulary. It is at the basis of all our thinking with regard to politics—creates a community substance of the *homonoia.* I have been showing you what is meant by "quest of the ground." It all comes back to the question: what is that ultimate purpose toward which we are rationally oriented? This leads us to the question of the nature of man, and to the answer that his nature differentially, as against all other creatures, is openness toward the ground. *That* is reason: openness toward the ground.[2]

With those clarifications, we can now go through the modifications of the quest of the ground in various types of cultures and civilizations. Let me give you some examples. There were, preceding philosophical culture as in Hellas, cosmological cultures, such as Egypt and Mesopotamia, that expressed themselves in terms of myths. Now, what is myth? There are many definitions, and I shall not go into that matter in detail. But the best authorities (people like Mircea Eliade, for instance, in his recent book *Myth and Reality*) agree that a myth is a technique of imputing a ground

---

2. See the discussion in "Anxiety and Reason," in *What Is History? And Other Late Unpublished Writings,* vol. 28, *The Collected Works of Eric Voegelin,* ed. with an intro. by Thomas A. Hollweck and Paul Caringella (1990; available Columbia: University of Missouri Press, 1999), 52–110, at 88. In the little volume from which the present essay is taken, the matter is further elaborated by Voegelin's emphatic words:

What *is* the reason after all? "Reason" did not exist in language in the history of mankind until it was formulated in the Greek fifth century as a word denoting the tension between man as a human being and the divine Ground of his existence of which he is in search. The consciousness of being caused by the divine Ground and being in search of the divine Ground—that is reason. Period. That is the meaning of the word *reason.* That is why I always insist on speaking of "noetic" and use the term *nous:* in order not to get into the problems of the ideological concept of reason of the eighteenth century.
The word *nous* is applied by Plato and Aristotle to the consciousness of being in search of the ground of one's existence, of the meaning of one's existence—the search, the *zetesis.* One is in the state of ignorance, of *agnoia;* one asks questions, the *aporein;* and the answer is that the divine *Nous* is the cause that moves me into the search. Not the mere fact that somebody is searching is reason, but the movement by the divine Ground that pushes me in that direction or pulls me in that direction. That is why in the *Laws* [644D–645B] Plato uses the mythological symbolism of the god who pulls man by various cords: the golden cord of reason and the other cords. Then, preserving human freedom, he *can* follow the golden cord of reason but he can also follow the other cords and be a fool. It is a divine pull that pulls you. It is not a natural movement. (*Conversations with Eric Voegelin,* ed. O'Connor, Conversation IV [1976], 138. On the divine puppet-master, see *OH* III, §3 [original edition, pp. 231 f.]—Ed.)

to an object of experience. That is, if I have experience of men, of the gods, of a piece of landscape, of a temple, or a custom, or an institution, and I want to know, "Where does it come from?" then I tell a story of where it comes from, and that where-it-comes-from is now the ground of it, the *aition* in that sense. That is now an answer. Everything comes ultimately from a transcendent Ground—for instance, a Creator-God, or, in a philosophical sense, the *Nous*. But in myth it comes from very specific things: A god has created it, a demi-god has created it, an institution has invented it, or a dynasty has a god for its ancestor. Various such *specific* grounds are given. Or in action: When you look at the Homeric epics, you will find that Achilles, just on the point of saying a few nasty things to Agamemnon, suddenly feels Athene lay her hand on his shoulder, asking "Would it not be better to restrain yourself?" and then he says something else. Here is a ground of action: a very concrete divine intervention.

This type of imputation of a ground, imputation of existence and manner of existence to a ground, one can now more closely formulate as: imputation toward another intracosmic object or action. There is a general experience of the cosmos; everything is *within* the cosmos, including the gods, and if you want to explain anything in the cosmos you can explain it only by telling a story: how it originated from something else in the same cosmos. That is what we might call intracosmic relating of things to their ground, to other things or actions within the cosmos; there is nothing outside the cosmos. Thus *myth* can be defined, I think fairly exactly and there are no exceptions to it, as imputation to other intracosmic things of a ground. It is myth when you tell a story of an intracosmic ground.

In philosophy there is obviously a refinement because the cosmos has dissociated through that experience of a *transcendent* Ground that now requires an entirely new vocabulary. Within the primary experience of the cosmos that is expressed by myth we can indeed speak of a cosmos (although that also has difficulties), but when that cosmos has dissociated and the gods now are outside the cosmos and there is a divine Being beyond the world, then we need new terms. This is because all gods are intracosmic, while the One God or the One Divine Being is outside the world. So the world and God, as the result of an experience of transcendence, are in a new pattern of understanding that has exploded the myth where the gods are all intracosmic. There can be a genesis of the gods also within the myth, but there cannot be a genesis of God in revelation. There can still be a story of the genesis of the world because there is one God, a Creator-God, but you cannot have a story of the genesis of God as you have it in the myth. Thus the term *world* should be reserved to the area of philosophy and revelation where the world has become immanent, i.e., something that is created by one Divine Being that is not itself the world but the chooser of the world. In this type of experience (whether philosophic or revelatory), the ground has become known as transcendent. I do not want to go into the details of the difference between philosophy and revelation; that would take too much time. But in both cases we have a transcendent divine Ground.

And now comes the matter that is, of course, of most immediate interest for us: What has happened to this transcendent Ground under modern conditions in modern political conceptions? All ideologies operate against the background of an understanding of the transcendent ground, since the divine ground is part of the cultural heritage. We are living in Western civilization, which has philosophy and revelation and Christianity and the Church as its background, and all our vocabulary is taken from there. We have no immediate mythical vocabulary; all our vocabulary is revelatory or philosophical. What has happened to the transcendent ground in that connection? It has become, let us say, immanentized. We still have of course, the quest of the ground; we want to know where things come from. But since God (in revelatory language) or transcendent divine Being (in philosophical language) is prohibited for agnostics, they must put their ground elsewhere. And now we can see, beginning about the middle of the eighteenth century, in the Enlightenment, a whole series of misplacements of the ground. The transcendent Ground is misplaced somewhere in an immanent hierarchy of being.

The first such misplacement would be making an immanent reason of man the ultimate ground. The eighteenth century has been called "the Age of Reason" because human, not divine, reason is considered to be the ultimate measure and ground of all action and everything within the world. This human reason, however, is empty of content. A transcendent Reason, the tension toward transcendence, gives you a criterion, because if you are oriented in your action toward transcendence and see that "here is the nature of man," then obviously certain things are impossible. If the nature of man is to be found in his openness toward a divine Ground, you cannot at the same time see the nature of man in having certain kinds of passions or in having a certain race or pigmentation or something like that. It is in the openness to the ground; there is a content in it.

With human reason, you have no content whatsoever, and therefore the immediate consequence of the introduction of reason has been the necessity of filling up reason from various immanent sources. You find, therefore, as an example of the meaning of reason, the profit motive in the economic sense. *Rational* would mean operating for the optimum of profit under the given conditions of economic action and out of that would result an optimum economic society. Or the rational motive would be striving for power in competition, which, if it does not lead to the overpowering of somebody else, will lead to something like a balance of powers in a competitive society. The balance-of-power motive is, since 1713 and the Peace of Utrecht in international relations and domestically in the theories of Jeremy Bentham and James Mill, the idea of restoring a balance within society, with the implication (fostered by Herbert Spencer but also in part by Bentham and Charles Darwin) that the survival of the fittest or a competitive situation will secure the best kind of society. Or you may place the ground, if not in an economic motive or strict power motive, then in generalized problems, of productive relations, as Marx did: There are productive relations and they produce all the so-called superstructure of culture in society. The productive relations would be objectified, would be "the cause"; whatever we can explain in culture must be reduced to the productive relations that determined this or that type of culture. Or you may explain the cultural phenomena, philosophy, religion, and so on, not through openness toward the ground but by various urges ultimately summarized in the Freudian term *libido*, the ultimate urge, the comprehended collectivity of urges, and you arrive at something like psychoanalysis. Or since the first third of the nineteenth century, you might look to race relations. People belong to this or that race and that makes for their general intellectual makeup; *that* is the cause, the ultimate ground, and will determine the whole course of history. Or you might adopt the very crude racial conceptions of Hitler.

There is a whole gamut of possibilities of misplacing the ultimate ground: from human reason down to such phenomena as the Nordic race and, in between, the *libido,* the production relations, economic or political rationality, and so on. I have given you only examples, but I have already introduced into the series of examples something like a certain order. If you reflect on the whole series (I could, of course, give more examples) you will find that there is a *limit* to such misplacements of the ground; you can misplace the ground only in more or less identifiable, distinguishable areas of immanent existence: human reason or animal urges or economic or political urges or the *libido* or sex relations or the color of the skin, and so on. But you can go only through: reason, psyche, body, inorganic matter. We can observe, over the last two hundred years, that every possible locale where one could misplace the ground has been exhausted. This expresses itself in the fact that we have, since the great ideologists of the mid- and late-nineteenth century, since Comte, Marx, John Stuart Mill, Bakunin (and so on), no new ideologist. All ideologies belong, in their origin, before that period; there are no new ideologies in the twentieth century. Even if one could find a new wrinkle in them, it wouldn't be interesting because the matter has been more or less exhausted emotionally. We have had it.

Here we come to an interesting fact: Without peering into the future we can prognosticate that when ideas have run their course and are obviously exhausted, we can say certain things about them. First, nobody will be a great thinker of the type of Marx or Hegel or Comte in the future, because that has all been done once. There will be no further ideological thinker of any stature. We have had them all. Further, one can say that once ideological misplacements of the ground are in the world they run for a while, because every one of those great thinkers has followers, has publicity, and has epigones. But you cannot have an indefinite sequence of those. In every new generation there are always some intelligent people who are bored with seeing epigones and who will sooner or later tear the epigones to pieces, intellectually and by criticism. This is, in fact, now done.

But one must not be too optimistic with regard to the exhaustion of the *power* of ideologies. Once ideologies are institutionally established—the Communist government in Russia or in China or in the satellite states, or in our society (established in academic institutions) certain intellectual ideologies that do not immediately become political (like positivism of the various kinds, or various kinds of Freudianism)—they last a long while, because there is a vested interest in them. Every new generation is brought into them through college education, and it takes a while until they snap out of it. The college teaching level is usually thirty, fifty, or more years behind what is going on. There is always a hangover, a lag, that we have to calculate. As far as science is concerned, there is no scholar living whom I know who is an ideologist. That does not mean ideologies or epigonic movements will disappear, or that where they are established their power will melt away from one day to another. But there will certainly be nothing *new* of the kind. That one can say.

Now for the phenomenon of exhaustion. In a sense, ideologies are criticized to pieces. We have in our time a very peculiar generation of scholars who all are clear about it: Ideologies are finished. Each one in his way has taken this or that ideology and criticized it so that nothing is left of it. Nevertheless, he does not quite see what to do afterward, so we have a peculiar fence-straddling generation. These people are very serious; but their having seen that all is wrong still doesn't mean they know what is right. For instance, there is Karl Löwith, author of *Meaning and History* (1949), who has in an earlier work, *From Hegel to Nietzsche* (1941), completely analyzed the problem of German Hegelian historicism and all its inadequacies. Nobody seriously today can any longer be an historicist on the scale of *From Hegel to Nietzsche,* including Löwith himself. It's out; everybody knows that. But that doesn't mean that Löwith now knows what to do. The situation has its comic aspects; but it is very serious for these people because it is not easy to find out how to get out of the mess. Or take a case like Philip Rieff, who has written a splendid book, *The Mind of the Moralist.* If you read that book on Freud and psychoanalysis you know psychoanalysis is finished. After that book nobody can be a psychoanalyst with a decent conscience. But Rieff doesn't know what to do now. Or in certain political utopias you find a peculiar kind of "negative utopia," so called. It isn't that; it's a satire, in the sense of the Menippean satires: Aldous Huxley's *Brave New World* or George Orwell's *Nineteen Eighty-Four.* The whole sense of utopia is shown up as the nonsense it is. But that doesn't mean that Huxley, or Orwell before he died, knew what to do next. They had known that all the utopian excrescences of their political creeds are nonsensical. But what now? Or take the famous case of a Nobel Prize winner, Albert Camus. If you look at his book *L'Homme révolté,* you find the ideological perversions of the nineteenth century analyzed into pieces. It would have been most interesting (had not Camus unfortunately been killed in an accident) to find out what he would have done now, whether he would only have become his own epigone. Camus was comparatively young when he wrote book *L'Homme révolté,* and there would have been plenty of time—twenty or thirty years in his life—to start on something new.

I have given you a few examples just to show that we have today, in those who are in their fifties, approximately, a generation of men who have done all the critical work on the ideologies that possibly can be done, work which, however, does not become effective because it leaves them with nothing at all.

But ideologies are finished. The symptoms show that after this generation nobody can be an ideologist if he is intelligent to any degree or a man of any stature. That one can say with certainty, but again I must warn: no optimism with regard to the actual power of ideologies. Things go on in China and elsewhere just as they did in the past, and they will go on for a long while. We have here an empirical rule that has been studied by Oswald Spengler and by Arnold J. Toynbee: Periods of great establishment, such as a Communist government in China or a Communist government in Russia, have a habit of running for two hundred and fifty years. They may be finished earlier through foreign intervention, but if they are undisturbed they usually need, for their exhaustion, about two hundred and fifty years. That goes generally for observation of the past. There is, however, one point to be noted that may speak in favor of a shorter period, especially in the Russian case. Russian Communism takes place on the general background of philosophical and Christian tradition. If there is established publicly a highly defective conception that neglects the life of reason, that doesn't permit you to find sense in your life by reflecting on problems of life and death—especially of death—then you get, sooner or later, disappointment that the things promised, like a perfect Communist realm, never come and the restlessness of this defectiveness. There is no sense in life because indefinite progress doesn't work. (If we had a blackboard here, we could show, by a simple mathematical formula, why progress doesn't work!)

That is enough about ideologies. Let me in conclusion say just a few words about the general importance of the quest of the ground in a larger context. What is being done today in various sciences—

by classical philologists, by comparative religionists, by archaeologists, by scholars concerned with problems of the ancient Orient, by medievalists, and so on—is a sort of convergent development of a science of general structures that are not peculiar to our Western civilization but have their root in the nature of man and are in their variants, therefore, to be found *everywhere,* in all societies. One can develop a sort of system of the structural common denominators in such matters; I have given you this evening just one example: the quest of the ground.

The work has progressed much further, however, and there are many other such structures, already fairly well known, which are to be found everywhere. This permits one to judge, to a certain extent, the point at which a problem has stalled in a society, or the point that has been reached or that can be foreseen in the future. What will happen is an acting out of certain types of ideas; and when they have been acted out, they are finished. Understanding of such units of ideas is so interesting for us now because some of them— installed at certain points, say in the period of Enlightenment— now after two hundred and fifty years approach their end at the end of our century. The considerable area of general structures known already will permit far more precise judgment, although it does not permit action, you see. It doesn't help for action to know these matters, because people act by emotions and not by reason. But it helps for understanding what probably are the processes that have to run their course before a particular kind of nonsense is completely finished and out. I have given you examples of the ideology problem so that you can see one really can say something about it if one looks for the phenomena—and one looks for the phenomena if one knows what to look for—for example, that certain misplacements of the ground are finished now.

Discussion[3]

E.O'C.: I've just been asked: Why hasn't Professor Voegelin finished his *Order and History*? Does this lecture partly show why he hasn't finished it?

---

3. Participants in the question period, designated in the transcript by their initials, were (in order of their first interventions): Eric O'Connor, Eric Voegelin, Stanislaus Machnik, George Furse, Richard Jacobsen, Martin O'Hara, Cathleen Going, Winston Arnold, Felix Karpfen. Q. designates five unidentified questioners.—Ed.

E.V.: To put it quite plainly, I *have* finished it, but it is a shelf [of books] in print, six more such volumes—and that is preposterous. So I will have only one volume on systematic questions of the type of which I have given you an example tonight, and I'm using historical materials only as representative examples. That enormous manuscript is unpublishable.

S.M.: In speaking of the ground you said that the grasp of causation, and therefore of the processes of reason, has formed a very substantial ground in many ways. I'm wondering whether a ground can be identified that is particularly appropriate to aesthetic preoccupations. I'm thinking particularly about what is manifest in Martin Buber's confrontations of individuals, their response to the liberty of existence. I don't yet see how this experience has any one of the grounds that you presented. Is my question clear enough?

E.V.: One can at least guess at what it is. I have talked about the ground only insofar as it is expressed in some sort of symbolism— either myth or philosophy or revelation or ideological construction —i.e., in the rational sphere where we speak expressly of imputation of a thing to a ground (or imputation of a ground to a thing, whichever way you want it). In art we have an entirely new problem: All art, if it is any good, is some sort of a myth in the sense that it becomes what I call a *cosmion,* a reflection of the unity of the cosmos as a whole. The odd thing about a work of art is that it is an intelligible unit even if it is only, in the most naturalistic sense, a segment of a reality that extends around it in all directions. Think of an impressionistic painting that gives you a bridge over the Seine: One bridge arch is there and then the wings go on and there is nothing; nevertheless it is a unit. How to produce such units and make them convincing models of the unity of the world—that is the problem in art. It's much closer to cosmological thinking than anything else.

S.M.: But to find an unconditional commitment to the particular—

E.V.: Could you give an example of what you mean by unconditional commitment to a particular?

S.M.: I contract a commitment toward this particular individual or group of individuals and preoccupations; come hell or high water I am committed to this way. It makes possible the operation of love, not in the sense of how the Divine is reflected but—

E.V.: Oh, I understand now. Especially in the nineteenth century you find a growing number of such surrogate religions—either on the erotic level or making art a surrogate religion or something else. There are famous cases. For instance, in spite of his positivism Comte had a mistress whom he venerated as the earthly divinity of the unity of mankind. In his apartment, which is still well preserved by Comtists in Paris, you will find the red plush chair on which the lady always sat when she called on Comte; that is the altar of the Comtist movement. It is covered by a slipcover and, according to Comte's testament, it should be revealed only on ceremonial occasions.

G.F.: About your statement that there can be no new ideologies: Is it possible that a synthesis of all the current theories on the structure and operation of the human psyche could produce a new concept of the nature of man? And would this not produce a new ideology?

E.V.: The nature of man is in principle known. You can't produce by new insights a new nature of man. The nature of man is open-ness toward transcendence. By no amount of science can you find anything overriding openness toward transcendence. What could that be?

G.F.: If the nature of man is known, it doesn't seem to be known well enough to be able to be controlled.

E.V.: You can't control openness toward transcendence, because that's controlled by God. Part of what openness toward transcendence means is that you know that you can't control the relation. That's very important. If you think you can, you have transformed your understanding of man from what I call a theomorphic conception into an anthropomorphic conception: a human controller. *That* is an ideology.

G.F.: Isn't that an unprovable statement—that man can be controlled only by God?

E.V.: It has nothing to do with proof. Either the openness is a reality and then you can't prove it—you can't prove reality; you can only point to it—or it isn't. Well it is. We know—we have documents of the experiences, they are in existence: the dialogues of Plato, the meditations of Saint Augustine on time and space, or the thornbush episode in Exodus. Here are the documents of the openness toward transcendence. You can't have more. There's nothing you can prove or disprove.

R.J.: You mentioned that certain civilizations can run a particular course for two hundred and fifty years and then switch and try another path. Now, what of individuals? They are born into a particular context. Has there been any study done to show that they must run through sets of errors and eventually come out of those? The examples you were showing seemed to imply that those people ended up knowing that everything was wrong before their time but not anything that was right, and that would imply that there hadn't been any study done in that direction.

E.V.: Such studies are done. There are various problems of that kind. For instance, to what extent is a man bound, if he is born into his time as we all are, by the errors of his time? That is a very important problem for judging such fantastic phenomena as National Socialism in Germany. For individual people who have done extremely stupid things—not murder, but things in support of Hitler—to what extent can one plead as extenuating circumstance that they were so grossly ignorant because nobody told them any better? That's what they learned in school, in the universities, in the newspapers, every day from everybody. You can only grant them that they are not super-geniuses who can break out of a rotten situation. That's a great problem.

One part of the rotten situation is a fantastic ignorance of the past. The *Principia Mathematica* published in 1910 by Bertrand Russell and Alfred North Whitehead has had far-reaching consequences. It was a great success in finding the logical principles of mathematics. But the metaphysics presented in the *Principia Mathematica*, the so-called "logical atomism," indicates that Russell and Whitehead were gloriously ignorant of philosophy. They didn't know anything about Plato and Aristotle. Are they to be blamed for not knowing? I don't know.

R.J.: Is it by accident, then, that one comes to know?

E.V.: That comes within the other question: It's a sort of meeting, it's not controllable. You can get over the "accident of your birth" (as George Santayana calls it) only if you have a desire to do so. But whether there is a desire or not, that is something that in theology is called *gratia praeveniens*. There is nothing *you* can do about it. If you have the desire and the energy to follow the desire, you can get out of the mess. Already in the nineteenth century, a generation before Russell and Whitehead, there was a man who knew all these problems perfectly—Gustave Flaubert. Just look at his *Tentation de Saint Antoine* or his *Bouvard et Pécuchet*. He knew all about the perversions of gnosticism; he established a central connection between *hérésie et cruauté*—in its tragic form and in its comic form. He knew, in *Bouvard et Pécuchet*, that such people had Ernst Haeckel for their bible as Hitler would have later. But who knows Flaubert? Who uses him as a source for understanding these matters? It's a very complicated cultural situation.

Q.: When in your books you spoke of a leap in being, were you referring to a society or to something possible for an individual?

E.V.: It is always done by individuals and spreads from there. We do not know of any collective leaps in being but only of experiences represented in concrete personalities. In the person of Confucius, as attested by his work, such a leap has taken place. Or in the life of the unknown author of the *Tao Te Ching* as attested by that text. Or in Plato's dialogues we can see it. But it's always a matter of individuals as far as we know.

Q.: How do you see the existentialism of Jean-Paul Sartre? As antagonistic to your position? Or as one of the criticisms of previous ideologies?

E.V.: Excuse my rough words—I don't mean to be disrespectful to the psychological analyses of Sartre (late in *L'Être et le néant*, for example)—but he is a vulgarian and an epigone. He's not interesting. He's not to be compared with Albert Camus; *he* was a thinker! Sartre is not on that level.

Q.: Professor Voegelin, what is *your* ground?

E.V.: What do you mean by that?

Q.: Your ideology.

E.V.: I have no ideology. I hope not. Why should I? Or do you consider it a general human obligation to have an ideology?

Q.: Is there a standard by which you govern your existence?

E.V.: Philosophy, first of all; then there are certain elementary guides contained in revelatory literature—the Ten Commandments, for instance—and so on.

M.O'H.: What do you mean by an ideology? I'm thinking particularly of what you said about Freud: You distinguished between Freudian ideology and the openness of Freud's work.

E.V.: Well, I have not defined ideology. I have only picked out the formulation of one element in it—the misplacement of the ground within an immanent hierarchy of being. I cannot of course now give a lecture on ideology; I can only enumerate what is part of it. In the first place, all ideology comes out of the classic and Christian background (beginning with enlightenment)—so one element always is the survival of apocalypse, the idea that this present imperfect world is to be followed by a more perfect phase. A second element is gnostic, that is, knowledge of the recipe for bringing about the more perfect realm. (That is gnostic: the recipe.) Third, immanentization, as distinguished from older apocalypses. In old apocalypse, the new realm—the Fifth Monarchy [Dan. 2:44]—is brought about by the intervention of God, or by a messenger of God, by an angel. In modern immanentist ideologies, it is always brought about by human action. That begins even earlier; you might say Oliver Cromwell's army takes the place, in apocalyptic speculation, of the messenger of the Lord in Revelation chapter twenty.[4] Then occurs a certain intellectual misplacement, due to the immanentization of this question of the ground. The temptation to extend "positively" a new science or immanent world physics as a model to other areas where the model doesn't apply—the element of scientism—is always there too, from Marx as a scientific socialist to Mary Baker Eddy and Christ-come-as-Scientist. These are some of the components you find always. And since you asked especially about Freud: He has the closest relation to Hegel's dialectics. I should say the nucleus in Freud is that famous sentence, "All *id* should become *ego*." Everything that is in the compactness of the unconscious should be unfolded into rational clarity—which is done by Hegel through the dialectical process and by Freud through analysis. In that sense Freud also is a gnostic ideologist. That gives you some possibilities of classification.

4. Cf. Voegelin's discussion in *History of Political Ideas*, CW, 22:167–73, for the Fifth Monarchy speculation; CW, 25:104–14, for Cromwell.—Ed.

C.G.: Thinking of what you were saying about the basis, in the ground of being, for political friendship, political love, I wish you would say a bit more—perhaps in terms of this question: Aren't there myths about the transcendent divine being that need to be broken before this kind of friendship can occur?

E.V.: Could you give an example of what you mean? It's very difficult to answer such an abstractly formulated question.

C.G.: Trying to ask more concretely: Are there not conceptions of a relation between a divine being and our world that distract us from concern for other human beings? I think of the phenomenon—at various stages in my own development—of a primitive and perhaps recurring strand of conception of the divinity that seems in fact *not* to ground political concern.

E.V.: You wouldn't let us know an example?

C.G.: Various Christian statements that seem to be speaking about escape from the community of this world.

E.V.: Ah! you mean something like the Christian doctrine of the *contemptus mundi*? In the Middle Ages every good person, including every good pope, had to write at least one treatise on *contemptus mundi*. That is of course a problem. If we mean by Christianity, in its origin, that sort of experience that has manifested itself in the writings of the New Testament, Christianity contains nothing about politics but only, apocalyptically, about your way out of this world through the Second Coming of Christ, which will occur next week or the week after next—in your lifetime, anyway. There is no particular interest attached to the order of life in community, and so you can't expect politics out of the Bible. If the church later has a lot to say about politics it is because it has compromised with the reality—given up the immediate expectation of the Parousia and developed the church itself for life in the world. That's a complicated process.

C.G.: The eschatological imagery turns into mythology then?

E.V.: It was never anything but mythology, of course—not in a pejorative sense but in the technical sense. *Myth* has a good sense.

Q.: What exactly would be the criteria for rejection of past ideologies? If we could develop standards to judge the situation then perhaps we might have a way out.

E.V.: Oh, quite obviously. I've given examples of how to define an ideology. An ideology has an apocalyptic element. Now "there is no apocalypse" means that change in the structure of being (what I technically call the *metastasis*; it is an ancient term), change in the nature of man, as we usually call it, does not exist. We have no empirical knowledge of it. Wherever there is an apocalypse in an ideology, that is wrong, nonsensical. There is no such thing. Is there a recipe for bringing about such a change? Since there is no such change, it is not a technical possibility. Every recipe is of course a piece of nonsense, whether it's Marxian revolution or Freudian analysis. Or there is misplacement of the ground in the immanent hierarchy of being: ground by definition is the Ground beyond the world; if you put it in the world you've made an elementary philosophical mistake. And so on. That's how it's done.

Q.: About that notion of apocalypse: Civilizations have eventually destroyed themselves. We might be able to stop that process if we could sum up past ideologies and leave them?

E.V.: Oh yes. If you follow your common sense and forget about the ideologies, you're already on safe ground.

R.J.: You referred to a person's having a desire placed in him so that he would strive. If he were willing to accept the technical aid others might give him, he might end up on a higher plane. An element of desire that some people have and some don't: Doesn't that seem a bit like occasionalism, in the sense of Berkeley's "God gives you the right things to do at the time he thinks you should do them," and in the sense that somehow there's no inherent control of human nature?

E.V.: Occasionalism is a seventeenth- and eighteenth-century doctrine that arose in connection with psychophysical parallelism. What I was talking about has nothing to do with that. I simply meant that we don't know why some people have such a desire and are willing to undergo the labor to work themselves out of a mess, and others don't. It just is so—I don't know why.

R.J.: Didn't we say that they are acting completely within a pattern and that if we were to help them out of that pattern then they would show the same desire we show ourselves?

E.V.: But as soon as you say this, perhaps you get in a mess psychologically. If you speak of attitudes of people who are living, as you call it, a pattern—then you get the idea: Can we help them out of the pattern? In most cases you can't because what you call a pattern is an attitude, a habituation of action, determined by all sorts of things—for instance, by inertia, or by just plain stupidity; it's too difficult to get out of it, it's much easier to follow an attitude. Or, in really interesting cases, it is a question of *L'Homme révolté*—the revolt against God—and you can't break it by explaining it to the man. There you get into the real metaphysical and religious questions of the "lost" soul. There are such people. Think of Samuel Beckett's *Waiting for Godot*. A man like Beckett is also one who knows perfectly well that all that agnosticism is blooming nonsense—but he can't get out of it. I don't know why.

W.A.: Your lecture has been in the context of traditional philosophy —you considered man and you emphasized the noetic self and man as having reason and responsibility—but contemporary philosophy attempts to deny that, or denies it outright. I'm wondering about one thing. You emphasized absence of ideology in the epigones: Is that an optimistic or a pessimistic note in your lecture?

E.V.: Oh, personally I'm quite optimistic. But you said: "contemporary philosophy denies that." That is true only if you identify as contemporary philosophy the "has-beens" while excluding the people who are good and do something new—for instance, Henri Bergson. There you have a great philosopher. And a Bergson is worth all contemporary philosophy of second raters.

Q.: What is your attitude toward British analysis?

E.V.: Well, British analysis is a funny affair. If you are interested, there is a brilliant book by J. O. Urmson, *Philosophical Analysis* (Oxford, 1956), which gives you the history of logical atomism and empiricism from Bertrand Russell's and Whitehead's *Principia Mathematica* into the period of the Second World War. It is dead since about 1940. People don't know yet that there is nobody in Oxford or Cambridge who has continued it. There are no new great people in it. But on the college level, the epigones are just now finding out about it and it is their strength, while in fact everyone who started it, including Russell, has given it up long ago as complete nonsense. Urmson does his book with British understatement, but it's a wonderful comedy.

Q.: You said there are no new ideologies because all were presented, developed, studied, and eventually proven not to stand serious criticism. Does this prove, in your opinion, that these theories are wrong or does it prove that man has the intellectual power to undo what he has done, thus showing the duality of any idea?

E.V.: I'm not sure that I got that clearly.

Q.: If I have an idea or ideology and it is destroyed by you, does it follow that my idea is wrong, or that you are able to operate in the ambivalence of man's world?

E.V.: You would have to get out of this whole vocabulary of ideas and ideologies and return to the commonsense attitude of philosophy that, in philosophy, you are talking about the exegesis of experiences of transcendence of a noetic type. Because it is to an exegesis of certain experiences that we owe our philosophical vocabulary, any one who misuses the vocabulary, because he doesn't know enough about it, is wrong. If he would keep quiet it would be much better.

Q.: But how do you protect yourself against the person who speaks well?

E.V.: Oh, by reading the classics, of course. That's the purpose of education—you must have the masters at your fingertips.

Q.: Professor Voegelin, still on that question of ideology: Do you think we've given an adequate trial to the idea that all our concepts of God are perfectly valid projections of an archetype within the collective unconscious and that therefore we'd do much better to look within the individual human unconscious to discover the nature of man?

E.V.: You are now trying to plead for Jung's psychology, if I get you rightly? If you want information, read the book on mysticism by Zaehner of Oxford.[5] There you find the whole problem explained and also a very interesting criticism of Jung' s psychology. Jung is finished after Zaehner.

5. R. C. Zaehner, *Mysticism Sacred and Profane: An Inquiry into Some Varieties of Praeternatural Experience* (Oxford: Clarendon Press, 1957).—Ed.

IN SEARCH OF THE GROUND

F.K.: I was sad to see that you were dismissing the apocalyptic element. I was wondering: If you get rid of it, how do you avoid ending up with a static civilization such as you might have in India?

E.V.: Civilizations as such are never static because every man is a new element of revolution in the world. Just stop being static and do something. But there comes again the question of the pattern: It's difficult to break out of it. Nobody is obliged to participate in the crisis of his time. He can do something else.[6]

S.M.: It seems that acting purposefully into the future requires that we anticipate a certain sense of order into which we act, or which we want to bring about. Now the conception of whatever order we take to be viable is going to turn into an ideology, if we take it as *the* order. However, it would seem that we have to act toward an anticipated ordering, which isn't so now. In other words, intelligence demands a sense of order that is worked out imaginatively and intelligently. Isn't it, therefore, desirable that there should be something like ideological commitment—but tentative and open to criticism and open to change?

E.V.: It is a sensible question on the surface but I don't think it will work out as soon as you come to concrete instances. One of the rules would be: concrete cases—because the concrete case usually explodes the lovely cliché jargon that we all use inadvertently. Concretely, a government that has a good tradition in operating politically (say, the British Foreign Office) knows that on the pragmatic level one can plan ten years, and never more than that. (In ten years all the conditions of the situation have so much changed that there is no sense in projecting beyond ten. But know your business within the ten years.) I can give other cases which I've seen myself. I grew up in the twenties in Vienna; there we had good training in law and in economics (with people who are now the great economists in America). Quite concretely we all knew that the productivity of society is better if there is a free-trade area. What does everyone do

6. This sentiment expresses a resoundingly defiant *motif* in Voegelin's philosophy, as one discerns especially in his inaugural lecture at Munich. Cf. Eric Voegelin, *Science, Politics, and Gnosticism: Two Essays,* intro. Ellis Sandoz (1959; English, 1968; reprint, Washington, D.C.: Regnery Publishing, 1997), 15: "No one is obliged to take part in the spiritual crisis of a society; on the contrary, everyone is obliged to avoid this folly and live his life in order."—Ed.

at the peace conference? Cut up the free-trade area of the Austro-Hungarian Empire and make small states with high protective tariff walls. If one knows that is wrong, why does one do it?

Every economist knew that if the enormous reparations demands made on the Germans were paid—assuming they could be paid at all—they would ruin completely the economies of the receptors. Therefore they had to be stopped. Why do you ask them in the first place?

Here are the concrete cases where you use common sense; you don't need an ideology. Most of the problems you have to handle are commonsense problems on the pragmatic level within contexts about which you perfectly well know what pragmatically can be done. Why shouldn't it *be* done?

Just think of certain things connected with the end of the Second World War. The same stupidities as after the First were done again. If you look in Winston Churchill's memoirs, for instance, you see his desperate attempt to make clear to President Roosevelt that one shouldn't, for heaven's sake, surrender to the Russians every capital in Europe. But it was done. Bucharest, Budapest, Belgrade, Berlin, Vienna—everything is surrendered to the Russians. Roosevelt didn't understand. Historical common sense is on the side of Churchill. You don't need an ideology for this.

I was caught in 1938 in Austria when the Nazis came because I considered it impossible that the French, the English, the Italian governments could ever permit Hitler to occupy Austria. We knew from history and from the general strategic problems in central Europe that if a German government has Austria also, it is in a position to win a world war in Europe. That would be a shift in the power position that no government of England or France could tolerate. Well, they *did* tolerate it.

E.O'C.: I think one of the problems moving here is this: You're not saying that persons shouldn't have ideas and imaginations about the future, but that they should not make those the ultimates. Obviously, without imagination and without patterns, without many possible ways of moving, one can't think at all. You're not denying that?

E.V.: No, no. One can do on the commonsense level (say, within a framework of the next ten years) all sorts of things. As soon as you have ideologies you usually obfuscate the structure of reality within which you have to move. That is the problem. Ideologies are highly dangerous because they make you lose contact with reality.

S.M.: It seems, though, that people cannot be energized into a major move to change this present state unless there is a presentation of some concretized image of what can be attained.

E.V.: That also is a serious problem, which has already been dealt with by Aristotle in his *Rhetoric*. It is the task of a politician to bamboozle his people into doing, for all sorts of reasons, things which should be done for the right reasons. That is the art of a statesman.

E.O'C.: I want to express our utter appreciation for Professor Voegelin's talk, and for his coming here, which I know was a great deal of trouble for him. I think the thanks have been given to Professor Voegelin by the type of questions he was asked.

Index

253

Study of History (Toynbee), 10, 100–114
Substantive communication, 47, 48
Suffrage. *See* Voting behavior and
    suffrage
Suggestio falsi, 58
Sumeric civilization, 106
Summum bonum, 55, 57, 97
Summum malum, 55
Superbia (pride), 35, 41
Superman, 55, 120
Suppressio veri, 58
Survival of the fittest, 235
Symbols: apocalyptic, 152; of Christ in
    Old Testament, 176; compact symbols
    for compact experiences, 176; of
    national state, 26; of objectifications,
    204; of transcendence, 138–40; of
    world, 145–46
Synoikismos, 202

Taoism, 136
Tao Te Ching, 243
Taubes, J., 130–31, 133
Technology, 66–69, 121, 127–28, 131–
    32, 146, 185–86. *See also* Industrial
    society
Television, 48, 50–51
Telos (end), 115, 117, 150–53, 155
Temporalia, 220
Ten Commandments, 6, 77, 244
Tentation de Saint Antoine (Flaubert),
    243
Terminiello v. City of Chicago, 63n3
Theism, 120
Themistocles, 201
Theoi eleutherioi, 136
Theologia civilis, 11, 36, 37, 41, 174,
    181. *See also* Civil theology
Theologia naturalis, 11, 181
Theologia supranaturalis, 174
Theology: of Bultmann, 156–77;
    Bultmann's definition of, 162–64,
    170–71; civil, 11, 36–46, 174, 181–83;
    Comte on, 174–75; conflict between
    civil theology and philosophy, 36–46;
    natural, 159–60, 181; Paul's theology
    of history, 165–69, 175, 177. *See also*
    Christianity; God; Religion
Theology of the New Testament
    (Bultmann), 162, 166–67

Theopolity, 8, 61–62, 203
Theoria, 115
Théorie de la fondation (Hauriou),
    194–96
Theory: of conscience, 46; Lindsay on,
    38; organic and mechanical theories
    of politics, 44–45
Third Realm, 3, 11, 181
"Third world," 93, 137, 143
Thirty Years War, 51
Thomas Aquinas, Saint, 28, 30–33, 116
Thucydides, 18
Tocqueville, Alexis de, 37n12
Tolerance and intolerance, 35, 36, 37,
    54, 62, 63, 84, 98–99, 182
Topoi, 124, 125, 126, 127
Topos, 194
Torah, 160
Totalitarianism: Arendt on origins of,
    15–23; change of human nature by,
    21–22; compared with liberalism,
    4, 22; D'Entrèves' anachronistic
    use of term, 30, 31–32; difficulty
    in exploration and theorization
    on, 15–16; and eschatology, 1, 21,
    31–32; and gnostic dualism, 41; and
    immanentism, 21–22, 32, 41; impact
    of, 15; institutional aspect of, 17,
    18; invitation to, 5; suppression of
    violence by, 152; victims of, 17, 18.
    See also Communism; National
    Socialism
Toynbee, Arnold J., 9, 10, 19, 83,
    100–114, 123, 127, 129–32, 135, 238
"Toynbee's *History* as a Search for
    Truth" (Voegelin), 10, 100–112
Transcendence: derailments of
    experience of, 204–6; Goldman on,
    119–20, 126; and Ground of existence,
    229–31; human existence as point of
    transcendental irruptions of history,
    172–73; human's relation to, 32;
    metastasis and elimination of, 133;
    openness of soul toward, 230, 241–42;
    and *psyche*, 229, 230–31; and soul,
    121; symbols of, 138–40; tension
    toward transcendent Being, 229–31,
    232n2, 234–35; transcendence-
    problematic, 76–77; transcendent
    Being, 116–17, 119, 150, 154, 229–31,